LATIN AMERICA ACTUALITY

by ALBERT WEISBORD

Latin American Actuality is a study in depth of one of the most pressing problems facing our country today. It is based not only on the factual data of the moment but on the fundamental trends that are revealed today and must play out their roles tomorrow. The book is both an excellent example of reportage and an historical, dialectical analysis from which the reader will be able to appreciate the basic contradictions that make Latin America such a turbulent scene. The emphasis of the book is on the present; history is called on to explain the present; the dynamics of the situation foretells the future.

The first part of the book, entitled "Chronic Crisis in Latin America," fully establishes that the crisis in Latin America is not an ephemeral phenomenon but enduring and chronic, inherent in the relations between the impoverished toilers and the traditional rulers, brought into sharp focus by the present efforts for industrialization, and made dramatic by the action of the military. In this part the author demonstrates the contradictions that struck Latin America in its capacity as chiefly a producer of primary exports for the industrial and capitalist world, how these exports did not keep pace with the exports of the rest of the world, how its exports were forced relatively to decline while its imports steadily rose both in regard to the rest of the world generally and in regard to the United States in particular. At the same

Continued on back flap

Albert Weisbord

THE CITADEL PRESS
NEW YORK

LATIN AMERICAN ACTUALITY

To VERA

FIRST EDITION

Copyright © 1964 by Albert Weisbord

All rights reserved. Published by The Citadel Press, 222 Park Avenue South, New York 3, N. Y. Manufactured in the United States of America by The Haddon Craftsmen, Inc., Scranton, Pa.

Library of Congress Catalog Card No.: 64-15965

CONTENTS

PART ONE

Chronic Crisis in Latin America

Latin America is in a chronic crisis so deeply rooted in the very operations of international capitalism as to make it impossible for the crisis to end without profound modifications of the economic system itself. To help solve the growing problems, efforts are being attempted, with little permanent results, by at least the following international organizations, agencies, and funds:

The World Bank (WB),
The International Monetary Fund (IMF),
The Export-Import Bank (Eximport Bk),
The Inter-American Development Bank (IADB) with its Social Progress Trust Fund (SPTF),
The International Bank for Reconstruction and Development (IBRD),
The Central American Bank for Economic Integration (CABEI) and Central American Free Trade Area (CAFTA),
The International Finance Corporation (IFC) with its Development Loan Fund (DLF),
The European Economic Community (EEC) with its Overseas Development Fund (ODF),
The Organization of European Cooperation and Development (OECD) with its Development Assistance Groups (Committees) (DAG(C)),
The Inter-American Fund for Social Development (IAFSD),
The International Development Association (IDA),
The Agency for International Development (AID),
General Agreement on Trade and Tariffs (GATT),

United Nations Economic Commission for Latin America (UNECLA)
United National Food and Agricultural Organization (UNFAO),
North Atlantic Treaty Organization (NATO),
Organization of American States (OAS) with its subsidiary bodies
such as the Inter-American Economic and Social Council
(IAESCOAS),
Latin American Free Trade Association (LAFTA),
International Institutes for Special Commodities (coffee, cocoa, tin,
etc.),
U.S. Peace Corps; U.S. Military Missions; U.S. Special Missions,
Soviet Bloc Agencies,
Japanese Agencies,
Numerous national, regional, and local agencies within each country,
etc.

All these organizations tend to operate on their own with little
cooperation or coordination among them. Each is proud of its own
autonomy. Each is openly or secretly pictured as a tool of this or that
foreign power. Each has its own purposes and motivations. Each has
its own criteria, techniques, and praxis. Some of these bodies are for
special and specific projects, others are general; some are *ad hoc* arrangements, some are permanent; some are commercial, some financial; some are economic, concerned with the structure[1] of society,

---

[1] By the term "structure" of a modern society we mean the economic organization dealing with the production and distribution of values or commodities.
This structure has three principal branches: industrial, commercial, and financial.
The industrial structure, in the broadest sense, consists of such divisions as deal
with extraction (mining, mineral wells, etc.), field products (agriculture, cattle-
raising, etc.), basic metals, chemicals, transportation and communication, energy
and power, machinery and producers goods, construction, production of consumers goods (necessities and luxuries) and various auxiliary pursuits. Similar
divisions can be made of the commercial and financial branches.
   The "substructure" is the foundational part of the structure, without which the
rest of the structure could not be built. It appears as the production of essential
consumers and producers goods. It consists of the wealth of the country and its
resources (meteorological characteristics, climate, topographical features, continental shelf, mountains, forests, rivers, lakes, seas, metals, minerals, flora,
fauna). It also consists of the labor force, including its size, distribution, demo-
graphic and ethnological features.
   The "infra-structure" deals with the ability of the human material, the labor
force, to handle and control the subjects and instruments of labor. The physical
aspect of the infra-structure which can be called social or public capital consists
of such items as highways, schools, sanitation systems, water systems, etc. Infra-
structure is concerned with the capability of the people to learn and communi-

others are social, concerned with infra-structure or super-structure, some attach conditions of self-help, or of development planning, or of economic and social reforms, others are without conditions; some give grants and gifts, others make loans or grant credits; some make only "hard" loans to be repaid in convertible money, such as dollars, and at a customary rate of interest, others make "soft" loans to be repaid in inconvertible currency, or in domestic currency, and still others make "hard" loans but at such generous terms of repayment as could not be obtained in the ordinary business world, etc. All want to give the impression they are functioning only to help out because of pure friendship, or humanity, but since their altruistic pretensions are not believed, they make confusion only worse confounded.

In the midst of all this has burst the bomb of the Cuban Revolution. This persistent Cuban Revolution has shown clearly the dire necessity and urgency for new measures to be taken if Latin America is to be saved for private business. It is plain that modern capitalism, if it wishes to survive, can not rely upon the large landholders (the *latifundistas,* or *latifundarios,* or Oligarchy, as they are called in different countries), or upon the *Juntas* composed of hardbitten military dictators. Furthermore, the control of any country by such antediluvian cliques maintains the political life of that country so rigid and aloof from the modern world as to make it impossible for up-to-date methods to flourish freely and develop in every direction as they should. The old regimes absolutely must be removed, both in order to prevent social revolution and in order to develop modern industrial capitalism, or they will be destroyed by revolution.

The Cuban Revolution has also shown that it is very difficult to convince the military *Juntas* and antiquated sections of the ruling classes that they must yield political and military power. This is all the more true since the newly arising progressive layers of capitalism have come on the scene very late. Untested, fearful, and cowardly, they are unable alone to cope with the unleashed forces of the people.

---

cate arts, skills, crafts, techniques, and training, and includes the areas of health (physical, mental, and moral) and language.

The "superstructure" embraces the totality of human relations flowing from the economic structure and includes religion and philosophical views, methods and contents of educational systems, literature and arts, scientific levels and achievements, ethnic and social groupings, trade unions, forms of sports and recreation, social organizations of control, political organizations, military-police systems, government, state, nation, etc.

It thus becomes imperative that the newer social layers of capitalism be aided by the dominant foreign power if they are to remove the older elements and take over. Otherwise civil war may result, in the course of which the masses may adopt their own methods, launch their own demands, and thus reach a social revolutionary stage on the level of Cuba. The problem of the United States and other strong industrial foreign powers is how to nudge out the worn-out older elements by a steady and persistent pressure without starting a civil war in which the masses can act on their own.

Furthermore, the pushing out of the older and the establishing of the newer systems of control must be accomplished as far as possible in such a way that the masses of workers are induced to believe the whole thing actually is mainly for their benefit and hence will actively participate in isolating the older regimes and in supporting the new. In supporting the new capitalist layers, the masses can also be induced to fight the Cuban Revolution and similar attempts elsewhere.

Here, then, are some of the basic motivations for the formation and activity of all these international "aid" organizations aforementioned. While they are all working to prevent more Cuban Revolutions from occurring, as well as to get what they can for themselves, they do not go to the heart of the problem. The basic fact is that they themselves are the heart of the problem since, as agents of imperialism, they are part of the very forces that have produced the chronic crisis in Latin America.

As a direct result of the Cuban Revolution the following escalation of political events has occurred in Latin American history:

The Act of Bogotá,
The Punte del Este Conference,
The Latin American Free Trade Association,
The Central American Free Trade Area,
Increased U.S. missions, such as those listed previously, strengthened U.S.-Latin American Chambers of Commerce, improved English-speaking press and other media in Buenos Aires, Rio de Janeiro, São Paulo, Mexico City, etc.,
U.S. interference in the Dominican Republic,
U.S. action in Haiti,
U.S. action in Nicaragua,

British action in British Guiana,
Invasion of Cuba,
Imminence of nuclear war between the United States and the Soviet Union.

In the world subdivision of labor, Latin America has occupied chiefly the role of producer of primary materials exported mainly for use by industrial countries, principally the United States and those in Western Europe. Each Latin American country has depended upon one or a few primary products, the export of which makes the country able to continue functioning in a capitalist world. Table 1 illustrates the situation:[2]

Table 1

EXPORTS OF CERTAIN PRIMARY COMMODITIES AS % OF TOTAL EXPORTS
IN EACH LISTED COUNTRY: 1958-1960

	Argentina	Brazil	Chile	Uruguay	Venezuela	Colombia	Ecuador
Coffee		56%				75%	44%*
Copper			67%				
Meat & Meat Products	41%			88%†			
Grains	24						
Nitrates			8				
Petroleum					88%†	16	
Bananas							42
Totals	65%	56%	75%	88%	88%	91%	86%

* includes cacao
† data for 1960

The situation illustrated in Table 1 is essentially a situation left over from the 19th century, when England dominated the import-export structure of Latin America. Then, supposedly, it was for the best interest of each country to export as much as possible of the goods wanted by others and by selling these exports buy all the imports needed. For Latin American countries this system meant complete dependence upon external trade and the stifling of home industries that could not compete in manufactured goods with a better-organized and more efficient England. Latin American countries exported then

[2] Most of the statistical tables given, unless otherwise stated, are from official United Nations sources (Annual World Economic Surveys, or Surveys of Latin America, etc.) or U.S. official publications (Statistical Year Books, Reports of and to the Joint Economic Committee, Congress of the United States, etc.)

not the surplus over and above what was needed by the country itself but as much as was necessary to buy what the country had to have to exist and grow. Such Latin American nations produced prime materials not because they themselves used them but because they could sell them. And in this process they often had to sacrifice production of what was needed at home. In those times, Argentina, for example, working only to raise cattle, imported flour and grain; Brazil still does so even now; so does Cuba.

This situation, of course, suited England, the prime importer-exporter of the world, which fattened on world trade and on the profits of world shipping, which was also in its hands. Under British guidance the Latin American countries did not sell very much to their immediate neighbors but rather to industrial markets situated thousands of miles away. If Argentina wanted to buy coffee from Brazil, Argentina would first have to sell its grain and meat to Western Europe through Britain, suffering the heavy charges of British freighters, and then with the proceeds buy the coffee, while Brazil would first have to sell its coffee in New York under similar conditions in order to buy wheat from Argentina.

For these reasons the Latin American countries were not stimulated to produce anything for themselves, rather even at times were prevented from starting such production. England in Latin America confined herself to investing in agricultural prime material production and in public utilities necessary to bring the stuff to market (e.g. railroads), while also dominating the commercial and financial institutions. As an importer-exporter, England was not at all necessarily concerned under what conditions the stuff was produced, so long as she could ship it and sell it. Thus England could not play much of a role as a persistent progressive force within Latin America. Progress and development passed Latin America by. The old landholders with their military cliques kept firm control. Even chattel slavery held on in Brazil until 1888.

Under such conditions, Latin America remained completely in the hands of those who controlled foreign markets in regard to both exports and imports. Each Latin American country, having only one or two principal exports, and these being primary materials which could not be easily changed or substituted, had little or no flexibility in bargaining. If England, for example, drank tea rather than coffee,

Brazil could not switch to the production of tea, but would have to stand by the falling coffee market. If France bought her coffee from her own controlled plantations in Africa rather than from Brazil, Brazil would just have to suffer. If the United States could develop instant coffee so as to use the green bean of coarser grades of coffee and thus switch from Brazil's coffees to other cheaper grades, Brazil could do little about it. If the use of instant coffee meant the feasibility of permanent storage of vast stocks, causing a chronic surplus, and market prices fell accordingly, Brazil would have to bear it.

Such a situation did not face industrial countries like England, or Germany, or the United States. If certain items or commodities were surpassed, the industrialists simply switched to other items or commodities that they could manufacture. One material or subject of labor could be replaced by another; one process could be shelved for another. In fact, this is precisely wherein lay the greatest strength of the industrial countries: persistent development, constant change, continual new inventions and discoveries. Such countries could play off one material against another, one market for another. Instead of steel they could use aluminum, instead of aluminum they could use synthetic plastics, etc.

As an example, consider tin production in Bolivia. Just when Bolivia felt it was getting along very well with an increasing demand for tin on the part of the U.S. canning industry, along came an invention that reduced by half the amount of tin covering that was needed, and the price of tin crashed drastically. Bolivia was helpless. It could not shift to another metal that did not exist within its borders. Similarly when, with the rise of the automobile industry in the 20th century, Brazil was beginning to develop a big natural rubber production in the Amazon country, the United States found it could use synthetic rubber and Brazil's natural product became superfluous. So it was with the synthetic fibres, such as rayon, nylon, dacron, and other material supplanting cotton, wool, and flax. And this is a situation that is bound to be reproduced repeatedly.

The rapid advance in scientific efficiency in the industrial countries has meant steadily improved processes, sudden switching from one material to another, cutting down of waste and scrap, making synthetic substitutes, vastly improved productivity of labor, etc. Under capitalism the arithmetic growth of the market can not possibly equal the geometric progress of scientific achievement. This law can be translated into the plain economic fact that the industrial countries of the world can improve the quantity and quality of their products without corresponding increases in the raw materials and labor supplies necessary. Thus the gap between the industrial countries and the primary producing countries tends to become ever greater.

Added to this is another point particularly pertinent to Latin America, namely, that in the 20th century the growth of industrial countries has come principally not in the field of soft consumers goods, such as textiles, shoes, or food, but in the field of durable consumers goods and, above all, of producers goods, such as machinery and equipment. The Latin American countries, however, (except Chile, Bolivia, Peru and Venezuela) in the main furnish the prime materials for the soft goods sector only and thus are bound to suffer the same stifling history as their counterparts, the manufacturers of soft consumers goods, have in the industrial countries.

The effect of all this on Latin America is reflected in the following data: In the period 1928-1958 total production in the industrial countries of the capitalist world (North America, Western Europe, and Japan) increased 113%, but in the primary producing countries only 46% (excluding petroleum). While world manufacturing exports increased by 103%, world primary goods exports (excluding petroleum) increased by only 14%.

Focusing on Latin America and using a still longer trend, we find that before World War I Latin American exports accounted for 10% of the world's total exports while in 1961 they accounted for only 6.5% of such exports, despite an immense population increase in Latin America during that period. A more detailed picture is given in Table 2.

After World War II, with its devastation of many export areas, Latin American exports (exclusive of Venezuela and Cuba) again reached 10.3% of the world's total exports, but by 1960 they had dropped to only 4.8%. If we take 1950 as our base index year, world exports grew 130% by 1960, while Latin American exports (exclusive of Venezuela and Cuba) stood only 11% higher at the end of that period. Latin America's rate of increase trailed behind all other areas, including Africa.

Since the Latin American markets are now dominated by the United

Table 2

GIVEN LATIN AMERICAN EXPORTS AS % OF WORLD TOTAL EXPORTS
OF SUCH COMMODITIES

	1939	1950	1960
Wheat	13.6%	16.0%	9.0% *
Meat	39.2	26.8	16.8 †
Coffee	85.4	83.0	71.1 ‡
Cacao	26.0	26.6	23.5
Wool	17.5	19.3	13.9 §

* of which Argentina furnished about 96% of the Latin American total in 1958-1960 instead of the previous 99% of the total, the loss being in favor of Uruguay.

† of which Argentina furnished about 83% of the Latin American total in 1958-1960 up from the 72.5% of the total in the 1948-1951 period.

‡ of which Brazil furnished about 54% of the Latin American total in 1958-1960 as compared to about 63% of the total in the 1948-1951 period.

§ of which Argentina furnished about 74% of the Latin American total in the 1958-1960 period up from about 64% of the total, its level in the 1948-1951 period, mainly at the expense of Uruguay.

States, it is meaningful to note how shifts of needs and improved processes have cut down per capita consumption in this country of primary goods exported by Latin America.

Table 3

U.S. PER CAPITA CONSUMPTION: 1955-1957
(INDEX BASED ON 1948-1950 ANNUAL AVERAGE AS 100)

Lead	91*	Textile fibres	84†	Beef & Veal	129*
Zinc	102*	Cotton	91*	Mutton &	
Copper	99*	Wool	52*	Lamb	100*
Tin	75*	Coffee	87	Tobacco	98*
Natural		Cocoa	93	Sugar	101*
Rubber	80†	Bananas	93	Wheat	64*

* Substantial U.S. domestic production; imports prevented by quotas and by tariff restrictions.

† Replaced by U.S. synthetic products.

From 1946 to 1957, Latin American imports to the U.S. fell from 40% of the total volume of imports into that country to only 25%. Whereas U.S. imports as a whole increased from 1950 to 1957 by 24%, raw materials imports increased only 10% and unprocessed foodstuffs 5%, which last two categories include what Latin America contributes (coffee, bananas, sugar, wool, hennequin, metals, minerals). During that time the percentage of the total U.S. imports allocated for foodstuffs and raw materials fell from 58% to 50%, while the share of Latin American foodstuffs fell from 52% to 45% and raw fibres from 8% to 2%.

Looking at the situation from the standpoint of Latin America, its exports to the United States, which had consisted of 46% of its total exports in 1950, shrank to 42% of its total by 1960.

Although U.S. disposable income rose 40% in the period 1950 to 1957, of the total coffee imports to the U.S. those from Latin America fell from 95% to 84%; of the total imports of cane sugar, those from Latin America fell from 87% to 79%; cacao fell from 670 million pounds to 513 million pounds; bananas from 51 million stems to 48 million stems. Similarly, of the total imports by the U.S. apropos the Latin American share of each commodity, copper fell from 62% to 59%, lead from 55% to 42%; tin from 60% to 53%, nitrogen fertilizer from 63% to 53%, raw wool from 46% to 31%, fibres from 88% to 76%. Only zinc rose in percentage and in absolute volume.

The slow expansion of world trade in primary commodities has been due only partly to a lag in consumption. The big impact is due to the trend toward self-sufficiency among the industrial countries. In the United States, for example, the consumption of imported primary commodities (excluding petroleum) advanced in the thirty years ending 1955-57 by only 17%, whereas U.S. per capita consumption increased by 35%. In Western Europe, in the same period of time, per capita consumption also increased by 35%, but imported supplies rose only by 9%.

The general trend to achieve self-sufficiency was sharply emphasized a) during the decade of the Great Depression in the 1930's and the rise of totalitarian autarchic regimes; b) during the period of World War II; and c) during the post-World War II period marked by the intensity of the cold war and by the rise of the European Economic Community (European Common Market).

But even before these great world-wide events the rise of aggressive American capitalism had terminated English hegemony in Latin America and brought an end to the free trade era favorable to Britain. American capitalism in its advances required vast sources of minerals and metals for its industries and in return needed huge markets for its steel and metal manufactures. It took over the nitrates and copper production of Chile, the lead, tin, and zinc mines of Peru and Bolivia, etc. Thus, unlike the English rule, American domination was marked by dramatic changes in production and productive methods, by emphasis on manufacturing and use of metal products. In Argentina, for example, the Americans pushed refrigeration development for meat products; in Central America they directly took over and modernized the vast fruit and agricultural plantations. Americans were interested in a sort of economic Monroe Doctrine in which the huge resources of Latin America would become exclusively an American domain.

All this was greatly furthered by the rise of the automobile and petroleum industries in the early 20th century. American capital was everywhere exploring and exploiting the natural wealth of Latin America, its petroleum vanguard stimulating automobile consumption and road building. Thanks to petroleum and to automobile production, Americans swept the entire field before them and easily became the dominant foreign force in Latin America. In automobiles, airplanes, chemicals, communications, machinery, and equipment to construct durable goods the Americans adopted what might be called a veritable crash program overturning all the old social habits and structures encrusted in the Latin American past.

Previous to the years of the Great Depression, the rise of American penetration had not as yet advanced so far as to change the basic situation in Latin America. Each country was still dependent on one or a few principal primary exports in order to buy needed imports. The prices of these exports on the world markets could and did vary suddenly and violently so that no Latin American government could really tell from year to year just what it could expect in terms of international trade and needed income. Such a situation has endured to the present and makes orderly planning and programming on the part of any administration extraordinarily difficult and even impossible.

How violently the market prices for primary products can fluctuate can be seen by the following typical examples:

a) Rubber: The New York spot prices in crude rubber in cents per pound varied from 17.6¢ in 1949 to 60.9¢ in 1951;
b) Sugar: The world price per pound in 1952 was 8 cents; in 1959, 2.6 cents; early 1963, 10 cents;

c) Coffee: New York spot prices per pound for Brazil coffee were 52.51¢ in 1950, 79.65¢ in 1954, 36.97¢ in 1960;

d) Cocoa beans: New York market price per pound averaged 57.7¢ in 1950 and 30.5¢ in 1957;

e) Copper: Electrolytic copper prices in New York per pound went from a peak of over 50¢ in 1955-56 to a low of 22¢ in 1958;

f) Tin: New York spot prices were $1.80 a pound in 1951 and 80¢ in 1954;

g) Zinc: This went from a high of 28¢ a pound in 1950 to a low of 8¢ in 1958;

h) Lead: Prices went from a high of about 18¢ a pound in 1952 to about 10¢ in 1960; etc.

(See World Commodity Year Book for examples.)

The advent of the world depression in the 1930's gave the first great shock to the international subdivision of labor that had been developed to such a point in all of Latin America. Previously, World War I had brought no more than an acceleration of the changes that had already been initiated by North American leadership before the war and only made stronger the hegemony of the United States. The great economic depression, however, affecting most seriously the very economy that was most dominant, that of the United States, and also equally that of Germany, Britain, and Western Europe, forced Latin Americans to make some efforts to change the very bad situation in which they found themselves.

This great world economic depression affected the Latin American and primary producing countries far more severely than it did even the industrial countries, hard hit as they were. Prices fell much more drastically in the market for Latin American products than they did in the markets for goods which Latin America had to import in order to live and work. Not only the volume of exports by Latin America fell but the prices for these goods fell even more sharply, reducing the terms of trade still further, and, with her rapidly increasing population, reduced the per capita capacity of Latin America to import to truly desperately low levels.

The great economic depression forced Latin America to try to industrialize itself in order to become more self-sufficient and thus reduce its expensive imports. This process was further developed during

World War II, when Latin America had such difficulty in getting needed supplies from the industrial countries then at war. In this effort such countries as Argentina, Brazil, and Mexico partially succeeded and laid the basis for the present trends in the same direction now operating in these countries.

One would have thought that with the advent of World War II the situation so unfavorable to Latin America as described above would have changed, what with the desperate need by the industrial countries at war for the raw materials which Latin America could produce. But this was not quite the case. Yes, Latin America could sell its raw materials and at high prices, but it lacked shipping and it could not get much finished goods in return, or when it did so, it was only at exorbitantly high prices. Thus Latin America had to retain her currency instead of getting capital goods with it, and had to wait until the war was over before it could cash in its savings for goods, now at even higher prices.

The following Tables 4A and 4B show the trends sufficiently. The index is based on the year 1937 levels as 100, fair enough since 1937 was the year when production approximately equaled the level it was before the start of the 1930 depression.

Table 4A
LATIN AMERICA: POPULATION AND EXPORTS
(INDEX BASED ON 1937 LEVEL AS 100)

Year	Population (millions)	Quantity Index of Export — Total	Quantity Index of Export — Per Capita	Export Price Index	
1929	104.3	108.7	124.1	113.2	Peak of Prosperity
1932	109.3	82.0	89.3	53.4	Depth of Depression
1937		100	100	100	
1940	126.5	85.7	80.6	85.5	Beginning of World War II
1946	142.6	111.6	93.2	171.3	End of World War II
1949	150.7	111.5	88.1	216.9	"Normal" Post-War

Notice that in the twenty years from 1929 to 1949 the population had jumped about 45%, or about 46 million, while the total exports remained at the end at about the same level as at the beginning. Thus the per capita exports fell greatly, about a third, from an index number of 124.1 to 88.1, or about 40% of the latter index number.

See how all during the Depression, and right up to the very start of World War II, the prices for imports to Latin America were relatively higher than the prices of the goods exported by Latin America.

Table 4B
LATIN AMERICA: TERMS OF TRADE AND CAPACITY TO IMPORT
(INDEX BASED ON 1937 LEVEL AS 100)

Year	Price Index		Terms of	Index Capacity to Import	
	Export	Import	Trade	Total	Per Capita
1929	113.2	117.0	90.7	105.1	120.0
1932	53.4	76.0	70.3	57.6	62.7
1937	100	100	100	100	100
1940	85.5	109.0	78.4	67.2	63.2
1946	171.3	163.0	108.1	117.3	99.9
1949	216.9	195.5	110.9	122.5	96.8

The expression "terms of trade" tells how much goods the exports of a country can buy in terms of imports (export price index divided by import price index). In 1940, for example, according to Table 4B, $100 worth of exports bought only $78.40 of 1937 imports. Thus, even if Latin America, in 1940, had exported the same volume of goods as in 1937, she would have received back in return only 78.4% of the 1937 total. But the fact is that in 1940 she could sell only 85.7% of the exports she sold in 1937 (because of disruption of trade during the war) and thus her total capacity to import (export price index multiplied by export quantity index) fell to only 67.2% of the 1937 level, while her per capita capacity to import fell even farther, to 63.2% of the 1937 level.

Table 4C
AMOUNT OF UNFINISHED PRODUCTS OBTAINABLE FOR A GIVEN QUANTITY OF
MANUFACTURED GOODS (ANNUAL AVERAGE OF 1876-1880 PERIOD
IS BASE LEVEL OF 100)

1911-13	85.8	1931-35	62.0
1921-25	67.3	1936-38	64.1
1926-30	73.3	1946-47	68.7

Abnormal war years left out.

Table 4C tells an interesting story. In later years, when the terms of trade became relatively more favorable to Latin America, during and after the War, the total volume of Latin American exports was only about the same as it was in 1929 (see Table 4A above) so that even with the higher prices the total income was not enough to match the growth of the population, with the result that the masses of people never could reach the level even of 1929 through foreign trade alone.

Immediately following the war, with the terrible destruction in Europe, Latin America had to shift her import buying as well as her export sales mainly to the United States. The United States, however, did not take this money spent by Latin America for U.S. goods and in return import Latin American goods. Instead, the policy of the United States consisted in making a large number of bilateral deals with countries throughout the world putting Latin American dollars to other uses. This meant a drop of U.S. imports from Latin America and this, in turn, meant that the total income received by Latin America was not great enough even to keep up with the much greater growth in population, not to speak of improvement in living standards.

The foreign trade situation for Latin America during and right after World War II could be summed up as follows:

1. The war called for a great increase in the exports of Latin America but reduced greatly her imports. The price of her exports rose, but not as high as that of her imports. But as Latin America could not import too much, she was able to save some money (for the military and politicians to steal and squander).

2. During and right after the war, Latin America was forced to deal mainly with the United States, both in exports and imports, on very unfavorable terms of trade.

3. After the war was over, the United States reduced her imports from Latin America, leaving Latin America unable to sell exports so as to buy either the necessary machinery and equipment that would bring her up-to-date or the consumers goods, especially durable goods, so badly needed.

It has already been stated that during the depression years the per capita income of Latin American masses had been very low. Latin America needed a far greater income not only to raise the standards of the people but to obtain necessary capital improvements. With the end of the war, however, while the terms of trade were indeed favorable to Latin America, the situation got no better, but actually worse because of the relative drop in Latin American exports due to cutting down of U.S. imports from Latin America. With a great increase in population not matched by an increase in exports equally as great, Latin America had an ever greater and hungrier labor force eager to work but no capital or markets to put it to work. It is during this time, to make matters worse, that Brazil had to destroy huge stocks of surplus coffee and Argentina to burn several grain harvests as furnace fuel. At no time was export volume high at the same moment when terms of trade were very favorable and imports high.

Immediately after World War II dependence of Latin America upon the United States grew steadily greater. Before the war, in 1939, the United States had taken 57% of Latin American exports to the industrial countries of North America and Western Europe. After the war this percentage rose to 68%.

In an effort to make itself less dependent on the United States, Latin America had to try desperately for increased capital imports. It spent its war savings, it went heavily into debt, it devalued its currencies, it did all it could to attract U.S. capital. In this it had some success, but it also succeeded in becoming more controlled by U.S. interests which were not always the same as the interests of the country receiving the capital. During this very period when it was starved for funds, for example, in the eight years from 1945 to 1952 inclusive, Latin America had to pay out in profit and interest alone to foreign, mostly U.S., capitalists the enormous sum of almost $6 billion! This sum was considerably more than the value of all the exports Latin America had sold in all the World War II years to the United States!

To this must be added the unceasing unfavorable balance of payments which, thanks to the relatively decreasing flow of exports, the unfavorable terms of trade and the outflow of investment and credit returns, caused Latin America (except Venezuela which depended on petroleum exports) to remain annually in the red and pay out more money than she received. To stave off bankruptcy, at least temporarily, Latin America had to place herself in the hands of U.S. bankers and investors.

From various issues of the *Survey of Current Business* published by the U.S. Department of Commerce we learn that the advance of U.S. direct investments to Latin America was $3 billion in 1946, $4.6 billion in 1950 and $9.3 billion by 1960, or a rise of over 300%. It must not be supposed, however, that this was the result of some single special drive on the part of U.S. investors. On the contrary the same sources show that during the same time the rise of U.S. direct investments to Africa was 600%, to Asia 450%, to Japan and Oceania and South Africa 750%, to Europe over 600% and to Canada over 400%, so that actually Latin America was the least favored in respect to rate of increase.

As viewed by the Latin American governments themselves it would seem that the task of maintaining a viable economy would depend on what success could be achieved in realizing the following goals:

1. Elimination of unnecessary imports so as to reverse the unfavorable balance of trade. The direct flight of gold and capital also had to to be prohibited.

2. Adequate supply of domestically produced goods, substitutes for the reduced imports. Production had to be greatly expanded not only because the population was expanding but also because needs for goods were rising with industrialization.

3. Expansion of exports so as to obtain more money with which to pay off debts and to import needed items. This called for an increase in both production and in productivity by means of improved machinery and methods.

4. Diversification of exports removing the complete dependence on one or a few items with the resultant rigidity and inflexibility in world markets. This meant a shift in exports to manufactured goods, where possible, as well as diversification of primary goods. Aid to domestic manufacturers implied protective tariff rates. Emphasis on manufactures also led to special inducements offered to outside capitalists to come in and industrialize the countries involved. (This last, however, was to become a two-edged sword, as will be seen.)

5. Development of a domestic capital goods industry that would put the Latin American country on the road to self-sufficiency in capital investment without necessary recourse to industrial countries abroad. This called for a rapid basic heavy industrialization of the country.

During the Depression in the 1930's, with the drastic fall in trade, some of the larger Latin American countries—Brazil, Mexico, and Argentina—began to develop their lighter consumer goods industries, such as textiles, food processing, shoes, and clothing. As the scarcity of consumers goods persisted during World War II, this domestic manufacturing trend was continued, although with the developing of metal and mineral mining, there also arose in the larger countries mentioned the beginning of a durable goods industry as well.

These trends found their reverberations in the political superstructures of the larger countries, illustrated by the rule of Perón in Argentina, and Vargas in Brazil, and also leading to the victory of the policies of Cárdenas in Mexico. There was a fear for a while that Perón and Vargas, following the autarchic policies of Hitler, Mussolini, and Franco would get too big for U.S. comfort, but with the defeat of the Axis Powers and the complete ruin and exhaustion of Western Europe the United States remained in full control of the situation.

It was not to the interests of the United States as a whole to stop the industrialization process now entering into full swing in the larger Latin American countries, since such industrialization provided a tremendous outlet for the machinery, equipment, and capital producing industries in the United States as well as a fertile field for financial investment.

What the United States had to do was to so direct the process so that it would operate primarily not for the country in which the capital was invested but for the investors of that capital. Again, just as in the 19th century the export-import free trade was designed not primarily to benefit Latin America but the exporting-importing industrial countries, so now in the 20th century the industrialization process was concerned not primarily to help Latin America but to provide a suction pump with which to drain that region dry of as much surplus value and profits as possible. This was done by means of U.S. government loans and grants to win over Latin American rulers, especially their military leaders, and by means of private investments, loans, credits, services, etc.

This was the basic trend that lasted for the entire decade of the 1950's. Only now is it being challenged with a dramatic turn away from the lead of the United States, manifested most by revolutionary Cuba, toward a new constellation of powers that promises a better way out.

The situation prevailing for Latin America in the 1950's could be summed up as follows:

1. In general production, the larger countries in Latin America began to grow at a very fast rate, not production for exports but production for increased domestic use to replace imports and to meet constantly increasing domestic demand, due to the great increase in population and the growth of a domestic market hitherto unknown under previous primitive methods. Thus, as a corollary to the above, the growth of manufactured products was far greater than the growth of agricultural production. Towards the latter part of the decade, the

growth of producers goods and capital goods grew even faster than manufactured goods as a whole.

The following tables illustrate the situation described above:

Table 5

GROWTH IN PRODUCTION: LATIN AMERICA COMPARED WITH INDUSTRIAL COUNTRIES 1958 (INDEX LEVEL OF 1950 IS BASE OF 100)

	Industrial Countries	Latin America
Gross Production	130	138
Industrial Output	133	. . .
Gross Production Per Capita	116	114

Table 6

WORLD COMPARISON: INDEX OF GROWTH IN MANUFACTURING OUTPUT (1950 LEVEL IS BASE OF 100)

	Manufacturing Output	Percent Distribution 1950	Percent Distribution 1960
Underdeveloped areas, including Latin Am.	189	15%	17%
Developed areas, including United States	165	85	83

Note: 1950 base in manufacturing output was relatively very low for underdeveloped areas as compared to developed areas.

Table 7

LATIN AMERICA (EXCL. VENEZUELA & CUBA): ECONOMIC GROWTH (ANNUAL AVERAGE OF 1945-49 PERIOD AS 100)

	Agro-pec*	Mining	Manufacturing	Total
1936-40	86.3	60.8	57.9	69.7
1941-44	95.0	69.1	73.7	80.4
1945-49	100	100	100	100
1950-54	114.8	138.1	129.8	125.2
1955-60	141.6	202.5	181.1	162.1

* agriculture and cattle-raising.

Table 8

LATIN AMERICA (EXCL. VENEZUELA & CUBA): CHANGES IN ECONOMIC STRUCTURE AS % OF GROSS PRODUCTION

	Agro-pec*	Mining	Manufacturing
1936-40	30.7%	4.1%	15.0%
1941-44	29.3		16.6
1945-49	24.8		18.1
1950-54	22.7		18.8
1955-60	21.6	5.9	20.2

* agriculture and cattle-raising.

Table 9 shows that the more prosperous the Latin American country appears, the greater the percentage of industrial production as compared to agricultural production, and the greater the percentage of manufacturing products.

Table 9

LATIN AMERICAN COUNTRIES: AVERAGE INDUSTRIAL DISTRIBUTION OF GROSS
DOMESTIC PRODUCT IN PERCENTAGE
(ANNUAL AVERAGES OF 1950-1959 AND 1958-1959 TAKEN AS BASE)

Underdeveloped countries	Industrial Production			Primary		
	Total	Mfg	Basic*	Con-structn	Pro-ductn†	Serv-ices
Category I‡	20%	11%	5%	4%	47%	33%
Category II‡	25	14	6	5	30	45
Category III‡	26¶	16	6	5	30	46
Category IV‡	28	17	6	5	27	46
Industrial Countries§	49	32	11	6	13	37
Brazil (II)	34	24	8	2	26	40
Mexico (III)	28	21	5	2	25	48
Venezuela (IV)	23	10	6	7	38	39
Chile (IV)	26	18	6	2	21	53
Argentina (IV)	28	22	-6-		20	52

DISTRIBUTION OF ECONOMICALLY ACTIVE POPULATION: AVERAGE RECENT CENSUS

							Unallo-cated
I	13%¶	9%	3%	2%	69%	15%	2%
II	17	11	3	3	64	17	2
III	21	13	4	4	50	25	4
IV	29¶	18	6	4	31	36	4
Industrial Countries	44¶	29	7	7	19	35	2

* Basic production includes transportation, storage, communications, electricity, gas, water.
† Primary production includes agriculture and mining.
‡ Category I includes countries with less than $125 per capita production
  Category II includes countries with per capita production from $125 to $249 inc.
  Category III includes countries with per capita production of $250-$374
  Category IV includes countries with production of $375 and more
§ Industrial countries are those with per capita production of more than $800.
¶ Rounded to nearest whole number and thus not equal to sum of parts.
Notice that Brazil is far above its category rating and shows the tremendous gap that exists between its industrial and its general agricultural production.

It is estimated that the domestic production of import substitutes during merely the period from 1950-51 to 1958-59 created a net savings in foreign exchange in Argentina of $184 million, in Brazil of $57 million, and in Mexico of $34 million.

2. Though the Latin American larger countries were becoming industrialized, their exports still remained primary, in large part agricultural, and agricultural production did not improve very much. As the Subcommittee on Inter-American Economic Relationships of the Joint Economic Committee, Congress of the United States, declared in 1962: The production per agricultural worker in the U.S. in terms of wheat units in 1954-55 was 4,220, as against 450 in Brazil, and 250 in Peru. The agricultural methods employed today in much of Latin America differed little, if at all, from those employed in the colonial period. "A low level of technology prevails. Large numbers of workers paid low wages are used rather than machines. Innovations are rare; tradition delimits the few choices available to the rural population."

The same Report goes on to state that the large holdings produce well below their potential and there is much mere subsistence agriculture. "Frequently the best land is used for the landowners' crops and the workers left to grow their own food on the poorer or more remote parts of the property." Absentee landlordism is the general rule on the big estates.

In Colombia, for example, agriculture is not growing because less than 10% of the agricultural land is cultivated, most of the best land lying idle or being used as cattle runs on very large estates in the hands of absentee landlords. Although it can raise wheat and cotton, bananas and sugar, it depends on one export crop—coffee. So it was with Cuba before the Revolution, where sugar was the chief export. In Brazil the per capita agricultural production fell, as measured by 1950 cruzeiros, from 1,298 in the period 1930-34 to 1,173 in 1956, while the percentage of this production which went for exchange rather than for consumption fell from 60% in the earlier period to 38% in 1956.

3. Exports did not grow in volume in some of the more important countries and there was not much greater diversification. Terms of trade continued to deteriorate in foreign exchanges as did the balance of trade. For example, between 1953 and 1957, world exports jumped from $73.3 billion to $98.8 billion, while the exports of Latin America remained practically stationary. Even when the mass of Latin American exports grew, the unit prices fell so drastically that the total value of the exports practically remained stationary, as can be seen from the following Table 10:

Table 10
INDEXES OF LATIN AMERICAN TRADE: (1955 LEVEL IS 100)

	Quantum of Exports	Unit Value of Exports	Total Value of Exports
1950	88	93	82*
1951	86	114	98
1954	93	106	98
1955	100	100	100
1956	108	98	106
1957	110	98	108
1958	112	91	102
1959	122	85	103

*Column three is the product of columns one and two multiplied as percentages.

That the Latin American export prices fell in relation to the export prices not only of the industrial world but of other primary producing countries can be seen by Table 11:

Table 11
WORLD EXPORT PRICES (1953 LEVEL IS BASE OF 100)

	1955	1956	1957	1958
Industrial Countries	99	102	105	104
Latin America (excluding petroleum)	97	95	95	87
Terms of Trade				
Primary producing/industrial countries	101	97	94	92
Latin America/industrial countries	98	93	90	85
Latin American Import Prices	102	116	113	115

4. Foreign investments, loans, grants, services, etc., continued to advance at a great rate, together with the repatriation of capital, remittances of amortization of capital, royalties, interests, dividends, incomes, and similar items. The net result was that added to a negative balance of trade was a great negative balance of financial payments in current accounts leading to a staggering negative balance of over-all payments. This is amply shown in the following tables which bear close study:

Table 12A
LATIN AMERICA (EXCL. VENEZUELA & CUBA): BALANCE OF PAYMENTS
(ANNUAL AVERAGES IN $ MILLION)

	1951-1955	1956-1960
Current Income of Foreign Exchange	$6372.5	$6926.6
Imports	− 6084.2	− 7054.8
Balance of Trade	288.3	− 128.2
Payments Abroad	− 461.1	− 577.0
Other Net Payments	− 452.3	− 250.3
Balance on Current Account	− 625.1	− 955.5

Thus, in the 10-year period, 1951 through 1960, Latin America had to meet foreign negative balances totalling close to $8 billion, payable in current dollars! The term "payments abroad" includes amortization or repatriation of foreign capital, income, and payment of interest on long-term loans, all representing direct or other investments. The following Table 12B gives this break-down.

Table 12B
LATIN AMERICA (EXCL. VENEZUELA & CUBA): PAYMENTS ABROAD
(ANNUAL AVERAGES IN $ MILLION)

	1951-55	1956-60	1961
Payments Abroad (Direct and Other Inv.)	−$461.1	−$577.0	−$793.0
Returns of Foreign Capital Income	− 364.5	− 387.9	− 503.5
Interest on Loans	− 96.6	− 189.1	− 289.6

How did Latin America manage to meet its obligations and pay its negative foreign balances? This was done by means of new loans and credits and new foreign investments as the following Table 13A shows:

Table 13A
LATIN AMERICA (EXCL. VENEZUELA & CUBA): BALANCE OF PAYMENTS
(ANNUAL AVERAGES IN FIXED 1950 $ MILLION)

	1945-49	1950-54	1955-60
Exports and Services	$7000	$7070	$9060
Imports of Goods and Services	− 5140	− 6440	− 7670
Balance of Trade	1860	630	1390
Payment to income factors abroad		− 825	− 1020
Balance of Payments		− 195	370
Net Foreign Financing		400	915
Losses in Terms of Trade in relation to 1950	− 1330	− 190	− 1280

(Note: Table 13A is not to be compared with Table 12 above, since the latter table is not in current but in 1950 dollars)

The last line in the above table shows that over and above the actual drains that foreign capital returns made on Latin America, the disadvantageous terms of trade took away vast sums of money that otherwise Latin America could have used for its upbuilding. The disadvantageous terms of trade reduced the purchasing power of Latin American exports by an average of a little over $1.3 billion a year during the ten-year period covered by the years 1945-49 and 1955-60, or a total of $13 billion!

A still more recent table is the following:

Table 13B

BALANCE OF PAYMENTS OF LATIN AMERICA WITH THE UNITED STATES
IN 1960 AND 1961 ($ MILLION)

	1960	1961
Exports to U.S.	$3619	$3299
Imports from U.S.	− 3522	− 3453
Balance of Trade	97	− 154
Service Deficit	− 717	− 825
Goods and Service Deficit	− 620	− 979
Private Capital Transfers from U.S.	597	463
Transfers and Loans from U.S. Government	280	864
Balance of Payments	$ 257	$ 348

We have seen above that Latin America can meet its obligations only by means of aid from foreign capital. This foreign capital inflow takes two distinct forms: a) non-compensatory capital in the form of direct and portfolio investments which are not be repaid as loans; b) compensatory capital in the form of private and public loans which are to be repaid at the end of the stated period of the loan. While these loans and investments stave off Latin American bankruptcy for the moment, they are designed to bring these countries more and more under the control of foreign capital.

The next two tables furnish some data on this matter.

Table 14A

LATIN AMERICA (EXCL. VENEZUELA & CUBA): CAPITAL MOVEMENTS
(ANNUAL AVERAGES IN $ MILLION)

	1951-55	1956-60	1961
Net Non-Compensatory Capital	$432.7	$979.2	$1494.3
Net Compensatory Capital			
Deferred import payments & loan repayments	131.2	118.8	164.1
Net Official Monetary Reserves	96.2	66.2	149.8
Totals*	$625.1	$955.5	$1486.3

* Note that the Totals include an allowance for errors and omissions, which allowance is very large due to the widespread cheating and hiding of foreign capital movements.

The United Nations Economic Commission for Latin America at its recent international conference held in the Spring of 1963 at Mar del Plata, Argentina, has furnished us with a summary balance sheet (page 31) for Latin America as a whole, exclusive of Venezuela and Cuba; showing that region's purchasing power or total capacity to import.

Thus, despite the vastly increased repayments on investments and

Table 14B
LATIN AMERICA (EXCL. VENEZUELA & CUBA): NET NON-COMPENSATORY
CAPITAL MOVEMENT (ANNUAL AVERAGES IN $ MILLION)

	1951-55	1956-60	1961
Direct Investments	$252.0	$543.1	$ 352.3
Total Net Long Term Loans	94.5	320.9	998.2
Private Loans	49.0	181.7	370.8
Public Loans	45.5	139.2	627.4
Official Donations	29.0	98.7	108.4
Other	57.2	16.5	35.4
Total	$432.7	$979.2	$1494.3

Table 15
LATIN AMERICA (EXCL. VENEZUELA & CUBA): TOTAL CAPACITY TO IMPORT
(ANNUAL AVERAGES IN $ MILLION)

	1951-55	1956-60	1961
Exports	$5455.3	$5519.8	$5603.0
Net Non-Compensatory Capital	432.7	979.2	1494.3
Investment payments	− 461.1	− 577.0	− 793.0
Payments on Deferred imports and loans	− 127.1	− 172.3	− 192.0
Sub-total	5299.8	5749.7	6112.3
Net errors and omissions	− 35.0	− 208.6	− 321.9
	5264.8	5541.1	5790.5
Imports and net services	− 5619.3	− 5898.3	− 6296.3
Balance	−$ 354.5	−$ 357.2	−$ 505.8

loans, Latin America plunges ever deeper into debt and with greater negative balances. Either imports must be drastically curtailed, and this would greatly hurt Latin America's economic development, or exports must be sharply increased, and this seems very unlikely of realization. Otherwise ever-increasing inflows of capital for investments and loans must cover the deficits—inflows which in turn lead only to greater payments of interest and repayments of the capital invested and loaned—if Latin America is to remain solvent for the moment. Sooner or later, bankruptcy and its political counterpart, social revolution, must burst onto the historic scene. Latin America is living on borrowed time bought by imperialism.

The defeat of the autarchic regimes of Hitler and Mussolini during the War by no means ended the drive for self-sufficiency on the part of industrial powers. The struggle now shifted to one between the United States and the Soviet Union. World War II had shown the United

States the great need for materials existing outside its borders and the great military and economic urgency for it to stock up on such strategic materials. This nation, therefore, did its utmost to stimulate the production of such primary strategic materials and to control them all over the world—in Latin America, in Asia, and in Africa. Once these stockpiles were safely stored within the borders of the United States, there could be drastic cut-backs in the production of such materials without any military harm to the United States, no matter how low prices would then fall on the international markets and how damaging such results might become to the Latin American and other countries that had been called on to extend unduly their production in such primary strategic goods. Later on, as the character of the potential war with the Soviet Union changed to that of a nuclear conflict calling for much less of such strategic materials than had originally been planned for, the excess stuff collected could be ruthlessly dumped on the market by the United States and her partner Great Britain.

Since it was necessary to aid an exhausted industrial Europe ruined by the War and at the same time contain communism in Asia, the United States found itself committed to purchase large supplies not only in South America but also in Asia—the Philippines, Malaya, Indonesia, Ceylon, India—as well as in the European African colonies. Later, when Europe had recovered, after the success of the Marshall Plan operation, these Asian and African former colonies were to be further developed to produce goods that Latin America had previously sold to Europe and under special terms that would prevent Latin America from competing.

The great unique advantage that the United States had over all previous world capitalist leaders was that she was not only the foremost industrial power but also the foremost prime material producing nation, with an enormous surplus of agricultural goods on hand that could destroy the competition coming from other primary producing countries, including Latin America. The United States now took full advantage of this agricultural superiority by seeing to it that indebted Europe bought agricultural products from her in exchange for its rehabilitation grants and loans, and that countries with strategic materials needed by the United States would exchange them for her surplus agricultural commodities. Thus the agricultural markets were still further disrupted, to the great detriment especially of Latin America. When the stockpiling deals had been successfully accomplished, by about 1957, the United States was ready to use her huge agricultural plethora to dominate the colonial world through capital investment.

By 1958, U.S. direct investments in Latin America totalled $8.7 billion, about as much as U.S. investment in Canada, and more than U.S. investments in all the rest of the world put together. Table 16A shows the spread of these investments; Table 16B gives the distribution of these investments among the principal Latin American countries.

Table 16A
DISTRIBUTION OF U.S. DIRECT INVESTMENTS IN LATIN AMERICA
BY INDUSTRIAL SECTORS: 1958 ($ BILLION)

Mining	$1.3	Public utility	$1.2
Petroleum	3.0	Trade	.6
Manufacturing	1.7	Other (agriculture, etc.)	.9

Table 16B
DISTRIBUTION OF U.S. DIRECT INVESTMENTS IN LATIN AMERICA
BY PRINCIPAL COUNTRIES: 1958 ($ BILLION)

Venezuela	$2.86	(of which $2.3 in petroleum)
Brazil	1.35	(of which $.7 in manufacturing)
Cuba	.86	(of which $.26 in agriculture, etc.)
Mexico	.78	(of which $.2 in mining and $.36 in manufacturing)
Chile	.74	(of which $.48 in mining)
Agentina	.52	(of which $.26 in manufacturing)
Peru	.43	(of which $.2 in mining)
Central America	.74	(of which $.55 in agriculture, etc.)

It is important to note that besides these direct investments there were portfolio investments and short-term loans and credits easily doubling the total given in the tables above.

By means of these strategic investments the United States was able to insure its stockpiling, conserve its own resources, give optimum direction to its surplus goods and capital, and keep the Soviet Union out of Latin America. In addition, in return for its investments there, the United States in 1959 alone recorded a net total of $700 in income receipts. What the unrecorded total was can only be surmised.

In addition to these private capital investments, the United States government gave direct grants to Latin American countries that totaled in 1959 more than half a billion dollars, distributed as follows:

Table 17A

TOTAL U.S. DIRECT GRANTS TO CERTAIN LATIN AMERICAN
COUNTRIES: 1959 ($ MILLION)

Bolivia	$134
Mexico	111
Guatemala	84
Brazil	54
Peru	45
Chile	42
Haiti	38
Total 7 countries	$511

On March 12, 1963, the U.S. press carried an Associated Press dispatch from Washington giving the final version of a report by the Agency for International Aid (AID) to President Kennedy, in which it is stated that from July 1, 1945, through mid-1962, total U.S. foreign aid had reached a total of $99.7 billion. Of this total $66.6 billion was called economic aid, of which $42.7 billion was in the form of outright grants. Of the $31 billion in military assistance practically all was given in the form of grants.

The report gave the following overall totals for Latin American countries, rounded to the nearest $ million (Table 17B):

Table 17B

U.S. AID TO LATIN AMERICAN COUNTRIES, JULY 1945 THROUGH
MID-JULY 1962 ($ MILLION)

Brazil	$1,953
Mexico	767
Chile	738
Argentina	641
Peru	471
Colombia	408
Venezuela	274
Bolivia	258
Guatemala	163
Ecuador	138
Haiti	101
Panama	101
Costa Rica	99
Uruguay	88
Nicaragua	69
Paraguay	59
Cuba	53
Dominican Repub.	45
Honduras	45
El Salvador	41
Total	$6,512

By the end of 1957, the stockpile program of the United States had been pretty well completed. The $9.3 billion target for the strategic and critical materials stockpile had been realized up to $5.7 billion worth by December 1957, when it was decided that nuclear warfare needed less stockpiling and that the maximum stockpiles should be planned not for five years' but for three years' use.

The United States supplemental stockpile of $400 million was realized in January, 1958, by materials obtained through sale of agricultural surpluses. Also realized was $750 million worth of inventories procured under the Defense Production Act, apart from the $1,750 million in Government commitments under contract. A stockpile of $200 million, mainly medicine for survival and relief of communities, had been secured for the Federal Civilian Defense Administration. There was also a machine tool inventory of $3.5 billion, inventories of equipment and supplies for the military, a national industrial reserve of plant and equipment, and big stocks of fissionable materials on behalf of the Atomic Energy Commission. Thus the margin left for further purchases from Latin America was quite small.

Furthermore, fearing this surplus, the United Kingdom out of its own stockpile dumped on the market between 1955 and 1957 100,000 tons of copper, 30,000 tons of lead, 100,000 bales of wool, and after 1957, 20,000 more tons of lead and 27,000 tons of zinc. All this, of course, was a further blow to Latin American exports.

The biggest blows of all, however, were still to come. By 1957 the United States had built up enormous agricultural stockpiles. In cotton the stockpiles had jumped from 3.7 million bales in January, 1950, to 6.5 million bales by the beginning of 1957; in wheat during the same period the increase was from 155 million bushels to 820 million bushels, and the value of the cost of the agricultural inventory, including crop loans outstanding, had risen from $2.4 billion to $7.4 billion.

In addition to these constantly growing agricultural stocks, the United States, in order to help farmers sell their stuff abroad in competition with such countries as Argentina, provided price supports for 20 major crops. In 1956 these directly supported crops had a cash value of $6.8 billion; other crops supported by import regulations had a total of $7.5 billion, while the total value of farm crops supported in one way or another by the U.S. Government amounted to the grand total of $31 billion! Of course, all these supports only created greater surpluses for the United States to dispose of and for Latin American competition to meet. Naturally, Latin American exports, export prices, and terms of trade fell. With Latin American negative trade balances increasing and debts rising, imports to Latin America were curtailed and, helpless to resist, Latin America fell more and more into the hands of the United States.

First the United States offered supplies to foreign governments all over the world in return for strategic material stockpiling—at the expense of Latin America. Then, the United States made grants of surpluses to distressed countries, thus seriously affecting world prices and Latin American markets. Third, the United States sold its surplus goods to foreign countries under Public Law 480 for local currencies, which it loaned back to those countries in such a way as to strengthen the domination of U.S. interests within those countries.

These "promoted" U.S. exports gradually increased in value from $500 million in 1952/53 to $2 billion in 1956/57, or to 43% of total U.S. agricultural exports. Apart from wheat and cotton, affecting most Argentina, Brazil, and Mexico, many other agricultural commodities were sold by the United States under government programs: some below cost (rice, barley, maize, dairy products), and others at cost (tobacco, fats, oils, and in some cases meat, fruit, and vegetables). All this had an adverse effect on market prices.

Says the Report of the Joint Economic Committee, Congress of the United States, in 1962: "For the period July 1954 through June 1961, Government financed programs supported $9.5 billion out of a total of $28.5 billion in agricultural exports. In that period the total agricultural exports outside specified Government-financed programs of $19 billion include many products subsidized domestically. Additionally, many transactions not directly financed by Government receive government assistance in the form of (1) extension of credits for relatively short periods, (2) sales of Government-owned commodities at less than domestic prices, or (3) export payments in cash or kind." The Report did complain that by forcing down the world export prices, for example, in cotton, American textile manufacturers were very much hurt, since foreign textile manufacturers could purchase cotton 8½ cents a pound cheaper than domestic manufacturers had to pay.

Table 18 gives the products and amounts in dollar values which had been dispensed by the United States under its Public Law 480 by December, 1957:

Table 18
TOTAL U.S. DISPOSALS UNDER PUBLIC LAW 480
BY DEC. 1957 ($ MILLION-ROUNDED)

Wheat	$ 852
Other Grain	300
Cotton	426
Miscellaneous	476
Total	$2054

No wonder that by 1957 the first really world-wide recession since the great Depression in the 1930's struck the economic world. In this regard the Economic Commission for Latin America in its Economic Survey issued for 1958 stated: "Over the past four years, the demand for many raw materials and foodstuffs has grown comparatively slowly, in many cases more slowly than the capacity for supplying this demand, and this explains the general and chronic weakness of Latin American export markets. So the recession of 1958 came at a time when commodity markets had already been undermined, and the income of primary producers fell sharply. This was the first post-war recession which justified the adjective 'world-wide.' "

Aggressive world-wide dumping of agricultural products is only one of the methods by which the U.S. economy tries to prevent a new depression and to maintain its production levels. Heavy import taxes and quotas are other means. The United States maintains protective duties on a number of products competing with those of Latin America including sugar, cotton, wool, tobacco, edible nuts, meat, linseed oil, canned fish, wheat, hides, and skins. The United States also protects its domestic minerals industry, particularly petroleum, lead, zinc, and copper.

In cases where the United States is a net importer, although a large producer as well, as for example in the case of wool, sugar, edible nuts and linseed oil, it uses the mechanisms of custom duties, subsidies to local producers (wool), and import quotas. Where the United States is a substantial net exporter (cotton and wheat), as we have seen it uses Public Law 480 and sells below artificially maintained domestic support prices, to the detriment also of American manufacturers who have to compete world-wide. Lead, zinc, and petroleum are subject to import quotas as well as customs duties. Those on lead and zinc, imposed September, 1958, limit their imports to 80% of the annual 1953-57 average. Also mandatory quotas were imposed on petroleum imports in March, 1959. Even when no such quotas were imposed, the U.S. oil companies preferred to import the cheaper oil from the Middle East to that of Venezuela, which is now in a great slump. Mexican and Canadian overland imports of oil have been exempted from the import quotas. Also custom duties have been placed on several other minerals imported from Latin America, including manganese, mercury, bauxite, and tungsten.

The United States, in its search for self-sufficiency and protection, is not the only country discriminating against the products of Latin America. The United Kingdom, ever since the last great depression in the 1930's, created a favored tariff system for its Commonwealth countries and for its former African and Asian colonies. If this favored system breaks down, it will be only to give way to a still more discriminatory system favored by the European Common Market.

Western Europe also has had discriminatory restrictions against Latin America affecting wheat, meat, bananas, coffee, cocoa, sugar, and tobacco. There are several motivations for this discrimination. First, Western Europe, especially now that it has organized itself into the European Economic Community, wants to become self-sufficient and to protect the stuff that its farmers are producing, such as wheat, meat, and sugar. Then there are fine revenues to be collected on such items as bananas, coffee, cocoa, and tobacco, running as high as 16% ad valorem on coffee, 20% on bananas, etc. Finally, there are the former African (or Asian) colonies of France, or of Belgium, or of Holland, to be favored so that a new self-sufficient world force can be built up around this European Economic Community. This means that African products in competition with those from Latin America will be favored as much as possible. Already Latin America is beginning to feel the blows of this Common Market and has bitterly protested this discrimination against the Western Hemisphere at various meetings.

Even before the Common Market had been organized, Latin America, in such products as coffee, for example, had felt the competition of post-War Africa and Asia. Before the War, Latin America's share of world production in coffee had been 90%; by 1957 it had become only 75.9%.

The competitive struggle is fierce in other products. In antimony it is West Africa versus Mexico, Peru, and Bolivia; in copper, Chile stands against Rhodesia; in manganese Brazil faces South Africa; in rubber Brazil has to meet Malaysia and Indonesia as well as Liberia; in cacao it is Brazil and Ecuador versus Ghana and the Cameroons; in coffee Brazil, Colombia, and Central America compete against Ethiopia and Madagascar; in cotton North Africa faces Mexico and Brazil, etc.

There is every indication that, thanks to Common Market favoritism, the share of Latin America's exports to that region will steadily and sharply diminish in favor of the African-Asian former colonies. According to the Common Market Pact arranged with 18 African countries—Burundi, Cameroun, Central African Republic, Chad, Congo (Brazzaville), Congo (Leopoldville), Dahomey, Gabon, Ivory Coast, Madagascar, Mali, Mauratania, Niger, Rivanda, Senegal, Somalia, Togo, and Upper Volta—African products will come into the Common Market duty free, European business will eventually operate in the African countries on a par with native business and a total of $730 million in European government aid during the five years of the Pact will be given. It is expected that the Pact will be ratified by all parties by January, 1964.

As has been emphasized, Latin American trade is principally with industrial countries (U.S.A. and Western Europe). What happens to the economies of these countries, particularly to U.S. economy, is of vital importance to all of Latin America.

Now since the end of World War II the United States has seen four different recessions. The first of these recessions occurred in 1948-49, before the Korean War which liquidated it; the second, in 1953-54 after Korea; the third in 1957-58; the fourth in 1960-61. The following features of these recessions should be noted:

1. The intervals between the recessions have been ever shorter. From the downturn in 1948 to the downturn in 1953 the period was 45 months; from the downturn in 1953 to that in 1957 it was 35 months; from the downturn in 1957 to that in 1960 the period was 25 months.

2. In each case when the economy did recover from the recession levels, however, the recovery levels were not very high, not high enough to make up for the losses incurred during the recession, so that the combined result was a net loss.

3. Each of the recessions was not too prolonged, however. The Ko-

rean War ended the 1949 recession; the 1953 recession was over in 13 months, the other two in about 8 months each.

4. During the recovery following the termination of each recession, the number of unemployed constantly reached a higher level than during the preceding period of recovery. U.S. unemployment in the peak quarter year of production following the termination of each recession was as follows:

a) In the second quarter of 1953 the unemployed was 2.3% of the civilian labor force and the average duration of unemployment was 8.3 weeks;

b) In the third quarter of 1957 the unemployed was 3.9% of the civilian labor force and the average duration of unemployment was 9.8 weeks;

c) In the second quarter of 1960 the unemployed was 5.4% of the civilian labor force and the average duration of unemployment was 12.5 weeks.

Tables 19A and 19B give pertinent figures on the unemployed in the United States and in Canada. The most recent estimates given by the U.S. government (February 1963) show unemployment to be considerably above 6%.

Table 19A

U.S. AND CANADA:

UNEMPLOYED AS % OF CIVILIAN LABOR FORCE

	U.S.	Canada	
1958	6.8%	7.1%	
1959	5.5	6.0	
1960	5.2	6.6	(first half)
1960	6.0	7.5	(second half)

Table 19B

U.S. UNEMPLOYMENT RATES BY

CATEGORIES OF WORKERS: 1961

unskilled laborers	12.5%
craftsmen	5.3
clerical force	3.8
sales force	3.7

The fact of the matter is that ever since 1957 the economy of the United States can be said to be in a state of stagnancy. The total rate of growth has averaged only about 2% a year for the past five years (as in the United Kingdom), not much above the growth in population. The United States, in the main, has met these recessions by cut-backs in inventories, and when imports were not reduced, by a drain of gold. Despite all efforts to terminate this drain, the net outflow still goes on and shows little signs of being able to be stopped without great difficulties in other fields accruing.

Of course these slumps in U.S. economy and their reverberations throughout other parts of the world have had adverse effects on Latin American exports both as to volume and especially as to price. Thanks to the 1957 recession, for example, Latin American exports fell from $5.8 billion to $5.4 billion and by 1960 and 1961 had just about recovered the level of 1956. Export prices, however, given 1953 as a base, had fallen from index level of 95 to that of 87 in 1958 and by 1961 were still only 95% of the 1958 level.

According to the *Commodity Year Book* of 1961 giving New York market prices, spot prices for Brazil coffee were 58.5¢ a pound in 1957 but only 36.97¢ in 1960; average prices for cocoa beans were 30.5¢ a pound in 1957 and only 20.8¢ in March 1961; spot prices for electrolytic copper per pound were 41.88¢ in 1956 and 28.82¢ in 1961 (March); lead had sunk to its low point of 10¢ a pound in 1960; tin was a little over its lowest point of 80¢ a pound and was about $1.00 a pound in 1960; similarly zinc had recovered somewhat from its lowest price and was 11¢ a pound, as copper also had done, moving from its low of 22¢ a pound to 30¢ in 1960. All these metal prices were far below their high level marks reached a few years previously.

Table 20

WORLD PRICE INDEX LEVELS OF STATED COMMODITIES (1955 EQUALS 100)

	1950	1953	1960	1962 (1st quarter)
Sugar	154	105	96	75
Bananas	97	98	86	—
Coffee	88	101	64	60
Cacao	81	96	74	59
Meat	—	87	100	103
Maize	95	109	83	81
Wheat	103	106	92	96
Hides	178	137	118	—
Wool	134	108	82	—
Linseed Oil	130	96	103	—
Zinc	113	89	109	76
Copper	57	77	86	66
Lead	88	89	79	57
Tin	101	101	106	—

There exists now, however, a qualitatively different sort of situation in Latin America than had existed before World War II. This different situation is marked by the following factors:

1. The industrialization process of the more developed countries, such as Argentina, Brazil, Chile, Mexico, and Venezuela can not be stopped or even slowed down without great danger. Although these countries still export in the main primary materials only, nevertheless already, except for Brazil, only a minority of the active working force works in agricultural occupations as shown in the following table:

Table 21A
LATIN AMERICAN COUNTRIES:
AGRICULTURAL LABOR AS % OF TOTAL LABOR FORCE: 1950

Argentina	25%
Brazil	61
Chile	30
Uruguay	22
Venezuela	41
Latin America as a whole	53

(Note: Compare this with Table 9 given above which shows that primary production in Argentina represented only 20% of total production and in Brazil only 26%)

As part of the industrialization process people are flocking to the cities in Latin America. In 1925 urbanization there averaged 33%; by 1955 it was 44%. The latest estimates show 63% of the Argentine population to be urban, 58% of the Cuban, 52% of the Chilean, 50% of the Uruguayan. The cities are very big as a rule. About 40% of the entire population of Uruguay lives in Montevideo; 25% of Argentina in Buenos Aires; 25% of Chile in Santiago; 15% of Mexico in Mexico City; and about the same percentage of Cuba in Havana. São Paulo in Brazil has passed the 4 million mark, Rio de Janeiro is rapidly reaching that level.

In contrast with the growth of industry and of the large cultural centers as an inevitable part of that industrialization, the hard meanness of the old oligarchical landlords monopolizing the land, the terrible misery and poverty on the countryside, the stagnancy, antiquated methods and general anachronism of the rural regions are accelerating the drive of the people towards the city and towards industry. New consumption patterns, centralization of government, rise of bureaucracies, an enormous increase in the middle classes, the rise of standards

Table 21B
LATIN AMERICA: POPULATION ANALYSIS (ROUNDED TO NEAREST MILLION)

	1940		1950		1960	
	number	%	number	%	number	%
Total Population (million)	124		156		206	
Rural	82	65.9%	95	61%	111	53.9%
Urban	42	34.1	61	39	95	46.1
Economically Active Popula.	42		53		69	
Agricultural	25	59.8	28	53	33	47.2
Non-agricult.	17	40.2	25	47	37	52.8

of living and opportunities all make return to the past absolutely impossible no matter how foreign trade goes. Any attempt to continue the past too long leads inevitably to a repetition of the Cuban Revolution.

2. The massive flow of U.S. capital into Latin America has gone through several phases in an irreversible evolution which must lead to a successful struggle to get rid of colonial disadvantages.

Generally speaking, U.S. investments began where the English left off, that is, they began with investments in primary production and in necessary public utilities. Investment in primary production took the form of large land holdings, such as those of the United Fruit Company in Central America, or of basic metal mining in Chile, Peru, Bolivia, etc., or petroleum exploration and exploitation as in Venezuela. In all these cases large quantities of materials were removed from the Latin American countries which, in the cases of metal and mineral extraction, were left with less and less of these resources and in return received sums of money in the form of royalties, or taxes, or fees, etc., from the U.S. companies removing the materials. The money received in payment was generally not well distributed, going mainly to the rich landlords or to the military and political leaders, with little remaining for the benefit of the people or for the development of the country.

A good example of what happens to the Latin American country under such conditions can be seen in Venezuela. This nation lives off her tremendous petroleum supplies, practically 90% or so of her exports being petroleum. She receives large sums of money for the oil thus extracted and taken away. In fact, the per capita income of Venezuela happens to be the highest in all Latin America. And yet, the sums of money given affect only about 10% of the Venezuelan population, the other 90% being on the same level as the miserable masses in the rest of South and Central America. The average Venezuelan receives about 10% of the income of a person in the United States. The Cuban revolutionists openly boast that the next country to feel the weight of social revolution will be Venezuela. This is echoed by a special Inter-American investigating committee report to the Organization of American States in which we find stated: "There is no doubt that the Castro Regime has selected Venezuela as its primary objective." (Cited in the *New York Times*, edition of June 8, 1963.)

The second phase of U.S. private capital penetration took the form of large-scale investment in the transformation industries, that is in manufacturing and similar enterprises. Here the story is different. The goods made are primarily not for export but to fill a domestic market. The greater the income of the people, the greater the sales can become and the greater the profits made. Hence, such American firms as Kaiser Industries, or General Electric, or Goodyear, etc., are a strong force favoring the rising standards of the people, at least of the growing middle classes.

Factories had to be built, roads for traffic expanded, labor trained and educated, and made healthy and strong to do the work well and cheaply. Such development meant a permanent strengthening of the country's structure and infra-structure. And now it was not the commodity that was exported but the profits, royalties, interests, dividends, incomes, amortizations of capital, capital gains, etc., made by manufacturing companies. In the previous phase the Americans had taken out metals or minerals and had left money from the sales of the stuff exported. Now the Americans took out money and left the machinery, equipment, plants, technical know-how, structural and infra-structural organization, constantly expanding it and staying with it.

At first such foreign-owned manufacturing companies tended to import most of their materials, supplies, machinery, equipment, capital goods, etc. But as the country developed they found it advisable and necessary to get their supplies, materials, parts, sub-assemblies, etc., from other manufacturers within the country. Just as they were no longer working primarily for exports, so they found that they did not need so many imports. Thus the drastic reduction in foreign trade which faced Latin America as a whole could be met in these more developed countries by the advancement of industrial development.

The problem arising from the reduction of foreign trade in goods, however, was solved only by changing the problem to one of a drain of gold and capital by means of imperialist suction. In other words, instead of the money obtained by the export of goods being used for the import of other goods either for consumption or for production, this money now could be drained off directly by the American firms while the goods could be made within the country instead of being imported.

How this suction pump operated can be illustrated by the following schematic example. X Company in the United States opens up a manufacturing affiliate in B Latin American country. To induce this capital to enter, B country declares that X Company may have a tract of land free or for very little money, near good concrete roads or railroad facilities, near a good port or a well developed city. The land will be tax-free for 10 years and taxed at half rate for the next five. Nor will there be any tax on the building or real or personal property for that period. Guarantees will be given for special police, fire, and other security protection. There will be no income tax or corporation tax levied for 5 years, no customs or other charges on any capital, machinery, equipment, supplies, and services brought into the country and needed for production, nor will there be any other competitor allowed to come into this particular market. All capital brought in can be repatriated either without restriction or on liberal instalments; all income can be remitted in foreign currency, as well as payment for technical services, amortization of capital, royalties and patent payments, etc. Wages will be kept low and cost of living controlled. If there is any revolution or confiscation of property, by treaty arrangements between the governments concerned, the X Company will be guaranteed its full capital. The United States may also speed the process along by granting through one of its institutions long-term, low-interest loans to X Company.

Under these conditions the X Company agrees it will invest, say, $1 million of which $300,000 will be in machinery and equipment, to be amortized in five years, $300,000 to be allocated for supplies and materials mainly imported, $100,000 for administration salaries for the first year with $200,000 more for wages and other administration expenses. $100,000 has been kept to pay annual interest fees at 10%.

At the end of the first year, with a guaranteed market, X Company makes 50% net profit on its investment (quite common in Latin America) and has thus $1.5 million. At the end of the first year it has remitted abroad the following sums:

$ 300,000	for machinery and equipment
250,000	for materials and supplies
200,000	for repatriation of capital invested
100,000	for interest payment on first loan of $1 million
150,000	for dividends (10% on $1.5 million)
50,000	on administration salaries paid to employees whose homes are in the United States or who intend eventually to return there
50,000	in royalties and patent fees
$1,100,000	Total sent abroad

In addition the following sums were spent at the place of production:

$ 50,000	for materials and supplies
50,000	part of the administrative salaries
200,000	wages
$300,000	Total spent in the Latin American country

The Company at the end of the first year now has at hand $240,000 worth of machinery and equipment ($60,000 or 20% has been lost in wear and tear), and $100,000 in undistributed profits. To continue business at the $1 million level it started with it must make a new loan of $660,000. Thus it now has a debt of $800,000 on the first loan (it paid off $200,000) and $660,000 on the new or second loan or an indebtedness of $1,460,000 with assets of $1,000,000 including the money received from the second loan.

During the second year it continues the same operations. During the second year it has the following expenditures made abroad:

$ 60,000	to replace machinery and equipment worn out
250,000	for materials and supplies
200,000	for repatriation of original capital
150,000	for dividends
80,000	interest payments on the old loan
66,000	interest payments on the second loan
50,000	administrative salaries portion remitted
50,000	royalties and patent fees
$ 906,000	Total spent abroad
300,000	Total spent in the Latin American country as in previous year
$1,206,000	Total spent

The Company, at the end of the second year, again has $240,000 in machinery and equipment and $294,000 undivided profit for total capital assets of $534,000. In order to proceed at the $1 million level it must make a third loan of $466,000. Thus it now has a debt of $600,000 on the first loan, $660,000 on the second loan and $466,000 on the third loan or a total indebtedness of $1,726,000.

During the third year, continuing operations at the same level, the Company spends abroad the following items:

$	60,000	to replace machinery and equipment worn out
	250,000	for materials and supplies
	200,000	for repatriation of original capital
	150,000	for dividends
	60,000	Interest on first loan
	66,000	Interest on second loan
	46,600	Interest on third loan
	50,000	administrative salaries portion remitted
	50,000	royalties and patent fees
$	932,000	Total spent abroad
	300,000	Total spent in the Latin American country as in previous year
$1,232,000		Total spent

The Company, at the end of the second year again has $240,000 in machinery and equipment and $268,000 in undivided profits for total capital assets of $508,000. If it continues business at the $1 million level it must borrow $492,000 on a fourth loan.

In its first three years, in the example given, then, the Company has spent abroad a total of $2,938,000 while the Company received from abroad in its first three loans a total of $2,126,000 making a difference of $812,000 which was the amount sent abroad over and above the amount sent in. With the new fourth loan of $492,000 the Company now owes abroad $2,018,000, while it is still operating with a capital of $1,000,000.

Insofar as the Company has produced in the course of the three years' operations goods to the value presumptively of $4.5 million, goods which were consumed by the people of the Latin American country involved, to that extent the Latin American country did not have to import such goods and did not have to rely on exports to get the money for such imports. If the goods were consumers goods they have been consumed and the country is no more permanently richer than if they had been imported except for the $240,000 worth of machinery and equipment which still remains and except for the development of the infra-structure of the country that such investments imply.

The example did not state that the machinery was overvalued, that it was not entirely new when it entered the country but was released by the parent company because it was out-of-date. The example further did not say that the patents and royalties were to the parent company which could not have disposed of them otherwise. Nor did the example explain that the commodities imported for production came from the parent company at a very high price in which the parent company made another 100% profit of $125,000. Nor was anything hinted about the fact that a 10% interest charge would be far too high in an industrial country, although not in Latin America. Furthermore, it was not divulged that the engineering and other technical services rendered and paid for at very high prices were really rendered by the parent company as a means of getting still further sums remitted. Finally, nothing had been said about whether the X Company was really enriching the basic industry of B country or perhaps just making non-essential items like perfume.

Tables 22A and 22B give an enlightening picture as to the relationship of direct investment capital outflow and net income receipts.

Table 22A

NET DIRECT-INVESTMENT CAPITAL OUTFLOW AND NET INCOME RECEIPTS
FOR LATIN AMERICA, INCLUDING WESTERN HEMISPHERE DEPENDENCIES,
BY INDUSTRIAL SECTORS ($ MILLION)

	All Industries		Petroleum		Mining & Smelt'g		Manu- facturing		Other	
	Net (1)	Net (2)	(1)	(2)	(1)	(2)	(1)	(2)	(1)	(2)
	Direct Capital Outflow	Income Receipts								
1957	1220	911	867	578	137	119	99	62	117	152
1958	329	688	163	395	81	112	70	47	15	134
1959	389	671	158	313	92	187	66	51	73	120
1960	149	719	24	331	− 60	235	125	64	60	89

(1) Net Direct Capital Outflow   (2) Net Income Receipts

According to a recent report printed in the *New York Times* of April 28, 1963, while the new direct investments in 1960 and 1961 by private U.S. companies amounted to $229 million, the profit and interest remittances totalled $1,307 million, or a drain on Latin America of more than $1 billion. The remittances, moreover, were not considered exorbitant, given the estimated present U.S. direct capital investment of over $10 billion.

Table 22B

LATIN AMERICA: TRANSACTIONS OF U.S. DIRECT-INVESTMENT
ENTERPRISES WITH THE UNITED STATES 1957 ($ MILLION)

Exports to U.S.	$1,563	Other	$ 444
Capital Flow from U.S.	1,163	Remittances to U.S.	950
Imports from U.S.	804	Fees & Royalties	70
Capital Equipment	360	Income	880

This situation, however, represents but the first aspect of this stage of investment development. There arise domestic manufacturers who can make the materials and supplies needed by the X Company and who insist that the X Company buy such goods domestically and not from abroad. The import licenses now become more difficult to get. Other companies, perhaps also U.S. owned, can also make the capital equipment that the X Company needs to replenish its worn-out machinery and equipment. The government can be expected to insist also that this capital equipment be purchased at home and not abroad. Finally, other moneyed men think that it is about time that the X Company took them into the profit making venture. The X Company should think twice before refusing to offer stock to native bankers and business men, and even to native middle-class elements who want to invest their money too.

With all this pressure on the X Company to turn native rather than remain completely administered by U.S. executives, strong bids arise for the use of native technicians and engineers so as to cut out expensive foreign services. Finally, the corporation asks the State to change its seat of incorporation from Delaware or Panama to the capital or central city of the Latin American republic so as to make the corporation a completely "nationalized" organization, although still an affiliate of the parent X Company in the U.S. To stimulate this desire for change of nationality in the corporation the State previously had decreed that only domestic or "nationalized" corporations would be allowed to share in State contracts. And as these contracts were becoming the dominant factor in the nation's economy the corporation had to decide what to do. This is the stage actually faced by American corporate affiliates in some countries of Latin America at the present time.

Should the United States and other industrial countries now discriminate against the exports from the more developed Latin American country, such as that given in the above example, then it will not only be the Latin American country as a whole that will suffer but also the U.S. corporation operating in that country, sucking out the money brought in by the exports, as well as the U.S. corporations at home that would ordinarily, as in the older days, have sold the goods that were imported by that Latin American country. A protective tariff in the United States indirectly prevents Latin America from buying U.S. imports and also prevents U.S. corporations in Latin America from making profit and remitting those profits to the United States as well. On the other hand, not to have a protective tariff in the United States might allow Latin America to undersell the United States at home. Because of relative economic stagnation at home, U.S. capital fled originally to Latin America where a fast 100% profit a year could be made; on the other hand, because of this same relative stagnation, American industry must be protected from that same Latin American export competition, thus making more difficult the fast 100% profit a year by American firms in Latin America.

3. Over and above the private industrial investment there is the government industrial investment that calls for huge projects to be constructed beyond the power or opportunity of private business to build. These projects also place severe strains upon the currency. Provided the Latin American country will buy the goods it needs at very high prices from the U.S., provided it allows the U.S. to be the most favored nation, and invites American businessmen to penetrate the country in the freest manner and on the most favorable terms, the United States and other industrial powers joined to the U.S. in a World Bank, International Monetary Fund, Export-Import Bank, International Bank for Reconstruction and Development, International Finance Corporation, and similar bodies will help with loans and credits. As Secretary of the Treasury Dillon stated before the House Committee on Foreign Affairs, 1961: "Our objective will be to insure that at least 80% of our foreign economic assistance will be spent on U.S. goods and services."

4. The final goal of U.S. private capital investment was domination: this was also the end of its "nationalization" process. It was not enough to produce everything within the country and not seek imports; it was

not enough to get the mass of stock holders and the mass of capital invested to come from native sources, not enough to employ only native executives, professionals, technicians and workers, or to change the corporation charter to have its seat in the Latin American country; these firms had to drive to extend the influence of their particular corporation to control a vast nexus of otherwise native firms. The American automobile concern, for example, becomes the center of a large group of several hundred auto parts establishments all native owned but dominated and really controlled by the American central ganglion.

Furthermore, while the American capital can only be considered generally a minority of the capital invested in a given country, at the same time nothing prevents that minority capital from controlling the majority of the key exports and the majority of the key imports needed by that country. In other words, it is very possible for the relatively minor American capital to become the very heart and soul of the capitalist system in the Latin American country. A study recently made showed that $87 million of U.S. capital apparently produced $4.8 billion in goods in Latin America, accounting for 30% of her total exports.

The final push in this direction came through the various military and economic development loans granted by the United States to the separate Latin American countries. Particularly important was the use of the sales of surplus agricultural commodities through U.S. Public Law 480 under the terms of which the United States was paid in local inconvertible currencies which were then loaned back to that government for developmental purposes approved by the United States.

In practice this often meant that the local currencies thus obtained were loaned to private industrial corporations, especially those run and dominated by U.S. citizens. By means of these favored loans the U.S. corporations could beat all competition and become the dominant factors in the economic life of the country; while firms that would not go along with U.S. hegemony would apply in vain for any of these loans or favors.

As a Congressional report has stated: "One of the criticisms of our development lending is that a disproportionate share of the external financing has gone to government projects and to large concerns that are able to borrow directly abroad or have close connections with governments. Small- and medium-sized industrial firms and farms are thus often starved for capital or must pay enormous rates of interest, while Government agencies and a few large firms obtain capital on terms even more favorable than private borrowers in industrial countries."

Thus, a U.S. corporation could now experience the following advantages over the domestic ones: 1. It could import capital goods without custom charges. 2. It was often free of taxes. 3. It could take full advantage of the fall in international exchange of the local currencies. 4. It could obtain unlimited loans and favors. 5. It had access to patents, processes, machinery, equipment, and markets that others did not have.

No wonder the native capitalists rallied round the American. This was all the more necessary because the native bourgeoisie had come late on the scene and did not feel great confidence in its own strength to win political power. Together with the U.S. business men, however, the native bourgeoisie felt it could better overcome the resistance and special privileges of the old agrarian classes standing in its way, as well as face the encroachments of the state.

All this frenzied search for profits through industrial development, however, does not solve the basic problems that remain. As we have mentioned, there still exist the relative export stagnation, the decline in volume and prices of exports, the adverse terms of trade, the larger and hungrier labor force, the growing debts, the fantastic inflation, the galloping cost of living, and the awful misery of the poor with ever-growing social unrest.

Given 1953 as 100, the index in the cost of living by December 1960 had risen to 622 in Argentina, 485 in Brazil, 945 in Chile, and 358 in Uruguay. (But these figures are so completely out of date at this writing as to be valueless.) Since then in some countries the cost of living has risen more than 60% in one year alone. This is not an accidental event; it may even be called a planned event. By means of this terrible inflation the whole cost of the capitalist growth in Latin America is thrown on the backs of the toilers and workers.

Galloping escalation of the cost of living is not the only sign that the costs of industrial development are to be placed on the backs of the poor. The taxation systems extant are other excellent illustrations. To quote from a Report of the Subcommittee on Inter-American Economic Relationships of the Joint Economic Committee, Congress of the United States, issued in 1962: "Whereas in the United States, about one-sixth of all taxes are property taxes administered at the local level, it is estimated that property taxes, speaking generally of South America, amount to no more than 3 to 5 percent of all government income. . . . In the countries of Latin America the 'mix' more generally approximates 70 to 75 percent sales taxes, excise taxes, and customs duties; 20 to 25 percent income taxes; and 0 to 10 percent property and other capital taxes. In the United States, on the other hand, the tax mix including all levels of government is about ⅔ income tax, ⅙th sales and excise taxes, and ⅙th ad valorem property taxes."

In the U.S., then, indirect taxes weighing most heavily on the poor are only 20% of the direct taxes on income and property which can be said in some manner to increase as the income and property increase. But just the opposite is the case in Latin America where the ratio of indirect taxes to direct taxes in 1955 was not 20% but as the following table shows:

Table 23A

LATIN AMERICAN COUNTRIES: RATIO OF INDIRECT TAXES TO DIRECT (1955)

Argentina	109%	Guatemala	265%
Brazil	296	Honduras	320
Chile	199	Mexico	113
Colombia	132	Nicaragua	667
Costa Rica	259	Peru	195
Ecuador	380	Venezuela	373
El Salvador	380		

How little the people can stand the weight of these taxes and inflation can be seen from the following tables estimating per capita income and cost of living. (The cost-of-living figures rise so rapidly as to be out-of-date when recorded.)

How this income is distributed in a given country is seen when the proportion of that income is given for the 10% of the population receiving the highest reported income as compared to the 60% of the population receiving the lowest income. This is shown in Table 24B.

Further light is shown on the distribution of income when the per capita income difference between the highest and lowest income regions of a country is given.

Table 23B
LATIN AMERICAN COUNTRIES: TAX DISTRIBUTION 1962
(% ROUNDED TO NEAREST UNIT)

Country	Corp. & Personal Income Taxes	Consumption, Sales & Similar Taxes	Export-Import Taxes	Other Taxes
Argentina	29%	33%	32%	6%
Bolivia	14	23	51	10
Brazil	32	43	12	14
Chile	32	42	22	4
Colombia	52	10	34	5
Costa Rica	17	14	58	12
Dominican Republic	18	23	44	16
Ecuador	16	11	41	32
El Salvador	11	20	61	8
Guatemala	7	21	54	18
Haiti	9	15	65	11
Honduras	15	29	56	—
Mexico	37	29	27	6
Nicaragua	9	18	61	12
Panama	19	19	44	19
Paraguay	12	25	21	42
Peru	47	22	21	9
Uruguay	7	26	37	30
Venezuela*	38	40	11	11

* Excludes royalties
Source: *Chicago Daily News* dispatch, March 18, 1963.

Table 24A
LATIN AMERICAN COUNTRIES: ESTIMATES OF AVERAGE ANNUAL
PER-CAPITA INCOME 1960

Guatemala	$100-$199	Argentina	$500-$599
Honduras	100- 199	Brazil	100- 199
Mexico	200- 299	Trinidad	400- 499
Panama	200- 299	Tobago	400- 499
Peru	100- 199	Bahama Isles	500- 599
Colombia	100- 199	Nicaragua	100- 199
Venezuela	600- 699	Ecuador	100- 199
Paraguay	100- 199	Haiti	under $100
Cuba	300- 399	Costa Rica	about $300
Chile	over $400		

From the following two tables it can be seen how inequable is the distribution of income both by economic strata of the population and by geographic regions. The figures given in these two tables for the Latin American countries mentioned are typical for all Latin America.

Table 24B

DISTRIBUTION OF INCOME IN RECENT YEARS COMPARING HIGHEST INCOME
10% OF THE POPULATION AND LOWEST INCOME 60% OF THE
SAME POPULATION IN GIVEN COUNTRIES

	Top 10%	Lowest 60%
Chile	37.5%	24%
Mexico	45.0	24
Venezuela	45.0	16
United States	31.0	34
United Kingdom	30.0	32

Table 24C

DISTRIBUTION OF INCOME IN RECENT YEARS COMPARING PER-CAPITA INCOME IN
HIGHEST INCOME REGIONS AND IN LOWEST INCOME REGIONS IN GIVEN COUNTRIES
(AVERAGE PER-CAPITA INCOME IN GIVEN COUNTRY EQUALS BASIS OF 100)

	Top Income Region	Lowest Income Region
Brazil (1960)	291	29
Colombia	185	17
Spain	219	50
Italy	205	40
United States	136	53

Table 25A

LATIN AMERICAN COUNTRIES:
COST OF LIVING INDEX (BASED ON LEVEL OF 1953 AS 100)
(FIGURES ARE OF DECEMBER IN EACH YEAR GIVEN)

	1957	1958	1960	1951
Argentina	183	275	622	84
Brazil	216	265	485	69
Chile	636	843	945	57
Peru	128	139	176	86
Uruguay	161	193	358	83

More recent figures are given in Table 25B:

Table 25B

LATIN AMERICAN COUNTRIES: CONSUMER PRICES (1955 LEVEL EQUALS 100)

	March 1960	March 1962
Argentina	496	645
Bolivia	804	952
Brazil	290	567
Chile	380	444
Colombia	154	172
Peru	148	166
Uruguay	247	365

And now, given the low incomes, the heavy taxes, and the general insufferable political conditions, we can appreciate why such an event as the Cuban Revolution could burst upon the scene.

In 1959, on its coming to power, the Cuban revolutionary regime issued a set of statements that it found 90% of the agrarians, the great majority of Cubans, in a state of plain malnutrition. The average span of life was only 40 years. Over 70% were infected with parasites of all sorts. Habitually only 2% ate eggs, 4% ate meat, 10% drank milk. It was estimated that a half million children had died of gastro-enteritis since the beginning of the century. The workers, ten to a shack, lived in miserable hovels, often made of waste materials, without potable water, except in some central locality, without toilets and 90% without electric light. There were few schools and 44% could not even sign their own names. For them there were generally no doctors, no hospitals, no clinics, no nurses. The agricultural laborers worked only part of the year, but then from sun-up to sun-down. They bought their necessities in company stores that mercilessly cheated them. Their clothes were made of gunny sacks or coarse fibre cloth. All this in a rich semi-tropical country filled with fruits and natural foods of all sorts. And Cuba was a Latin American country supposedly better off than most.

Table 25C
WORLD COMPARISON: DAILY PER-CAPITA CONSUMPTION (RECENT YEARS)

	Calories	Proteins (gr)	Fats (gr)
Latin America	2450	67	61
Europe	3000	88	94
North America (U.S. & Canada)	3100	93	142
Oceania (Australia & New Zealand)	3250	94	137
Argentina	3090	98	118
Brazil	2580	67	57
São Paulo	3058	89.4	88.3
Recife	2096	65.2	28.5

Table 25D
WORLD COMPARISON: EXPECTATION OF LIFE IN YEARS (RECENT YEARS)

	Men	Women
Brazil	39.3	45.5
Argentina	56.9	61.4
Mexico	37.9	39.8
United States*	66.4	72.7
United Kingdom	68.1	73.8

* Average statistics in the United States distorted by effects of Negro discrimination

The Cuban Revolution accomplished two great things: 1) it forced the U.S. and the Latin American governments to understand that not only an industrial revolution but a social revolution was on the agenda; and 2) it impelled all of Latin America to make a painful orientation toward the Soviet Bloc.

Soon after the victory of the Revolution a quarantine was placed around Cuba. Because the conditions leading to the victory of Castro in Cuba also existed elsewhere in Latin America, a strenuous effort was launched for the very backward agrarian countries in the Caribbean and in Central America to clean house. The U.S. saw to it that the dictator Trujillo and his tribe were ousted from the Dominican Republic and democratic elections held there. All aid was withheld from the dictator President Duvalier in Haiti and pressure put for his ouster. The British refused to grant, as promised, independence to British Guiana until they were sure the regime established would not be too far out of line and have kept steady pressure on the leading party of that country to prevent it from following too revolutionary a policy. The Somoza dictator family in Nicaragua was warned that it would have to change its face if it wished to continue in power there.

In order to bolster up the tottering dictatorial regimes in Central America, the U.S. fostered a Central American Free Trade Area, along lines vaguely resembling the Common Market in Europe. A Central American Bank for Economic Integration was set up that would develop the economy of Guatemala, Honduras, Nicaragua, Costa Rica and El Salvador as one entity so that each could help the other in case of attack from a common enemy.

The pertinent data pertaining to this Middle America region is given in the following table:

Table 26

MIDDLE AMERICA: SOME BASIC DATA

Country	Population (millions) 1961	1960 Gross National Product $ mill.	per cap.	1950-61 Annual Rate of Growth	Agri- cultural production 1961/1950	Leading Export %	
Costa Rica	1.2	$ 402	$343	5.4%	178%	coffee	53%
El Salvador	2.7	490	188	—	191	coffee	67
Guatemala	3.9	679	180	4.4	175	coffee	69
Honduras	2.0	384	197	4.8	143	bananas	49
Nicaragua	1.5	310	210	5.9	313	cotton	37

Table 26 (Continued)

MIDDLE AMERICA: SOME BASIC DATA

Country	Population (millions) 1961	1960 Gross National Product $ mill.	per cap.	1950-61 Annual Rate of Growth	Agricultural production 1961/1950	Leading Export %
Total Common Market	11.3	2265			200	
Panama	1.1	418	396	5.4	165	bananas 66
Mexico	35.7	10750	310	4.9	179	
Total Middle America	48.1	13433			192	
Total 20 Lat. Am	204.1	58842	295	4.1	144	

The assistance rendered Middle America from international organizations is summarized in the next table:

Table 27

ASSISTANCE FROM INTERNATIONAL ORGANIZATIONS TO MIDDLE AMERICA

JUNE 30, 1962 ($ MILLION)

	Total Middle Am.	Total Lat. Am.	Total All Countries
Total Assistance from Int. Org.	$228.6	$644.2	$1430.7
IBRD (1)	169.0	412.0	882.3
IFC (2)	1.1	10.7	18.3
IDA (3)	5.6	31.0	134.1
IDB (4)	48.6	153.9	153.9
UNTA (5)	1.7	10.3	48.7
UNSP (6)	2.7	20.8	70.7
EDF of EEC (7)		5.5	113.7

(1) International Bank for Reconstruction and Development (loans to either governments, government enterprises, or private firms with government guarantees).

(2) International Finance Corporation commitments to invest in private enterprises.

(3) International Development Association.

(4) Inter-American Development Bank authorization to government, government enterprises, or private firms from (a) ordinary capital; (b) fund for special operations.

(5) United Nations Technical Assistance: project costs under (a) regular and (b) expanded programs;

(6) United Nations Special Fund, allocations toward cost or preinvestment surveys.

(7) European Development Fund of the European Economic Community.

(Note that the Central American Bank for Economic Integration is not listed in this table. Its capital is composed of $4 million each from Guatemala, El Salvador, Honduras, and Nicaragua and $20 million from the U.S.)

U.S. aid is shown as follows:

Table 28

ASSISTANCE UNDER U.S. DEVELOPMENT PROGRAMS AS OF JUNE 30, 1962
($ MILLION)

	Total Middle Am.	Total Lat. Am.	Total All Countries
U.S. Assistance under Development and Aid Programs	$230.0	$1328.9	$6721.7
Total all programs	49.1	474.8	2528.4
Food for Peace, Pub. Law 480	9.4	134.5	1629.1
Social Progress Trust Fund	47.3	224.4	224.4
Eximport Bank	117.8	253.9	584.2
Other economic programs	2.6	120.0	204.2
Military Aid	3.8	121.3	1551.4

How loans to Middle America have grown since the Cuban Revolution is seen in the next table:

Table 29

U.S. AUTHORIZED LOANS, OFFICIAL SOURCES, TO CENTRAL AMERICA AS OF
JUNE 30, 1962 ($ MILLION)

1958	$10.5
1959	31.9
1960	47.2
1961	94.3
1962	31.1 (nine months only)

What has been accomplished so far by this Central American Common Market is summarized in the 1963 report of the Subcommittee on Inter-American Economic Relationships of the Joint Economic Committee, Congress of the United States:

"The so-called 'Central American Common Market' in the few years since its first beginnings has established itself as a viable, going institution including (since mid-1962) the five countries, Costa Rica, El Salvador, Guatemala, Honduras, and Nicaragua. The movement can already list among its accomplishments the elimination of trade barriers on half of the trade of the member countries; the standardization of external tariffs on over 80 percent of all commodities; the beginning of a regional development bank; and plans to spur investment in the area as a whole on an 'integrated' basis. As a regional movement, its motivation and objectives, to say nothing of its size, are, however, so different that any attempt to liken it to the rise of the European Common Market would only be misleading." (italics in original)

"The program for industrial integration of the area is intended to step up intraregional trade which up to the present has been quite small, although expanding. Trade among Central American countries as measured by imports from each other of $8 million in 1950, doubled by 1957 to $16.5 million, and doubled again in the 4-year period to 1961, to over $37 million. Intraregional trade, once largely confined to border 'spill overs' of locally produced consumer goods, now accounts for 26 and 30 percent, respectively, of the total imports of the five countries of foodstuffs and nonfood raw materials."

About the same time as this action was being taken in Central America, similar plans were being laid in South America through the Latin American Free Trade Association organized in the Treaty of Montevideo and for all Latin America by the Act of Bogotá. All this is in the period after the victory of Castro in Cuba but before the definite entrance of Cuba into the Soviet Bloc and Cuba's announcement that she was a socialist state.

The Montevideo Treaty signed on February 8, 1960, by representatives of Argentina, Brazil, Chile, Mexico, Paraguay, Peru, Uruguay (with place left for Bolivia), was still entirely on the economic plane. (Since then Colombia and Ecuador have also joined.) The contracting parties agreed through mutual negotiations, generally bilaterally arranged, to eliminate within 12 years in respect to reciprocal trade, such duties, charges, and restrictions as may be applied to imports of goods originating in the contracting party. At the end of each 3-year period the reductions were to amount to 25% until there was complete free trade, with certain exceptions and safeguarding clauses provided, among all the contracting parties.

The 1962 LAFTA Conference held in Mexico City reduced tariff barriers of 7000 items and lowered by a total of 30% the tariff rates that had existed among the members. Thanks in part to this new orientation, intra-regional trade in 1962 rose by 20%; Argentine exports to LAFTA increased 39%, Mexican exports 112% (of which 70% were manufactured items), while Mexican imports to LAFTA rose 48% and Peru's exports and imports to and from LAFTA rose 60% and 53% respectively. Especially important was the Mexican-Brazilian trade which rose from 3,000 tons in 1961 to 54,000 tons in 1962, causing a regular shipping service to become inaugurated.

The end result was to be quite along the lines to be achieved by the Central American Common Market so far as free trade was concerned, although the whole arrangement was more flexible and originally restricted to trade than to integration looking toward a common community. But with the great growth of U.S. capital investment in all these countries any trend toward economic integration and mutually supporting production would only strengthen the hold of the central position of the United States and would bind the South American countries in a further alliance against any possible communist encroachment. Furthermore, the opportunity to sell in a broad Latin American market will undoubtedly attract a greater volume of U.S. capital than ever before, just as the creation of the European Common Market attracted capital from the United States.

Emphasis on social development in U.S. aid programs is of rather recent origin. As the 1961 Report to the Joint Economic Committee stated: "The determination of the administration to provide a larger role for social development in its foreign assistance programs is a consequence of a perhaps belated realization that unless social progress goes hand in hand with overall economic growth, the political objectives of economic programs will not be realized. If, for example, industrial output continues to expand in the industrial centers of Latin America and agricultural productivity is increased on the large farms and plantations, but at the same time the ring of slums surrounding the industrial centers continues to grow and the lot of the Andean or northeastern Brazilian peasant does not improve, or even declines, the political battles will be lost."

The Act of Bogotá, signed in September, 1960, by a special committee of the 20 Latin American nations plus the United States, proposed new and broad measures for social improvement and economic development in a pan-American framework. By this time the United States and the Latin American governments had become thoroughly alarmed at the social and political implications of the Cuban Revolution and its tremendous reverberations throughout all of Latin America. Thus, the Act of Bogotá emphasized not the economic aspects but the theme of social justice and welfare. It was not so much the economic structure as the social infra-structure that needed speedy treatment. Something must be done and quickly for the poor unfortunate toilers and workers of that region.

We cannot give at this place all the measures for social improvement laid out in the Act of Bogotá. Suffice it to say that the Act included measures for the improvement of conditions of rural living and land use, measures for the improvement of housing and community facilities, measures for the improvement of educational systems and training facilities, measures for the improvement of public health, and measures for the mobilization of domestic resources.

As part of the Act of Bogotá the United States immediately offered to establish a special Inter-American Fund for Social Development, with the Inter-American Development Bank to become the primary mechanism for the administration of this fund. All this was later approved October 11, 1960, by the entire Organization of American States. The $500 million allocated to this Inter-American Fund for Social Development was seen to be completely overshadowed by the $20 billion fund later offered by the United States under the Charter of the Alliance for Progress Program but was nevertheless an important step in a new form of investment by the United States aimed primarily at the development of Latin American infra-structure.

The program contained in the Act of Bogotá was a pilot project of a far more ambitious program yet to come. It immediately displayed a great weakness in that all Latin American ruling cliques were very eager to seize the money offered but only in order to squander it on themselves rather than spend it for the benefit of the people. The United States was compelled to contain this avariciousness and, in the Alliance for Progress, to insist and make clear that certain conditions would have to be met before any part of the new $20 billion fund would be doled out.

The crisis becoming intensified despite these efforts, the United States was finally impelled to give full attention to the Latin American problem. The result was the Punte del Este Conference held in August, 1961, and the adoption there of the Charter launching the Alliance for Progress *(Alianza para el Progreso)*. The Charter contained a number of features constituting a new departure in U.S. policies toward Latin America.

1. The charter goes into considerable detail in setting forth the specific targets for economic and social development, including, among others:

a) The achievement within a reasonable period of time of a minimum rate of per capita growth of 2.5%;

b) The elimination of illiteracy and, by 1970, assurance of access to six years of primary education for each school-age child;

c) An increase in life expectancy at birth by a minimum of five years, to be achieved by specific health measures such as adequate water supply and drainage, etc.;

d) In the field of agrarian reform, the transformation of unjust structures and systems of land tenure into an equitable system;

e) Reform of tax laws so that the burden will fall more on the wealthy;

f) Achievement of balanced diversification in national economic structures, both regional and functional, making them increasingly free from dependence on the export of a limited number of primary products and the importation of capital goods while attaining stability in the prices of exports or in income derived from exports.

2. The United States Government made specific pledges of assistance subject to the undertakings of self-help measures by the Latin American recipients. The Charter states in effect that the United States, for its part, pledges its efforts to supply financial and technical assistance in order to achieve the aims of the Alliance for Progress. To this end the United States will provide a major part of the minimum of $20 billion, principally in public funds, which Latin America will require over the next ten years from all external sources in order to supplement its own efforts. Latin America itself is to provide a much greater sum for the goals of the Alliance, perhaps up to $80 billion more.

So now the U.S. is pledged to a long-term commitment to make available to Latin America a minimum of $20 billion over the next ten years. This sum will not all be given as an outright gift but will include funds allocated to the Inter-American Development Bank, the Export-Import Bank, the Development Loan Fund, the International Co-operation Administration, as well as funds from international lending agencies such as the International Monetary Fund, the World Bank, and private funds from investors from various parts of the world. It looks like a big sum to the Latin Americans but considering that the money will be spent over ten years, that it is to cover all of South and Middle America, that much of it will be in the form of loans to be repaid, that many other lending countries will be involved as well as the United States, and that the money will not be spent unless certain conditions are met, it can be seen that the shrewd Yanqui hand is very competent to get the most for the least.

3. The United States has by now considerable experience in handing out money to less developed countries run by greedy military oli-

garchic elements who, while prating about "honor" and "nobility," like to grab all they can although accomplishing nothing for which the money was given. The U.S. policy is committed to nudging these elements out of control, if possible, and to confide in the new capitalist elements.

This newer bourgeoisie, however, is just as greedy and selfish as are the older anachronistic groups. They would like to use the money for their own particular development regardless of what would happen to the older ruling classes who, however, dominate the military and alone can put down the masses. Sections of the newer groups, especially those allied with the older, would be willing to share the loot with the military but do not wish to share the wealth with the masses of workers and toilers who are susceptible to revolution à la Cuba. Such newer capitalist types would like to use the money for capital investment and reinvestment, for industrialization of the country and for modernization of agriculture. They wish to get better terms of trade and win new markets, even driving out the United States from these markets, if they could.

The United States, in its wisdom, however, had in mind a better and more balanced utilization of the fund:

a) Part of the money would go for agrarian reform, to modernize agricultural methods and techniques, to change the social structure on the countryside. This would not necessarily lessen the power of the agrarian groups since they could now get rid of some of their lands at very good prices, they could improve their production and productivity and get better returns, they could get greater social advantages, they might still keep their political powers if they would merge forces with the newer elements, etc. To assure these agrarians that no great harm would befall them, the United States made the commitment that it would help stabilize world agricultural prices, such as coffee, for example, and would thus be pledged to keep prices higher, at the expense of the U.S. consumer, than they would ordinarily be. This was, in truth, in violation, at least in spirit, of the obligations the United States had assumed in GATT and was fostering international monopoly action in the worst sense of the word—price fixing.

b) A considerable part of the fund would have to go for industrial development on a long-term and massive basis. The bulk of the money would be dispensed not to individual capitalists but to the government for the creation of large scale projects. But these projects could not be accomplished haphazardly. They would have to be preceded by careful national and long-term planning, for which not the shrewdness of profit manipulators was needed but the wisdom of scientists, engineers, economists, and technicians of all sorts. These last were all trained in the ways of the United States and were to be supplemented by large staffs of experts coming from the United States. The private capitalists who would be involved would be mainly those from the United States, strongly entrenched in the Latin American countries; the goods that would have to be bought would in large measure (at least 80%) come from the United States (at a good profit to the United States). The principal share of the money would be given *not* to the newer native layers of native capitalism, but to the government —not to the government in its political and military capacity, but to the government's particular entities and corporations set up to run the special projects envisaged. These entities and corporations would be under the immediate review and control of the United States and would come to dominate the affairs of the country, in the same way as, for example, the Steel-Coal Community, or Euratom, controls in Western Europe.

The utilization of such public entities would also tend to deter the intellectuals from adherence to any revolutionary cause, as such intellectuals were aligned in Cuba, for instance, in the fight by Castro against Batista. As a Congressional Report stated in 1962:

"The technique of the public authority with mixed public and private attributes such as our port authorities, turnpike authorities, and multi-purpose valley authorities, or the Port of London Authority, was suggested as a potentially useful device for the kinds of development called for in Latin America. It provides a managerial device for dealing with a specific problem, housing, land reform, or the like; is especially adapted to local or regional projects, e.g. northeast Brazil; and 'avoids vast encrustations of bureaucracy' which are likely to characterize remote control by the Central Government. It could 'attract, for the top management, nonpolitical figures' and the 'highly trained younger generations of technicians throughout Latin America' who at the present time 'lack the power of political decision.' With its more precise and limited aims, it would offer, too, some measure of isolation from the investment vicissitudes of national political instability."

The new careful approach now made by the United States has the following features:

1. The United States does not directly deal with any Latin American national body but works through an international agency that approves the plans, makes the loans and credits available, supervises and criticizes the performances on the part of the recipient governments and puts pressure for payment.

2. The loan is made not to a hungry bureaucratic state apparatus which works without civil service rules, is heavily overstaffed and infested with nepotism and favoritism, but to a modern business-like corporation.

3. The recipient body is one not directly tied up with parliamentary vicissitudes and political instability that might affect the national governments involved but has its own life and continuity independent of what administration is in control.

4. At every stage the U.S. government itself keeps far in the background having, apparently, no direct hand in the proceedings.

c) Naturally, if a good part of the money granted by the U.S. was to go to the newer capitalist layers and their intellectuals, just as a good part had to go to the older groups controlling the armed forces, at the same time a considerable portion would also have to be given to the masses or new Cubas would be the result. The development of the infra-structure of the country would have to become the primary goal of the Alliance for Progress. Such action was essential from every standpoint: to improve the lot of the people, to increase a domestic market, and to satisfy the rising demand for an industrial proletariat that knew how to read and write and could be safely grouped together in large numbers without being decimated by disease or stirred by agitators, etc.

In order better to accomplish this last point, the social control of the proletariat, the Alliance for Progress determined to make the maximum use of the trade union movement in the United States. The leaders of this movement had already done yeoman work during the Marshall Plan in Europe in infiltrating the ranks of the European workers, in splitting their ranks where they were controlled by Stalinists, or where they were going revolutionary on their own, in setting up new organizations, in coordinating and mobilizing all the reformist organizations into world-wide and regional centers controlled by the United States, etc. One of these regional organizations, the Inter-American Regional Organization of Workers (ORIT), had been formed precisely for this purpose in Latin America. This organization was immediately blown up to large size with unlimited support from the Alliance for Progress people.

In return for the servility expected from this "labor leadership," the Kennedy Administration of the U.S. Government meant to pay very well, as could be gathered from a rather recent announcement that in Ecuador alone the Alliance for Progress would build two "labor temples," one in Guayaquil and one in Quito, estimated to cost $560,000 for which the United States share would be $350,000. Two costly labor temples in a country where the per capita income averaged $100-$200 a year!

4. The vast sum allocated by the United States will have to be matched by another sum coming from the Latin Americans themselves. But how will the Latin American ruling classes raise this second amount? It is certainly not to be expected that they will tax themselves, if they can possibly avoid it. The agrarians will try to see that the industrial capitalists are taxed, the latter will try to throw back the burden on the former and on their generals. The generals will fight to keep their privileges and perquisites. The wealthier groups will levy heavy indirect taxes on the petty bourgeoisie and the salaried elements, etc. All this may lead only to more disorders and revolutions.

5. Clearly the money offered by a zealous President can not be handed out directly by the United States. This is no longer the approved technique. The people of each recipient country must be made to feel that the money comes thanks to the acumen and justice of its own ruling classes. These ruling classes must be called together and the whole plan worked through them. Hence the plan was first sent to the Organization of American States for approval and the money was to be spent through the International Development Association and the Inter-American Development Bank.

6. The big question to be settled was how the plan would be implemented. Although each country was to prepare its own program, a central reviewing body would have to exist to pass on the proposals made by each government. For this the Organization of American States had proposed a standing committee of experts to receive, discuss, and evaluate as well as to follow the progress of the plans during the course of their development and implementation in each country.

These proposals were met by resistance on the part of the *políticos* in the larger Latin American countries. They did not think their development should be controlled by any outside body. Their militarists did not believe there was much danger from a Cuba or from a communist take-over. They were not going to become accountants for the United States with their books carefully scrutinized and audited. On the other hand, the smaller countries of Central America, in the main utterly dependent upon the United States and feeling the breath of the Cuban Revolution hotter on their necks, were fully in accord with the U.S. position.

The result of this disagreement was a compromise, finally adopted and incorporated into the Charter, under which the review or development programs of individual countries would be made by independent experts drawn from a panel of nine high-level experts nominated jointly by the Organization of American States, Inter-American Development Bank, and the United Nations Economic Commission for Latin America. Each government, if it so desired, might present its program for economic and social development for consideration by an *ad hoc* committee composed of no more than three members drawn from the panel of experts, together with an equal number of experts not on the panel. This committee would study the country's development program in consultation with the interested government with a view to possible modifications and "with the consent of the government, report its conclusions to the Inter-American Development Bank and to other governments and institutions that may be prepared to extend financial and technical assistance in connection with the execution of the program."

From the U.S. point of view this sort of review was still not quite good enough, since it did not provide for specific review of underlying projects to be financed. Nor did it deal adequately with the urgent problem of coordination of external assistance activities at the country level, which might prove to be a major weakness of the program. For a better check-up the U.S. Government had to rely on its own Agency for International Development, its various special missions, and its "from below" observations of its "Peace Corps" emissaries.

As a U.S. Congressional report cautioned: "Our aid administrators cannot sit behind their desks and review projects for economic and social development as they are presented by governmental agencies or private organizations in the developing countries. They must play an active part in influencing the character of development programs at various levels, from the determination of the broad outline or pattern of a country's future growth to a consideration of specific projects to be financed."

From its original design, the new set-up was to place the United States in a commanding position to control the internal conditions of all the affected nations receiving aid. From such a position it could dictate what social reform measures should be undertaken, what should be the tax structure, the share of the social product to be distributed to each economic class, the rate of growth, the degree of industrialization, the level and character of international trade, the cost of living, the level of prices, the strength of trade unions, etc., etc.

That the Alliance for Progress program must fail in its grand design to stabilize the Latin American regimes, to eliminate the threat of communism and of social revolution, and to make the countries in the Western Hemisphere the satellites of the U.S., is certain. The grand design overlooks the role of the United States itself, the historic nature and character of the ruling groups in the Latin American countries, and the forces driving the masses to revolution. It also overlooks the tremendous appeal of the Soviet Bloc.

Let us first deal with the role of the United States. If the United States really wanted to help, it could declare the entire Western Hemisphere a free-trade area and let down all import barriers. This is completely in accord with the ideals expressed in GATT, of which the United States is a part, and is expressly stated as one of the obligations of the United States in the Charter. The Charter reads that it is agreed that "Importing member countries [of which the United States is clearly one—AW] should reduce, and if possible eliminate, as soon as feasible, all restrictions and discriminatory practices affecting the consumption and importation of primary products, including those with the highest possible degree of processing in the country of origin, except when these restrictions are imposed temporarily for purposes of economic diversification, to hasten the economic development of less developed nations, or to establish basic national reserves."

Apropos this saving through lowering import barriers, a recently published study[3] has indicated that the elimination of U.S. import restrictions would result in increased sales up to $1.7 billion by Latin America annually. If the petroleum quota alone were abandoned, increased imports from Latin America could be as much as $1 billion a year.

Is it really practically thinkable that the U.S. will remove import quotas, customs duties, subsidies and special treatment that favor the U.S. producers of wheat, corn, grains, tobacco, sugar, wool, cotton, meat, and other agricultural products, petroleum, zinc, lead, tin, copper, and other metal products, textiles, shoes, clothing, and other manufactured products? Such a situation would bring about a veritable revolution in the United States, a tremendous development of Latin America, and a vast outflow of U.S. capital.

Most of all, it is practically unthinkable because it would eventually equalize the United States and Latin America and bring them to a common level, and this would mean the end of domination by the United States, the end of imperialism. Only a U.S. ruling class gone insane would consent to such a fate. Among the most bitter opponents to such equal treatment of United States and Latin American products would be the American workingmen themselves organized in the American Federation of Labor-Congress of Industrial Organizations. Their very high relative standards are in part based upon the misery and poverty of the Latin Americans and the dominant role of their own employers.

But even were such an eventuality thinkable, the Western Hemisphere is only part of the world, after all. There would have to be erected a huge tariff wall all around the Western Hemisphere, as in the case of the Common Market in Europe, if Latin American goods were to be favored over those of Africa, or Asia, for example, since it is very possible that Rhodesian copper, African coffee and cocoa, Malayan rubber, Ceylonese tea, etc., could economically supplant Latin American commodities.

And what about the most-favored nation treaty clauses that insure that one country, say Japan, will be given the same treatment by the United States as the United States gives to any other nation? To believe that any such results could be practically realized for all South America is to believe that capitalism is not capitalism, but socialism, and imperialism is not imperialism but world brotherhood.

[3] Louis O. Delwart: *The Future of Latin American Exports to the United States 1965 and 1970;* National Planning Association, Washington, D. C., 1960.

And if United States and Latin American economies were to join forces, where would the truly staggering surpluses go? Barred by the Common Market Bloc taking in Western Europe, Africa, and part of Asia, barred by the Sino-Soviet Bloc embracing Eastern Europe and much of the rest of Asia, such surpluses would be unable to circulate, making the smothered economies involved a prey to all the social revolutions these countries intended to avoid.

Let us next deal with the historic nature and character of the Oligarchy. One of the great contradictions of the Alliance for Progress Charter is that it wishes to do away with the hegemony of the old large landholding oligarchies and yet must work through a government and an army controlled by such elements. The Charter thus gives money and support to the very people who are responsible for the evils it wishes to eradicate, and for conditions which the very rulers thus supported have fostered and without which they could not rule.

When first discovered by Europeans, Latin America was taken over by ruling groups who were not at all interested in production and trade but first in looting the country of gold, silver, and precious jewels, and then in enslaving the native populations and bringing in African slaves on big centralized plantations for their profit, while they frittered away their time in Europe or in the capital cities they built for their pleasures. Whatever they accumulated in wealth they either had to send abroad to their kings and emperors or they squandered on themselves. When Portugal and Spain were reduced to third or fourth rate powers because of the failure of their ruling classes to modernize themselves, their Latin American colonies could break away and form independent countries run by their own ignorant, vainglorious, and immensely backward ruling groups. These groups soon found themselves under the guidance first of English commercial and industrial capitalists who understood the world market only too well and soon had the South American yokels firmly in their debt.

The shattering of the Spanish empire meant the political fragmentation of Latin America. Large landholders everywhere became leaders of armies first to defeat the armies of Spain and to declare their countries independent, and then to seize vast areas, provinces, states, *capitanias,* for themselves as complete masters. These men were often not nobles or knights trained in the chivalry of the old country but rough bosses who built armies around themselves in a way resembling the methods in later days of the large U.S. mining and steel companies who organized their private coal and iron police. The boss was the state and the law. Nothing else mattered. Thus was the Latin American *caudillo* or "leader" born and nourished.

The early Latin American "revolutionary" leaders were of the George Washington type who in their fight for independence against Spain used the vague phrases of the French enlightenment popularized by the French Revolution in order to get the people to fight for them and their top group.[4] To this category belonged such "liberators" as Bolivar, Belgrano, San Martín, and others. They represented wealthy families which wanted to rule the Western Hemisphere countries for their own benefit. Establishing vast *latifundias* with large numbers of peons and slaves working for them, the strong ones among the oligarchy formed their own private armies (caudillism) and ruled their regions with an iron hand, no longer held responsible by others for their actions. Some of these regions actually became artificially created independent states, as, for example, in Central America. The fact that the countries were now independent, with all former social controls absent, led to fights among the ruling families themselves as to who should be on top. In many families were sons with self-given titles of "colonel," or "general," who staged one governmental revolt after another. So far as the masses of toilers were concerned their lot was improved not at all.

From the beginning Spain had introduced into the new world the *Fuero Militar,* under which the military were a privileged caste exempt from public liability and civic responsibility. With independence, the armed forces assumed political functions. The Latin American officer, living on civil war and the fight for power, tended to lose contact with the people. Militarism became triumphant when the landed oligarchs indicated their readiness to utilize their armies against the people and the liberators turned upon the liberated. The victory of the oligarchs was a victory of the landed estates over the intellectuals, the victory of the countryside over the cities, the original centers of disaffection from Spain.

Prior to 1850 no politically ambitious officer of any standing ever threatened a basic principle of the oligarchy's system of values. The *haciendado* (large estate owner) had complete control. The masses, dragooned into the armed forces, had no political, or economic, or

---

[4] See Edwin Lieuwen: *Arms and Politics in Latin America* (1960).

social rights that the officers had to respect. The *haciendados,* however, who controlled the central governments, were not always effective against provincial *haciendados* who were local *caudillos.* Ruthless landlords commanding private armies of peons, as well as desperadoes dominating large territories of land for other landlords, were the general rule in the interior.

About the middle of the last century new trends of capitalism entering Latin America changed some of the formulas of the military "revolutionists." The entrance of commercial and financial capital and the rise of a bourgeois world made increasingly felt the need for definite rules. This called for constitutional government that would allow for the interplay of bourgeois forces and would permit the newer wealthier elements to become fused with the old oligarchy. The formation of constitutions entailed a division of labor between the executive and the legislative branches of government. While the army tended to become professionalized, within it there was still room for the tiny military conspiracy. The military coup d'etat with personal parties gathered around some military conspirator remained to dominate the workings of the constitution.

The military statesmen, having considerable wealth, were economic traditionalists. The constitutions adopted favored their property and the property of their class. Thus they created tax systems that depended overwhelmingly upon customs duties and levies upon exports, the revenues of which were easily collected and the burdens of which fell in regressive fashion upon the great mass of consumers. They were also for free trade favoring English and European imports and stifling the development of a domestic industry that might have eventuated in a different ruling class than the agrarians. Thus the military rulers never wanted to change the existing social and economic system.

Big changes, however, did occur, concomitant with the entrance of American capital into the scene after the end of the American Civil War. Between the middle and the end of the 19th century Latin America experienced not only a vast increase in the influx of foreign capital but also a vast immigration of foreign labor, especially hastened by the end of the slave trade in Brazil in 1850 and the final emancipation of the slaves there in 1888.

Millions of people came from Spain and from Italy and other countries to seek home and fortune in the countries of this hemisphere. Some became farmers and agricultural laborers, others small business men, professional men, workers in the growing cities, and such. Some of them even went into the army to play a role there as "majors" and "colonels." Now the more developed of these nations were faced not only with the matter of establishing basic rules in a constitutional framework but of granting these middle class elements and immigrants the right to vote. Hence new military conspiracies, new vague general programmatic phrases and new promises with a multitude of personal parties arising controlled by this or that strong individual and his clique combined with the military to take over power. It became appropriate to take on a radical coloration, *Radicalism,* in the name of the people. Batista in Cuba, Carranza in Mexico are only two among the many military leaders who could thus be classified.

This was a period when the old landholding oligarchy were also developing into other sorts of economic masters. Their sons were turning to commerce and finance on their own. The younger generations were going to universities not for religious studies, philosophy, and law but also for science and engineering. The militarists were turning "professional," receiving training from abroad (England, Germany, France). Army schools were sometimes the only institutions of higher learning offering courses in pure science. The cruder forms of bullying "caudillism" were being contained in the provinces and coming to an end.

As in the case of Russia under the Czars, the military leaders were perforce unquestionably on the side of modernization of the army and of the economic power of the country so that the military could be properly equipped to fight in the arms race and to defend the very rule of the backward Oligarchy that refused change. Roads, railroads, armories, metal plants, modern arms manufacturing works, and the large number of other vital tools and equipment had to be constructed or a military would lose the race and their Oligarchy would be destroyed. Victory by the army depended no longer on the genius of this or that Napoleon or *caudillo* but on pooled organized staff effort like that of the modern corporation.

As we have seen, after World War I and during the great depression of the 1930's, manufacturing and industrial development took measurable steps forward in certain larger of the Latin American countries. Latin American militarists were also witnesses of the new army sprung from the Russian Revolution and those that arose from fascism during the depression, all of which spoke to the people in terms of social goals. Learning their lessons well, these Latin American militarists also began to speak against foreign imperialism and foreign interests, to favor autarchy and self-sufficiency, and to expand their totalitarian principles to win over the mass of toilers.

Fascism was very popular among the military gentry and Oligarchy in Latin America, while Franco and Mussolini were much admired by Vargas in Brazil, Ubico in Guatemala, Benavides in Peru, Perón in Argentina, and Villaroel in Bolivia. Supporting them in their support were such political organizations as the Integralists in Brazil, the Senarquists in Mexico, the National Socialist Party in Chile, the Herreristas in Uruguay, etc.

Military interventions and coup d'etats in Latin America were now not in the name of some charismatic leader, but in the name of the armed forces as a whole, the *Junta,* with army, navy, air, marines all combined in it. The *Junta* was often preceded by the officers' conspiratorial club that would organize the coup d'etat as the Santa Cruz Lodge in Bolivia, in 1936, the Group of United Officers in Argentina, in 1943, and the Patriotic Military Union in Venezuela, in 1945. The army men, when they took over the governments directly, did not hesitate to use the schools, the church, the trade unions, and other social institutions. Economic sanctions were sometimes used even against the moneyed elements, while demagogic talk of "social planning" and national "socialism" filled the air.

The military now insisted on national self-sufficiency, at least so far as the vital interests of the armed forces were concerned. In Brazil, Vargas was pushed into producing airplanes; in Argentina, Perón came out for military heavy industry and metal plants. In a number of Latin American countries the military leaders insisted on taking charge of many industrial agencies that ordinarily would be in the hands of civilians and saw to it that they got a large share of the national budget.

It must not in the least be supposed that despite the efforts of the leaders of the armed forces to modernize their equipment and methods that they were still not close to the Oligarchy or would do anything to remove it from power. It is clear to most students of the problem that genuine agrarian reform in Latin America is perhaps impossible without the destruction of the officer corps, recruited as it has been from the upper-middle social ranks and top ranks of an oligarchy which believes firmly in the sanctity of private property and would do nothing to overthrow the existing system of control.

Furthermore, political exigencies have impelled the United States to favor and cater to these military leaders. Thanks to World War II, the United States was able to drive out the Axis military missions infesting Latin America and substitute its own, rendering a great deal of assistance to the Latin American militarists in order to secure bases, raw materials needed, etc. In 1942, at Rio de Janeiro, the United States got all American republics, except Argentina, to agree to sever relations with the Axis and set up an Inter-American Defense Board to get joint action. The Latin American military leaders, however, were eager to accept the hand-outs but not to carry out their pledges. Chile did not sever relations with the Axis, Argentina remained neutral practically to the very end; only Brazil declared war on the Axis and the Defense Board could coordinate only through bilateral agreements with individual countries.

After World War II, with the beginning of the "cold war" against the Soviet powers, the United States made new efforts to rally the Latin American military. In 1947 a new Rio Pact was signed by all Latin American states, with the United States calling for collective security on the promise that large monetary grants would be handed out by the United States. In 1951 Congress passed the Mutual Security Act granting both military aid and also general aid on a reimbursable basis provided the Latin American regimes would agree to prohibit trade in strategic materials to the Soviet Union and give the United States exclusive access to strategic resources. Mexico refused to agree and received no aid. By 1959 twelve Latin American republics had obtained $317 million in grants for military aid and nineteen American countries received $140 million in reimbursable aid. At the present time in Latin America the United States has exclusive military missions, gives exclusive military training, is the exclusive supplier of arms, etc. But only Colombia responded with aid in the Korean War.

The breaking out of the Korean War greatly accelerated the process of U.S.-Latin American military cooperation. The Organization of American States signed the Act of Chapultepec in which it was stated that an attack on one of the republics in the Western Hemisphere would be considered as an attack on all and the Inter-American Defense Board was made permanent.

As a result of these U.S. commitments to the Latin American militarists the Charter of the Alliance for Progress faces a most serious dilemma. The Charter states that agrarian reform is most necessary. To obtain this agrarian reform it must fight the Oligarchy. The Oligarchy controls the armed forces. The United States, up to now, has greatly favored the militarists. The army acts as a state within a state in Latin America. Should the armed forces be destroyed, popular revolutions would follow immediately.

The strength of the armed forces in Latin America can be seen in the following table where the figures are given for 1956:

Table 30

LATIN AMERICAN COUNTRIES: TOTAL ARMED FORCES: 1956

Argentina	147,500
Bolivia	12,000
Brazil	107,200
Chile	41,500
Colombia	16,700
Costa Rica	none
Cuba	23,400
Dominican Republic	18,500
Ecuador	19,800
Guatemala	8,400
Haiti	4,950
Honduras	3,700
Mexico	47,800
Nicaragua	11,300
Panama	3,500
Paraguay	7,300
Peru	37,500
El Salvador	6,900
Uruguay	6,450
Venezuela	17,200
Total	541,600

How entrenched the military are can be noted from the following table which gives the share of the national budget the armed forces received in 1954:

Table 31

LATIN AMERICAN COUNTRIES:
ARMED FORCES: SHARE OF NATIONAL BUDGET 1954

Argentina	23%
Brazil	33
Chile	23
Ecuador	40
Venezuela	16

These figures are mere illustrations, since they are subject to sudden and drastic changes depending upon national circumstances. Ordinarily the armed forces receive 25% to 30% of the national budget and would overthrow the government were they to receive less.

Up to now militarism must be considered a basic fact of life in Latin America. Since World War II only Uruguay, Costa Rica, Chile, and Mexico have been free of serious military meddling. Many of these countries have had military rule most of the time since their independent existence. Between independence and World War I the Spanish American republics experienced 115 successful revolutions and many times that number of abortive revolts. Between October 1945 and the end of September 1957 alone de facto regimes were overturned by the military in all but five of the twenty republics.

Recent successful military revolts can be enumerated as follows: Argentina—1955 and 1961; Brazil—1954 and an attempt in 1961; Colombia—1956; Cuba—1959, with a popular army replacing the old; Dominican Republic—1961, 1963; Haiti—1956; Honduras—1956, 1963; Guatemala—1954, 1963; Peru—1962; Venezuela—1958; Ecuador—1963. Presidents were assassinated in Panama (1955), in Nicaragua (1956), in Guatemala (1957). In Peru the President was exiled by the military (1962), also in the Dominican Republic (1963) and in Honduras 1963; in Brazil pressured to commit suicide (1954) or to resign (1961), in Argentina imprisoned (1961-1963).

Between 1930 and 1957, 56 military men held the presidential office in 20 Latin American republics for as long as one year. Many of these were young officers of the reform type interested in the industrialization of the country and using popular phrases to win the mass of people, especially the workers. A few are herewith enumerated:

Chile	Major Ibanez (1930-31)
Argentina	Colonel Perón (1945-55)
Paraguay	Colonel Rafael Franco (1936-37)
Paraguay	General Felix Estigarriba (1939-40)
Bolivia	Colonel German Busch (1936-38)
Bolivia	Major Gualberto Villaroel (1943-46)
Colombia	General Rojas Pinella (1953-56)
Panama	Colonel Antonio Remón (1952-55)
Guatemala	Major Arbenz (1950-54)
Mexico	General Lázaro Cárdenas (1934-40)
Cuba	Sergeant Fulgencio Batista (1933-44)
El Salvador	Major Oscar Osorio (1948-56)

One writer has summed up the matter as follows: "Duly elected civilian presidents were generally powerless to call erring generals to order . . . Also, with few exceptions, the armed forces were in fact not strictly professional, no matter what the law said; rather they were highly political groups. They 'deliberated' on all matters, particularly 'on matters relating to the service' . . . Finally, they frequently flouted the constitutional rights they were supposed to 'guarantee' and ignored the laws they were pledged to enforce. Whatever role the armed forces played in a revolution itself the new civilian government was never permitted to alter the armed forces' 'traditional' role as the ultimate arbiters of political disputes, nor to trim the customary share of the budget, nor to interfere with their pay benefits, discipline, and promotions. Reform regimes were obliged to confine their activities to non-military matters . . ." [5]

At present the military in Latin America consider themselves above the law and the state and change governments at will. In Venezuela in 1948 the military removed a popular government and, when defeated in 1952, refused to quit. Peru in 1948 and Cuba in 1952 witnessed military leaders overthrowing duly-created governments and keeping themselves in power in face of popular opposition.

With supreme arrogance these military men, utterly ignorant in most matters, considered themselves competent to handle all kinds of posts. The extreme was reached in Peru when General Odrio had an all-military cabinet in which colonels headed the ministries of public health, education, labor, interior, treasury, and justice, and a Rear Admiral conducted foreign relations. In Brazil, in the spring of 1959, the armed force officers held the following positions in public agencies relating to industrial development:

Minister of Transportation and Public Works,
Director General National Mails and Telegraph Services,
President, Radio Technical Commission,
President, Merchant Marine Commission,
Administrator, Leopoldina Railway Company (state owned),
President, National Petroleum Council,
President, National Steel Company,
Superintendent, National Oil Tanker Fleet,

[5] See: *The Role of the Military in Underdeveloped Countries,* edited by John J. Johnson (Rand Corp.) 1962, pp. 150-151.

Director General, Civil Aviation,
Secretary General, National Coordination Council of Food Supply,
President, National Executive Commission for Coal Production
   Planning,
Director, Food Supply Service,
Chairman, National Price Control Board,
President, National Commission on Nuclear Energy,
President, National Transportation Council, etc.
plus very many subordinate posts.

Naturally, military leaders and dictators do not operate for love. In the volume edited by John J. Johnson already cited it is stated: "In the five-year period from 1954 to 1959 it was estimated that Latin America's fleeing military dictators carried out of the area upward of one billion dollars." Perón of Argentina is put down for $700 million! Perez Jiminez of Venezuela for $250 million; Batista of Cuba for $200 million (the Cuban regime says the Batista clique took $500 million); General Trujillo of the Dominican Republic $30 million a year (he stayed in power many years); the Somoza family of Nicaragua an untold amount; General Juan Vicente Gomez "hundreds of millions," Eleazar Lopez Contreras $13 million, Isaias Medina Angarita $13 million, all three from Venezuela; Rojas Pinella of Colombia, Magloire of Haiti and others, "large fortunes." And this is only a very small part of the loot which the followers of these men were able to steal and hide away.

In the light of these facts is it not ridiculous to suppose that these military vermin and their oligarchic class interests can be easily put aside by the Alliance for Progress program? Such people are quite willing to take a million oaths that they will carry out a million reforms, but nothing will happen and any money given to them is bound to go down a drain without sides or bottom.

Why are the U.S. policy makers so insistent on supporting this venal and disgracefully ignorant group of militarists? Certainly, from the hemispheric point of view military defense of Latin America is not a pressing problem since the area is not subject to invasion by the Soviet Union. With the advent of nuclear weapons, is it not silly to think that the armies of Latin America and their leaders who know only how to kill their own unarmed people will be of any use in a real war? What value, then, has the U.S. standardization program of modern weapons, or the so-called military missions of the United States?

In all this the United States simply ties itself up with the worst reactionaries in Latin America, feeds the hostility of the masses, helps the rise of militarism, and encourages a foolish arms race among the Latin American rulers. The Pentagon helps the army keep its dominant position in the political field and become of greater service than ever to the agrarians who must be ousted if Latin America is to advance even in a capitalist, not to speak of a democratic, sense.

In the meantime, while Latin America begs for capital help from the United States and their rulers constantly plead poverty and "underdevelopment," at the same time billions in cash are stolen and hidden away in Europe not only by the dictators but by their class masters, the landed Oligarchy. This flight of cash and capital is not new for Latin America but it is only in 1962 that the Joint Economic Committee, Congress of the United States, could report in reviewing the first year's work of the Alliance for Progress:

"The testimony brought disturbing evidence of a reluctance on the part of some wealthy Latin American investors to risk private investment in their own countries. This reluctance is, indeed, reported to have taken the form of a substantial 'flight' of local capital to Europe or the United States. Estimates presented to the subcommittee of the amount of this expatriated 'flight' capital ranged from $5 to $15 billion. The $10 billion estimate ascribed to one Latin American Minister of Economics is probably as good a figure to use as any." (italics in original)

To emphasize their own lack of faith, the rulers of most Latin American countries have decreed that only income arising from sources within the country is subject to taxation and earnings on investments outside a country are thus free of tax, even though the owner is a citizen and a resident. Such a policy obviously only enhances the attractiveness of sending money abroad.

Allied with Latin American militarists, already the U.S. Government is showing every indication of backing down on any serious agrarian reform. It will be remembered that one of the targets of the Charter called for the transformation of unjust structures and systems of land tenure into an equitable system. How this is to be interpreted and carried out is a most important matter.

Here is how the international labor organization, ORIT, attached to the AFL-CIO conceived the matter in its special conference held in São Paulo from August 17 to 19, 1961, right after the Punte del Este Conference. Keep in mind that the Cuban Revolution can best be contained if the workingmen can be persuaded to help the Alliance for Progress and this job was up to the American organized labor leaders. Their statement declared:

"The starting point for progress in the sovereign countries of Latin America, and also in those that are still under colonial rule, must be a program of rapid, radical transformation of their agrarian economy. The basis of progress in the under-developed parts of America must indeed be land reform. Whatever the particularities and differences that can be found in the various countries, common to all of them is the need to transform the structure of their rural economy, juridically and socially, that is to begin to put into practice processes of land reform.

"*We understand by land reform the return of the land to those who till it, and a recognition of their right to receive in full the fruits of their labor. In other words, a fundamental condition for progress lies in the elimination of the system of feudal holdings which, together with their political power, has plunged our peoples into misery and slavery.*" (italics in original)

This did not prevent these labor leaders from violently denouncing the Cuban Revolution in a separate Political Declaration issued in their full ORIT Congress held in Rio de Janeiro immediately following their Economic Conference in São Paulo. According to these sciolists, then, all Latin American countries needed land reform, but not Cuba; the starting point must be a program of rapid, radical transformation of agrarian economy, but not in Cuba; the land should be returned to those who till it, but not in Cuba; those who till the land should receive the full fruits of their labor, but not in Cuba; the system of feudal holdings must be eliminated, but not in Cuba; the feudal holders must be eliminated from political power, but not in Cuba; the Latin American peoples have been plunged into misery and slavery, but not in Cuba; throughout Latin America there is excessive oppression, despotic oligarchies, military police and terrorist machines, but not in Cuba; etc.

Such a ridiculous point of view, of course, can not be shared by the U.S. Government. On the contrary, the Government has to question whether the statement in the Punte del Este Charter did not go too far and whether the masses in Latin America would not thereby be aroused to realize the target set by the Alliance for Progress by revolutionary Cuban methods. Hence the reports to the Joint Economic Committee, Congress of the United States, contain such statements as the following:

"The meaning and objectives of 'agrarian reform' in the context of the Alliance for Progress, especially the interest and role of the U.S. Government as a participant in the Alliance, has tended to become confused as simply a tenure problem, but properly conceived should have as its primary objective increased agricultural productivity by a variety of means . . . Thoughtful persons in the United States are a bit uneasy, moreover, that the objectives of 'agrarian reform' are punitively directed and that we are lending our tacit support, if not encouragement, to a program whereby property rights under law are being interfered with."

What sort of measures the U.S. Government advocates is given in another report to the Joint Economic Committee issued 1962: "6. The objective of land tenure changes is not to be punitively directed against large landholdings or absentee landowners as such; on the contrary, existing property rights under law are to be respected." "11. As a first step in land reform and possible redistribution, the respective participating countries should look first to public lands and lands not presently under appropriation. To this end (1) an accurate survey of acreage and usability of the public domain, (2) an appropriate adaptation of the U.S. provisions for land grants in the aid of schools and colleges dating back to 1859, and (3) the so-called homestead acts dating back to 1891 are recommended for consideration."

The report also praised the plan applied in Venezuela which calls for the following order in expropriation of land: a) unused land; b) land indirectly developed in the owners' permanent absence, through temporary tenants, sharecroppers, or squatters; c) land kept idle for five years; d) farming land used to a disproportionately large extent in the raising of livestock. But none of this can be done until all public land is first disposed of.

Thus the U.S. Government fails to stress the important point in agrarian reform in Latin America which consists in the absolute necessity of removing the parasitic hand of the Oligarchy and its armed guards from the political control of the nation. It is not a matter of placing ex-peons on far-removed public lands, equipped with the poorest tools and unable to survive any great length of time, reaching finally the result that the very best lands of the wealthy landowners will only be further enhanced and the poor farmer eventually thrust out completely. It is a matter of destroying the old antediluvian oligarchic structure that sucks the very life blood of the nation and prevents all progress.

As a matter of fact, Latin American republics do not really need U.S. loans and credits. These lands are "underdeveloped" only because their agrarian rulers 1. squander enormous unnecessary sums on their armed forces; 2. refuse to tax themselves to any appreciable extent; 3. hide their wealth abroad; 4. suck out the gross national product for conspicuous consumption for themselves.

All that these nations need to do is: 1. reduce the military budget to 10% or less of the total national budget; 2. enforce a tax of 15% on all real property and a larger tax on all unused real estate; 3. enforce a stiff, progressive income tax; 4. prohibit the flight of money and compel the return of all such money sent abroad; 5. place a heavy sales tax on all articles of luxury consumption strictly enforced. Then there would be plenty of funds for rapid development, both of the national structure and of the infra-structure. But this, of course, is precisely what can *not* be obtained without revolution, to which both native rulers and U.S. politicians are opposed.

Instead of the above actions, what the United States wants the Latin American regimes to do is: 1. restrict wages; 2. drastically reduce the number of employees both in the government and in government operated enterprises (such as railroads); 3. eliminate the barriers to free trade; 4. permit free foreign exchange; 5. help the agrarian large landholder increase his efficiency.

We can now turn to the historic nature and character of the new bourgeois classes in the more developed Latin American countries: Argentina, Brazil, Chile, Mexico. Can the developing native industrial bourgeoisie take control of the armed forces, push aside the landed Oligarchy and modernize the country along the lines adumbrated in the Alliance for Progress Charter? This seems hardly possible.

In the first place, the landed aristocracy or Oligarchy have been entrenched in power for centuries. Their sons and relatives manipulate the army, control politics and, by expansion and infiltration, now control considerable masses of capital in industry as well. A large section of industrialists is now solidly tied to the agrarian wealthy.

In the second place, the agrarians, traditionally, have been supported by the leading imperialist powers, first England and then the United States. It was the agrarian wealthy who furnished the mass of primary exports needed by imperialist countries and who swept aside all barriers to imports of finished goods from imperialist countries. These are the people who have sent their sons abroad and who have great sympathy for the ruling groups of Spain, or of Portugal, or of England, etc. It is only relatively lately that imperialism has concentrated on industrialization and developed interests different from the agrarians, its former partners.

In the third place, the native industrial bourgeois elements come very late upon the historic scene. They are weak; they are relatively poorly developed; they are timid. They can not fight the army; they can not displace the agrarian Oligarchy. They can fuse with the Oligarchy, get some favors, and become partners in government, but they cannot remove that Oligarchy.

Besides, any real fight will bring in the masses who can not be relied on merely to fight the battles of the bourgeoisie. The Latin American workers and toilers have strong revolutionary traditions and are well used to bitter struggles. In the eyes of the native modern bourgeoisie by no means can the workers be trusted not to fight for their own interests and bring about another Cuba.

It is true that now that American capitalists have entered the scene *en masse* the industrialists have much greater support and have a chance with American help greatly to advance their interests and assume the dominant position. But here they are retarded by the fact that the interests of American capitalists are still not the same as those of the native industrialists. The entrance of American and foreign capital places the native industrialist in second place, as a sort of auxiliary worker for the benefit of that capital. This is not the kind of role favorable for political leadership. As lackeys serving American capitalism the native industrialists lack prestige; they can not take control and the Americans can not take control without them.

There is, however, a third and more radical grouping, a grouping foreshadowed by Vargas in Brazil, Perón in Argentina, Cárdenas in Mexico. This grouping has as spokesmen a large group of intellectuals, economists, writers, engineers, and other professionals who insist that following America and the capitalist West is only slowing down the rate of growth which more developed Latin American countries can achieve. With hungry eyes they have looked toward the Soviet Bloc and wish to utilize the procedures that have brought dramatic results there.

This grouping is not against state development of massive industries and plants. They do not wish to proceed only or even basically with private industrial capital at the helm. These intellectuals in their own search for power know that they would not become top beneficiaries by tying themselves with domestic corporations controlled by large family groups with their notorious nepotism. They want the state to act and to get the funds through taxation. They are also acutely aware of the numeric weakness of their group and they insist on an extensive development of the infra-structure to allow for mass education and scientific development on a grand scale.

These people do not follow the line of policy that avers that first the country must be agricultural, then it must develop light consumers industries, and then heavy, basic industry and only after a long period of time, centuries if England is taken as an example, will the country become mature and ready for international competition in all fields. They do not know why they cannot accelerate that process and move directly according to some basic plan, not from light to heavy industry, not from small to large plants, not from consumers goods to producers goods, but straightforward to heavy basic industry that would produce capital goods for the operation of light consumer goods factories as well as for the development of the primary resources of the country.

They have before them two very significant experiences. On the one hand they witness the development of the Common Market in Europe. Latin America had been taught traditionally to believe that as capitalism grew and flourished in the industrial countries the primary producing countries would be called on to furnish more goods. It had also been taught to believe that with industrial development the finished goods it needed would become cheaper and more plentiful.

What Latin Americans now witness is, however, something entirely different. They notice an enormous growth of Western Europe's economy with practically no increase in Latin American exports to that region. What is prosperity for the industrial countries of Western Europe is not at all prosperity for Latin America. Instead Western Europe displays a constantly clearer tendency for self-sufficiency with higher tariff walls instead of freer trade. Why should Latin America, then, continue to play this nonsensical game to its detriment?

In addition they have recently experienced the further unorthodox fact that though since 1957 the United States has been suffering from economic stagnation, U.S. steel prices have not fallen, wages in U.S. manufacturing industries have even risen, while their own prices have fallen both absolutely and relatively. Meanwhile their countries are sinking deeper into foreign debt. In 1958 the foreign debt in Brazil had reached the astounding total of $1.5 billion; in Argentina $1.4 billion; Chile, Colombia, and Peru well over a quarter of a billion dollars each, etc.

On the other hand they look at countries, like Romania and Bulgaria, no more developed than the leading Latin American countries were at the end of World War II, now galloping ahead industrially after emerging from the War practically ruined. Bulgaria and Romania have long-term plans. They start directly emphasizing heavy, basic industry. They develop their capital goods and from there move to satisfy consumers needs. No wonder the Latin American intellectuals grow discontented when they compare their own rates of growth with the figures given for the Soviet Bloc countries as shown in the tables on page 88.

These Latin Americans realize very well the suction pump operations of foreign capital. They are repelled by the fact that they who need capital most are forced to export capital (money and capital goods) and that they are rapidly losing all control. Instead of importing foreign capital as now done they would place a heavy graduated progressive income tax on individuals and on corporations and a special excess profits tax. This, they believe, would give them all the capital they need for new investments and development of the infra-structure. At the same time they would prohibit the repatriation of foreign capital, except for the original capital, and forbid any remittances abroad of incomes, dividends, interests, or profits, while carefully screening all entering industries as to the need for their existence and their contribution to permanent national development according to plan.

The economic theorists in Latin America in favor of all-embracing economic and social planning centrally directed are well aware of U.S. opposition to such efforts as evidenced by such views as the following made in a report to the Congress of the United States:

"A major effort of U.S. policy toward Latin America should be to

Table 32
SOVIET BLOC: ANNUAL RATE OF GROWTH:
PERCENTAGE OF NATIONAL INCOME 1950-59

	Total Growth	Industrial Growth
Czechoslovakia	7.5%	9.4%
East Germany	8.8	11.1
Soviet Union	10.1	12.6
Hungary	6.2	9.3
Poland	8.0	12.3
Yugoslavia	6.3	9.5
Romania	10.3	14.0
Bulgaria	8.7	13.3
China	15.2	28.0

Table 33
SOVIET BLOC: INDEX OF GROWTH BY VALUE OF OUTPUT
(PREWAR BASE EQUALS 100)

	Industry		Agriculture	
	1950	1960	1950	1960
Czechoslovakia	143	404	87	104
Soviet Union	173	520	99	159
Poland	231	778	98	124
Hungary	158	420	89	115
Romania	147	505	81	124
Bulgaria	309	1228	84	150
Yugoslavia	172	450	83	146

Table 34
SOVIET BLOC: ANNUAL RATE OF GROWTH IN INDUSTRIAL OUTPUT PER MAN,
AVERAGE 1950-59

	Total	Machinery & metal products	Chemical
Czechoslovakia	7.8%	10.2%	10.5%
East Germany	9.1	11.1	7.6
Soviet Union	7.4	11.0	8.9
Hungary	4.0	5.9	3.0
Poland	8.7	13.7	12.8
Romania	8.2	13.0	9.8
Bulgaria	6.6	13.6	11.3

Table 35
SOVIET BLOC: MACHINERY EXPORTS AS PERCENTAGE OF
TOTAL EXPORTS: 1950 & 1960

	1950	1960
Czechoslovakia	26%	45%
East Germany	28	48
Soviet Union	12	21
Hungary	23	38
Poland	12	28
Yugoslavia	2	15
Romania	1	12
Bulgaria	0	13

point up the merits of and assist these countries to develop a reliance on private enterprise and the processes of private investment decision-making. Every time we encourage reliance on centralized planning, we risk playing into Soviet hands, by showing a distrust of our own characteristic national method and encouraging the technique of our ideological competitors. If formalizing the role of government in economic decision making is to be our recommendation, it would not be surprising if the developing countries turned to the Soviet's example as notorious practitioners, and hence best equipped advisers in that line. We ought, in short, to be wary of trying to fight communism on the world stage by turning to socialistic and authoritarian instruments in the developing nations."

Historically, the United States is not in a very favorable position vis-a-vis Russia, so far as possible influence is concerned. Starting with the end of the 19th century the principal policy of the United States, up to the beginning of the 1930's, was one of contemptuous direct military intervention, as in Cuba (1898-1902 and later up to the 1920's with the possession of Guantanamo Naval Base), Haiti (1915-1934), the Dominican Republic (1916-1924), Panama (1903-1933), and Nicaragua (1912-1925, 1926-1933).

Then came the "Good Neighbor" policy of President Franklin D. Roosevelt, and various alliances during World War II, followed by a strengthening of the Pan-American Union and the Organization of American States—all this to the immense advantage of the North American state.

The third stage has been marked by the massive penetration of U.S. capital through a large number of international institutions, agencies, banks, and funds, with the resultant capital suction pump operations already described and the steady weakening of Latin America's relative position.

Now a new and ominous stage is opening up marked by the threats of invasion of Cuba by the coordinated efforts of all the old regimes of Latin America spurred on by the United States.

The Soviet Union has no such history. It has never invaded any Latin American country. It did not use them for its war purposes. It never subordinated any Western Hemisphere country economically. It has come to the aid of Cuba. It is the strongest opponent of U.S. imperialism.

Already various Latin American governments have been approached by the Soviet Bloc, a) for the sale of strategic materials; b) for the purpose of selling oil drilling machinery; c) for the purchase of petroleum at very low prices by Latin America; d) for acceptance of long-term very low-interest loans and credits; e) for help in planning for Latin American development; f) for acceptance of engineering missions to develop the resources and basic metals of the region; g) for full trade reciprocity; h) for cultural reciprocity, etc. Up to now Latin American governments have rejected these approaches as being in opposition to their obligations toward the United States. But these objections are becoming less and less strenuous.

In 1961, while Latin American exports fell in value 1% worldwide, and 8% with North America, they rose 55% to the communist world. The figures from 1959 to 1961 are as follows: Exports to Latin America from Communist Bloc countries were in 1959—$135 million; in 1960—$234 million; in 1961—$375 million. At the same time imports from Latin America to Communist Bloc countries moved from $154 million in 1959, to $307 million in 1960, to $475 million in 1961. In 1950 the Soviet Bloc took less than 1% of Latin American exports; in 1960 it took 2.8%, and the percentage is steadily increasing.

To Latin America, Cuba is the decisive test. Cuba was originally one of them, like them. If Cuba, now that it has entered the Soviet orbit, can have proper planning, develop its basic resources and industries, transform itself from a one-crop export country to diversified exports and become more or less self-sustaining, while moving at the same rate of speed as Bulgaria or Rumania in improving its infrastructure, there will be an immense appeal to all of Latin America to follow this example. That is why it is so important to the United States to counter Cuba and to destroy its new social system now.

In a special report to Congress it was stated: "The primary task of American diplomacy today is to weld together a large coalition of free nations on the basis of a common appreciation of the Communist threat and on the basis of a series of common undertakings to blunt that threat and assert the value of our own civilization." It is precisely this task that is threatened with non-fulfillment in Latin America.

PART TWO

Revolutionary Crisis in Argentina

Judged by orthodox criteria, Argentina has entered into a deep crisis from which there can be no exit save revolution. First of all, the biting economic crisis peculiar to this country comes superimposed upon a basic chronic crisis affecting all of Latin America, including Argentina. The economic crisis is of such a nature that it is practically impossible for Argentina to emerge from it without revolutionary methods. Second, there rages a deep political crisis manifesting clearly that the ruling classes of that country are unable to rule as of old because they can not solve the sharp problems distressing the nation. The ruling classes are so split up that the government is held together only by the most stringent military dictatorship, representing the executive committee of the bourgeoisie as a whole. Third, there surges a tremendous social crisis in which the working class and poor toilers are demonstrating unusual activity which can not be put down.

The revolutionary period into which Argentina is entering may start as a military coup d'etat but must become a democratic revolution, a social revolution, a people's revolution, perhaps even a proletarian revolution. Far riper for such a revolution than even Cuba, Argentina can well lead the way for all of Latin America really to snap the bonds of capitalism-imperialism for a break-through to a new social order.

How well this threat is generally realized was illustrated on June 5, 1963 when the United States and Argentina signed an Investment Guarantee Agreement whereby new U.S. investments in Argentina will be protected against losses that may result from inconvertibility, war, revolution, and expropriation. According to the press, requests to the

Agency for International Development (AID) for such guarantees immediately ran in excess of $400 million in value.

In the world subdivision of labor, Latin America occupies fundamentally the role of producer of primary materials which are mainly exported for use by the industrial countries, particularly the United States and those in Western Europe. In the case of Argentina the chief exports are grain and meat products. The shipments of these exports are mainly in foreign ships so that the freight charges weigh very heavily against Argentina.

Since each Latin American country, including Argentina, depends on exports of only one or two primary products, none of these countries has much bargaining power or flexibility, especially in comparison with the industrial countries. A versatile industrial country like England, for example, can shift its production and exports quickly from one article to another depending on the market situation, but should England buy its meat from Australia and its grain from Canada instead of both from Argentina, Argentina could not shift its exports to something else. It has no flexibility in that regard since it can not change to another prime material which does not exist within its borders. During the great depression of the 1930's such a frightening circumstance is exactly what happened.

Markets for prime materials may also decline not in any particular country but generally because industrial countries tend to become more and more efficient and can produce more and better finished goods with ever less materials, as in the case of minerals such as tin. Apropos Argentina this market decline can result from the importing country producing ever more food supplies for itself and becoming ever more self-sufficient. Argentina is also affected by the political needs of the industrial countries not to impoverish their own farmers to such an extent as to make them discontented and revolutionary.

Again, severely affecting Argentina, there has been a definite shift in the prosperous industrial countries away from bread and grains to fruits and vegetables. This can be seen in Tables 1 and 2.

In regard to meat, a recent issue of the *Meat Trades Journal* in London reported that Argentina supplied in 1962 only 7% of Britain's needs whereas it was 20% before the last war. Before the war

Table 1

FALL IN PER CAPITA CONSUMPTION OF WHEAT AND RYE (IN KILOGRAMS)

Country	1934-38	1954-55
Sweden	85.1	72.6
Denmark	85.8	83.9
Gr. Britain	88.2	85.1
Netherlands	96.7	86.0
Switzerland	97.6	89.5
Norway	106.6	89.7
W. Germany	108.0	91.5
Belgium	106.8	98.1
France	117.6	102.4
Austria	126.5	107.3
Italy	127.9	132.6
Greece	140.6	132.7
Turkey	152.7	147.6
United States	72.2	59.3

Table 2

DEGREE OF SELF-SUFFICIENCY IN WHEAT AND MEAT IN WESTERN EUROPE
(EXCLUDING GR. BR.) AND IN GREAT BRITAIN

Ave. of Yrs.	Wheat Western Europe (exc. Gr. Br.)	Great Britain
1905-13	64%	74%
1934-38	76	85
1952-55	84	91
	Meat	
1934-38	85%	103%
1950-52	95	109

Argentina sent 436,000 tons of meat per year, the figures for 1961 showed about 186,000 tons to Britain.

In the 30 years ending 1955-57, the per-capita consumption in Western Europe increased by 35% but imported supplies rose only by 9%. And now, with the rise of the Common Market protection of its own farmers, the situation threatens to become much worse for such countries as Argentina. Even where the per-capita consumption of beef jumped in the United States from index number 100 in 1948-1950 to index number 129 in 1955-57, this was counterbalanced by the fact that Argentine imports of meat were prohibited from entering the United States.

Furthermore, even when the total volume of exports does not fall, the prices may change in such a manner as to make the terms of trade very bad for Latin America and for Argentina. The following table illustrates the situation in both good times and bad, the year 1937 being taken as normal and equal to 100 in the index.

Table 3

ARGENTINA: POPULATION, EXPORTS, IMPORTS, TERMS OF TRADE, CAPACITY TO IMPORT

Year	Popu-lation (millions)	Quantity Index		Price Index		Terms of Trade Index	Index of Total Capacity to Import
		Exports	Imports	Exports	Imports		
1929	11.5	104	125	90.2	100.6	89.7	92.8
1932	12.4	92	57.6	60.5	93.2	64.9	59.7
1937		100	100	100	100	100	100
1940	14.9	69	69.9	89.6	137.6	65.1	44
1946	16.0	73	68.3	235.5	219.2	107.4	78.4

As this table repays careful and close study, it might be well for us to make a few explanatory remarks. The year 1929 is chosen to represent the peak of prosperity, the year 1932 to represent the depth of the depression. The year 1937 can be taken as normal since by this time the depression was well on the way to liquidation especially because of the coming world war and the necessary preparations for it. (The fact is, however, that the 1937 level was about 10% below the 1925-29 average level before the great depression broke.) The year 1940 is the first year of the war, the year 1946 the first post-war year, 1949 the year when the immediate economic effects of the war were over and the world was entering upon a relatively normal phase of its existence, although a recession was seemingly beginning. Since the year 1937 has been taken as the base year all columns in the table above are calculated as percentages of that base year index, except the column on population.

In further explanation it may be added: a) the price index of exports, and that of imports, is obtained by weighting the prices of all the principal items making up exports and imports and getting an average price as compared to the average that existed in 1937; b) "Terms of Trade" means the cost of the imports in terms of the cost of exports, this figure being reached by dividing the price index of the exports by the price index of the imports; c) the index of the capacity to import is obtained by multiplying the terms of trade by the index of the volume of exports. When the terms of trade are favorable it means that a given volume of exports may buy more imports—in the above table this being shown where the figures are over 100 as compared with 1937. When terms of trade are favorable, the capacity to import can then be gaged by estimating the volume of exports which can take advantage of the favorable terms of trade—in the above table being compared with the base year 1937.

Now the above table shows us:

1. The year 1929 was a better than normal year, it was, in fact, the peak of prosperity before the crash of the depression. The volume of exports was 4% above normal (1937). The prices that Argentina received for her exports, however, were about 10% less than normal while the prices which Argentina had to pay for imports were about normal, so that the terms of trade were against Argentina as compared with 1937 in that the same amount of exports could bring in only 10% less imports, or, in other words, to bring in the same amount of imports Argentina would have to export about 11% more. Since Argentina in fact that year exported a total volume of only 4% more than normal this meant the total capacity to import on the part of Argentina was only 92.8% of normal. Since Argentina in fact imported 25% more than its import capacity, it apparently went further into debt.

2. The data for 1932 illuminate what happened during the depression. The population since 1929 had increased by almost a million. Since Argentina exported food which people must have even in a depression her exports did not diminish too much in volume, falling only from index number 104 to 92, but the price index fell from 90.2 to 60.5. This meant a total loss in capacity to import of about 40%. Since such low prices were less than her cost of production, Argentina took the expedient of burning her grain harvests as fuel! Actually, that year the index of import volume fell to 57.6% of normal, most likely because Argentina's creditors were withdrawing their capital. Thus, during the depression Argentina could not import much finished goods, either means of production or means of consumption.

During the depression Argentina tried to make up the loss of consumption imports by developing her own factories in light industry, such as textiles, shoes, etc. She could not make up import losses in machinery and in means of modernization, however, and thus Argentina lagged behind in productive capacity. Possessing a very considerable gold reserve saved from previous good years, Argentina very foolishly allowed the military conservative leaders who had then seized control of the government to agree to pay the country's debts in gold reserve funds, illegally, it seems, during a depression when gold was worth enormously more than when the debts were originally contracted. This was no less than a betrayal of the country's interests, since no other capitalist country was doing this and the result was enormous unnecessary losses for Argentina.

While export prices were falling during this period to but 60.5% of normal, the prices of goods that Argentina had to buy were lowered only to 93.2% of normal, thus the terms of trade were heavily weighted against Argentina. The industrialized imperialist countries were exerting their pressure against the colonial primary material countries all over the world and Argentina was certainly no exception.

3. Then came World War II and all Argentine exports to Europe were cut off. This meant a drastic blow to Argentina first because she could not sell to some of her best customers (e.g. Germany) and thus buy back needed machinery and finished goods from them; second, because she could not buy from the United States and Great Britain since they were entirely engrossed in the war and could not spare means of production goods or much of any finished goods; and, third, because the price of imported goods rose very rapidly beyond the reach of Argentine purchasers.

All this is shown by the figures for 1940. The population had now increased to about 15 million, but the volume of exports was only 69% of normal, as was the level of the volume of imports. With such a glut of grain and meat on her hands Argentina had to keep prices low, to about 90% of normal, while the items she had to purchase went to about 138% of normal. Thus, with total exports low and with terms of trade bad, Argentina had theoretically the capacity to import only 44% of normal. If the table above shows in fact Argentina did import 70% of normal, this meant again she went further heavily into debt.

4. During the course of the war, however, Argentina was able to profit by the great losses of the Allies, as illustrated by the 1946 figures. While her exports rose to 73% of normal in 1946 the export price index had risen to the fastastic level of 235.5, far higher than the index level of import prices, so that the terms of trade now became quite favorable (107% of normal) and Argentina had a lot of money in reserve (only to be stolen and squandered in part by dictator Juan

Perón). The 1946 figures significantly show that try as she would Argentina could not at that time increase her imports to more than 68.3% of normal, although she had the capacity to import considerably more, mainly because the industrial countries would not, or could not, sell her more.

During all this time, while imports were relatively falling away, the population of Argentina was steadily increasing. For one thing this meant that goods, more urgently needed than ever, would have to be produced at home. Again there was a great spurt of home manufactures during the war years and this time not only of consumers goods but of light metal goods especially needed under the impact of the war. Native workers were brought in from the interior of the country to accomplish this industrialization which in turn led to a tremendous political and social upheaval within the country.

The pressure of imports can be seen from the following table:

Table 4
ARGENTINA: PER CAPITA IMPORTS
(ANNUAL AVERAGES IN 1925-1929 PERIOD EQUALS 100)

Years (ave. of)	population	import volume	import volume per capita
1930-34	113.2	68.4	60.4
1935-39	127.9	77.1	60.3
1940-44	138.3	42.0	30.4
1945-48	146.9	82.5	56.2

The above table shows that twenty years after the base years, that is after the five years of prosperity before the depression, Argentina was importing only 82.5% of the volume it had previously imported while, on the other hand, the population had grown to such an extent that the imports per person were only about half of what they had been a generation before.

To sum up, during the depression Argentina could not buy because the terms of trade were weighted so heavily against her; during the early years of the war she could not buy because she could not sell to her previous customers and the terms of trade were still bad; during the later years of the war and post-war period the terms of trade were favorable but she could not buy because no one could or would sell to her. In any case she was in difficulties so far as her industrialization or modernization was concerned.

Argentina's failure to modernize is exemplified in the following table showing not only the loss in acreage of production but also in returns per hectare (a hectare is roughly about 2½ acres; a kilogram 2.2 pounds):

Table 5A
ARGENTINA: AGRICULTURAL PRODUCTION (HECTARES)

	Ave. yr. 1930-34	1958/59	% loss
Wheat	7,065,300	5,176,000	27%
Corn	4,132,500	2,412,000	42
Linseed	2,550,700	1,011,000	60

Production per Hectare (in Kilograms)

Wheat	1,067 kg	1,256 kg	18% (gain)
Corn	1,874	1,824	3
Linseed	1,737	593	66

These Argentine figures should be compared with those in other countries that show a growth of 50% in yield per hectare in the same period. Argentine cows average annually only 106 litres of milk per head while in other countries they average over 1000 litres per head. Ranges properly seeded could hold three or four times the number of animals Argentine ranges do. In Argentina 12% of the cattle have brucellosis, 15% tuberculosis, 25% ticks, etc.

In all fairness, it must be said that Argentina's failure to modernize in agriculture must not be understood in an absolute sense but only in a relative one. On the one hand, Table 5B below shows the increase in tractors on the land, the greater increase in the horsepower of these tractors and the great reduction in the area of land per tractor horse-power. On the other hand, Table 5C shows that primarily because this modernization was not enough to meet the far better modernization in the United States, Canada, Australia, and other countries elsewhere Argentina's quota of land cultivated for grain crops steadily fell in favor of other forms of agricultural development.

Table 5B
ARGENTINA: TRACTORS: HORSE POWER PER UNIT AND
RELATION TO TOTAL HECTARES

	Tractors		Million	Hectares*	Hectares per
	Numbers	H.P.	Hectares	per tractor	tractor H.P.
1947	29,150	25	27.9	960	38.4
1952	49,759	27	28.0	560	20.5
1960	104,200	38	28.9	280	7.3

* Apparently rounded to nearest ten.
Source: Republic of Argentina: Secretariat of Agriculture: National Farm Census, 1960.

Table 5C

ARGENTINA: LAND UTILIZATION (EXCL. TIERRA DEL FUEGO)
(MILLION HECTARES)

	arable farming amount	%	pasturage amount	%	wood & forest amount	%	others amount	%	total
1937	19.7	11	104.3	60	37.2	21	12.4	7	173.6
1947	15.5	9	112.5	65	29.3	17	15.0	9	172.2*
1952	16.4	8	132.0	66	35.3	18	15.4	8	199.0*
1960	13.5	8	123.5	71	21.6	12	15.4	9	174.0

* Totals off due to rounding.
Source: Republic of Argentina: Secretariat of Agriculture: National Farm Census, 1960.

In the case of Argentina the chronic critical situation was made worse by her relation to the United States. The United States has been the chief rival of Argentina in regard to exports of meat and grain, and in more recent years has pressed home her great advantage against the less developed South American country. On the other hand, Argentina must buy from the United States many of the things that the importer must have, a truth brought home all the more sharply during and immediately after World War II when Europe was exhausted and bankrupt.

The following tables illustrate the situation:

Table 6

PERCENTAGE OF ARGENTINE TRADE TO AND FROM U.S., EUROPE,
AND THE WESTERN HEMISPHERE (EXCL. U.S.)

Year	United States exports	imports	Europe exports	imports	Western Hemisphere (excl. U.S.) exports	imports
1929	9.8%	26.3%	81.5%	56.9%	7.3%	11.7%
1932	7.8	11.9	82.2	65.1	7.2	14.3
1940	17.7	30.0	65.0	38.1	13.3	22.0
1946	15.0	28.5	62.3	35.0	16.1	30.8
1949	10.8	14.8	69.0	60.0	20.0	20.0

Table 7

ARGENTINE TRADE TO AND FROM THE U.S., THE U.K.,
AND THE COMMON MARKET. 1958 ($ MILLION)

United States Exports Am't	%	Imports Am't	%	United Kingdom Exports Am't	%	Imports Am't	%	Common Market Exports Am't	%	Imports Am't	%
$128.4	13.6	$202.6	16.4	$234.2	24.9	$102.1	8.3	$339.3	36.1	$313.9	25.4

In 1958 total Argentine exports amounted to $939.9 million, total Argentine imports, $1,232.6 million.

It can be seen from the above that as soon as possible Argentina shifted her imports away from the United States and bought from those who bought from her. This was bound to affect her political relations as well. While other Latin American countries merely supplemented the production of the United States and, in the main, exported to her food and raw materials she did not have herself (fruit, coffee, minerals, etc.), in return the United States furnishing the bulk of the finished goods needed by those Latin American countries, this was not true for Argentina. As we have seen, Argentina does not sell the main part of her exports to the United States, nor does the major share of her imports come from there either. Although Argentina is not so directly affected by what takes place in the United States as are the other Latin American countries, nevertheless every action affecting the United States vitally concerns Argentina.

In 1957, for example, the United States entered its first post-Korea recession with reverberations felt all over the world. Immediately the price of wool fell from 89 cents a pound to 69 cents. If we take the year 1951 as a base called 100 (a prosperous year because of the Korean War) the index of prices fell from 100 to 33 for wool, to 35 for leather, to 63 for cereals, and went to 104 for meat. The total loss to Argentina on this basis amounted to about $2 billion from 1951 to 1957. In 1958 the terms of trade were only 68% of those of 1937 given as normal in Table 3 above.

At this time, too, the United States began an intensified policy to sell its greatly accumulated surplus grain stocks in competition with Argentina. First, the United States offered supplies to foreign governments in return for its strategic material stockpiling. Then the United States made grants of surpluses to distressed countries, thus seriously affecting world prices and Argentine markets. Third, the United States sold surplus goods to foreign countries in return for local currencies "loaned" back to those countries.

Very much affected by all this was Argentina. Table 8 shows how Argentina's share in world exports has fallen.

Not only does the United States prevent Argentine exports (wheat, maize, and meat) from entering its borders, not only does it make special dumping export deals on the world market damaging to Argentine export prices, but the United States has actually prevented other Latin American countries from making barter agreements with Argentina

Table 8

ARGENTINA'S SHARE IN WORLD EXPORTS OF MAIZE, WHEAT, LINSEED, WOOL, AND MEAT AND COMPARISON WITH U.S. SHARE (1000 TONS)

Ave. of Years	Maize Tons	%	Wheat Tons	%	Linseed Tons	%	Wool Tons	%	Meat Tons	%
1934-38	6256.8	61.4	3340.5	19.3	1541.5	67.6	77.4	11.7	468.6	39.7
1945-49	1828.0	42.8	2079.6	8.7	243.5	30.5	110.9	14.0	396.4	35.0
1950-54	1029.0	21.0	2186.3	8.6	480.2	43.5	71.3	10.0	176.0	18.7
1955	362.3	7.5	3714.0	14.7						
1956	1065.1	17.2	2568.0	8.1						

U.S. SHARE IN WORLD EXPORTS OF MAIZE, WHEAT AND LINSEED

	Maize Tons	%	Wheat Tons	%	Linseed Tons	%				
1934-38	797.7	7.8	1259.4	7.3	1.2	.1				
1945-49	1661.9	39.0	11203.5	47.1	42.1	5.4				
1950-54	2560.0	52.4	8982.7	35.3	253.9	19.0				
1955	2752.6	57.3	7390.0	29.3						
1956	2976.4	48.0	12669.0	39.8						

(as, for example, Brazil, Chile, Peru, and Bolivia in regard to wheat and flour, with Chile, Bolivia, and Peru in regard to oils, with Colombia, Chile and Ecuador in regard to cotton).

Argentina is no small country.[1] In area it is the seventh largest in the world, equal to all of the United States east of the Mississippi River, with 2,500 miles of coast line and with an area equal to France, Germany, Belgium, Poland, Czechoslovakia, Austria, Hungary, Denmark, and Bulgaria put together. It is one of the few countries in the world with climates extending from the arctic to the tropics. At one time it was one with Chile, Uruguay, Paraguay, and Bolivia.

On this land mass she has now discovered a vast amount of mineral wealth, including petroleum, iron, coal, zinc, lead, manganese, lithium, bismuth, tin, silver, wolfram, antimony, beryllium, copper, gold, salt, clay for baking, caolin, quartz, asphalt, barium sulphite, talc, mica, arsenic, magnesium, ferrous and sodium sulphates, sulphur, gypsum, borates, alum, asbestos, calcium, granite and quartz rocks, various valuable sands, volcanic materials, marbles, basalt rocks, mineral waters, limestone, etc.

Up to now this mineral wealth has not been much exploited mainly because Argentina, reacting to imperialist pressure, found this exploitation not the line of least resistance. For one thing, no one cared to look for these resources, as they were in out-of-the-way places. Second, when they were discovered, the British did not think it feasible to

[1] See Marcello Isacovich: *Argentina Económica y Social* (1961).

extend their railroad lines to these places and the Argentine political rulers were too much aristocratic loafers, unwilling and unable to develop their country except under conditions which would give them the greatest immediate profit for scandalously sumptuous consumption in the metropolis and abroad.

In the case of coal, Britain did not want that either discovered or developed for it would have meant the end of British coal imports and much of British shipping of coal at great profit. When coal was finally discovered—and the Rio Turbe region alone has 400 million tons of coal—coal operations were put under state control where the various administrations favorable to Britain could sabotage production to death.

Such sabotage also affected the electrification of the country accomplished by means of harnessing the "white coal" of the force of the great rivers, instead of using costly British coal for that purpose. The result of this sad situation is that 85% of the electricity produced is now centered in Buenos Aires and Santa Fé, and 11% in Córdoba, Mendoza, and Entre Rios. The rest of the country has only 4% to use—and this in 1960!

While some electricity is produced by the State, two private firms control the electricity in Buenos Aires and, with three others in the rest of the country, produce about 70% of the total. The private companies had become legally obliged by the original terms of their contract made fifty years prior to turn over all their operations to the government but in 1936, after the conservative military coup d'état, the termination date was postponed for another forty years. A tremendous popular clamor then forced the repeal of this renewal but, in spite of this, in 1959 President Frondizi signed a pact with those companies by which a new mixed private-government corporation was formed, guaranteeing 8% dividends to the private owners while the rates were raised greatly.

In the case of petroleum, from the time of the discovery in 1907 and the organization of the State Enterprise, *Yacimientos Petrolíficos Fiscales* (Y.P.F.) a bitter struggle for its control was pursued by Standard Oil and British interests. In revenge for losing the battle to Standard Oil, the British supported the drive for the nationalization of petroleum. In return, Standard Oil supported the conservative military revolution in 1930 overthrowing President Yrigoyen who had favored Y.P.F. As a result the State administrations consistently sabotaged

Y.P.F. operations. (Even as it was, however, Y.P.F. forced the price of gasoline down from 43 cents a litre to 20 cents.) Many more wells could have been profitably drilled. The great sums of money spent on petroleum imports could have been avoided. The tremendous waste by loss of natural gas could have been saved. The refining could all have been done by the government instead of leaving 45% of it in private foreign hands, just as Argentine tankers could have made all the shipments abroad.

In 1930 the Soviet Union offered to sell to Argentina oil for 11 cents a litre, far below the price set by Shell and Standard Oil, but then came the conservative military coup d'etat overthrowing Yrigoyen. General A. P. Justo instead signed an agreement with the foreign oil concerns not to increase Y.P.F. production. In 1949, when the United States refused to sell drilling equipment to Argentina, Perón declined to buy such equipment elsewhere, instead spending the money for imported oil. Nor has much attention been paid to the great possibilities potential in the petro-chemical field.

Under Frondizi new contracts were signed with Esso and Shell to drill on 8 million hectares of the best oil lands—in 1958 the known petroleum and gas reserves in Argentina were estimated at 800 million cubic meters. At this time the Soviet Union offered Y.P.F. $100 million credit for drilling equipment, but this was only partially used. The concessions made to the U.S. firms call for a price per litre greater than the import price from Arabia or from the Soviet Union!

In the meantime petroleum consumption has inordinately increased in Argentina, resulting in tremendous imports that squander all her monetary reserves. In 1958 petroleum consumption increased to almost 1.4 million tons, a jump of well over 100% over the average ten years previous and about 2½ times the amount produced. In that year petroleum imports amounted to over 10 million cubic meters.

That Argentina with its relatively small population and poorly developed industries should be the sixth petroleum consumer in the entire world, seems fantastic. Rational consumption should be no more than 7 million tons at most. Of Argentina's total energy consumption, 71.5% comes from petroleum, 5.3% from coal, and 1.2% from hydro-electric sources, while industrial countries that need petroleum far more than Argentina have a far better balance and use much less petroleum proportionately.

Argentina has a tremendous continental shelf filled with fish, but not exploited. The consumption of fish per capita in 1954 in Argentina was but 4 kilograms whereas at the same time it was 53 kilograms for Norway, 45 for Portugal, 29 for Canada, 20 for Venezuela, 16 for Germany, etc. Freezers for fish are lacking in Argentina and the canneries are all in the hands of foreigners.

Argentina has immense forests so woefully abused that in the period of 1954 to 1958 she had to import $100 million worth of wood. Argentine rivers can produce 11 million kilowatts of electricity; instead they actually produce but 2.4% of that figure.

We have already touched on some of the aspects of the agricultural situation in regard to grain and cattle. In 1962 it was revealed that per capita production of grain in Argentina had fallen from about 1,200 kilograms to about 700 kilograms, or about 44%, in the past 20 years alone. The International Monetary Fund has been forced to warn Argentina that she must absolutely put an end to the poor methods of soil cultivation now prevalent there.

The persistent shrinkage of productivity in the corn growing zone is principally due to soil erosion caused by reckless farming. There has been a practically uninterrupted decline in fertility of the soil with an inadequate system of sowing because of lack of contour plowing. The situation now is very much worse than in 1884 when Dr. Ameghina had written: "I know of square kilometers completely denuded by rains which have swept away all the black soil leaving the Pampa-red earth on the surface." The Soils Institute has carried out investigations showing that in San Antonia de Areco there were 22,200 hectares eroded, or 32% of the total; in Baradero 85,000 hectares, or 75% of the surface; in Bartólome Mitre, 100,000 hectares eroded, or about 50% of that Department.

Much can also be said about the miserable condition of the country's rather extensive railroad system. This had been from the start mainly in the hands of the British who had operated it in a high-handed and expensive manner. The railroads were not built with the over-all needs of the country and its general development in mind, but only with the specific purpose of hauling cattle and grain to the ports, chiefly Buenos Aires, for shipment to Britain and abroad. Thus the railroads spread out fanwise from Buenos Aires regardless of the needs of the interior of the country. Furthermore, the roads have three different widths causing great inconvenience and delays. In 1928, comparing the U.S. and Argentine railroads, both had the same stock values per kilometer of track but on this track the United States had 150% more locomotives, 30 times more freight cars, and could move 3½ times more tons per kilometer of track.[2] Yet the rates in Argentina were much higher than they were in the United States or Canada. For a similar distance the charges of 100 kilograms of wheat in Argentina was $1.70, in the United States $1.08, in Canada $.75.

It can not be too strongly emphasized that the control of a country's railroad system by a foreign power gives that power tremendous control over the life of that country. By their control of Argentine railroads, the British dictated which parts of the country would be developed and which by-passed, the life and death of settlements, the pace of development, the growth of industry, the degree of competition possible with other countries, what the transportation rates would be, what sort of service would be rendered, etc., etc. As a result, Argentina's development was greatly hindered and the country thrown repeatedly into profound convulsions. No wonder Argentina was bound hand and foot for a long time as a British colony.

When Britain returned the railroads to the country in 1946 they were in wretched shape and needed extensive repairs and modernization. A survey made in 1960 showed that while the railroads had averaged in 1925 to 1929 an annual total of 50 million tons, in 1958 they were carrying only 34.6 million tons. Of the 4,090 locomotives, 80% were over 25 years of age, 40% were over 40 years of age. There were only 653 diesel engines of which 200 needed repairs. Of the 84,000 freight cars more than 22,000 were out of service. Most of them were old style, heavy cars with no air brakes. Of the 44,760 kilometers of track only 1,760 could be rated good, 17,000 kilometers average, while 26,000 were in a deplorable state, resulting in rolling equipment being worn out three times as rapidly as in Europe.

A despatch from Washington dated July 11th, 1962 stated that an international consultative organ of the Organization of American States had recommended the acquisition of 831 locomotives and 35,000 freight cars, as well as passenger cars as part of a ten year program for the modernization of the Argentine railroad system. According to this report, the railroads could be rehabilitated only if the government dropped the uneconomic branches, raised tariffs of freight

[2] See Scalabrini Ortiz: *Política Britanica en el Rio de La Plata* (1957 ed.).

and passengers and took measures to secure efficient work by personnel. The study called for the replacement of all steamers still in use by diesels and an extensive modernization of the rolling material. It demanded modification of the legal structures of the railroad system to permit better functioning as a commercial enterprise, to free it from political interference and to assure competent administration. The cost of the ten year program would be about $1,450 million. To improve, construct, and modernize 40,000 kilometers of road needed a budget of $793 million. Then there was the cost of removal of 12,800 kilometers of track and the building of 6,400 kilometers of new roads and an improvement of the river transportation system. The study was financed by a special fund of the United Nations.[3]

Already on January 1, 1959 the Frondizi government of Argentina had entered into an agreement with the International Monetary Fund calling for the following objectives, among others:

1. The Government deficit was to be ended by 1959 by means of the reduction of workmen in the Government to the total of 15%.

2. Public works were to be stopped until the deficit was ended.

3. Railroad rates were to be raised by an average of 150%.

4. 15% of the railroad workers were to be dropped from the rolls.

5. Anti-economic railroad branches eliminated.

6. Electric rates substantially increased.

7. Wages were to be frozen for two years.

8. Prices of petroleum derivates, including imposts, were to be raised an average of 200%.

9. Termination of both consumption and production subsidies.

10. New internal taxes destined to raise three billion pesos.

11. Export taxes of 20% on the majority of agricultural products, 10% on meat products.

12. Import taxes on manufactured products, 20% on semi-manufactured products, parts, and accessories.

13. Over-all tax on petroleum derivatives to raise six billion pesos.

14. Restriction of credit, with banks required to have reserves equal to 30% of sight deposits (hitherto it had been 20%).

[3] A full three-volume report has been issued by the Republic of Argentina: Ministry of Public Works and Services under the title: *A Long Range Transportation Plan for Argentina* (1962). For opposition to this Report, see the official organ of the Argentine Railway Workers Union: *El Obrero Ferroviario,* issues of May 2 through July 1, 1962, for example.

15. Free foreign exchange.

This agreement, strongly illustrative of the methods by which foreign capital tries to bring Argentina to heel, has become a basic source for economic, political, and social irritation, substantially contributing to the revolutionary situation in which Argentina now finds itself.

To understand the social pressures leading to the economic distortions and the abuse of its resources that prevails in Argentina, it might be well for us briefly to go into the country's economic and political history.

After its *conquistadores* had seized most of the lands in South and Central America and Mexico, Spain organized four Vice-Royalties: the earliest centered in Mexico, 1535, the next in Peru, 1543, the third in Colombia, 1717, and the last in Buenos Aires, 1776. Argentina was being settled by two principal streams of colonists, one based in Peru, flowing down the western borders close to the Andes Mountains and making Córdoba and Tucumán its chief centers, the other arriving directly from Europe and settling in or near the port of Buenos Aires. Thus, from the start there were in reality two Argentinas: one based on the interior peopled by Spaniards intermixed with Indians, living mainly off the cattle that had been left to turn wild on the splendid grazing ranges of the land supplemented by home manufactures; the other, a mixture of various Europeans—English, French, Spanish, Italian, German—who came to the port to trade needed goods, to defend and govern the country, or to give it necessary services. The nobility, the military officers, and the clergy all retained special privileges so that they could not be tried in the ordinary courts or be held responsible to the ordinary people for their actions. Under the Spanish colonial system all disposable lands were concentrated in the hands of a few. Unlike Brazil, Argentina did not tolerate slavery. It was a wild and "free" country.

Spain's difficulties with Napoleon in Europe gave the Latin American colonies their chance to become independent. Buenos Aires revolted in 1810, and after sending an army toward Tucumán and Córdoba under General Belgrano, with the aid of Libertador General San Martín, was able to secure a declaration of independence in Tucumán, the two Argentinas thus becoming free of Spain. At the same time, however, the Argentines lost their connections with Chile, Peru, and Bolivia and, thanks to the false actions of the Buenos Aires leaders and to the pressure of the English who did not want Argentina to extend on both sides of the River Plate, lost also Uruguay and Paraguay. Thus the independent history of Argentina starts with a great loss of territory and with a split within Argentina of the two distinct social entities, the East and the West, the Port and the Interior, the Metropolis and the country, the European and the native, the trader and the *gaucho,* the importer and the domestic handicraftsman, the "civilized" and the "barbarian."

By the time of Argentina's independence from Spain there existed not only a port on the coast, Buenos Aires, but also river ports in the regions of Santa Fé, Corrientes, and Entre Rios. Most important of all, the large landholdings that had been granted as *encomiendas* by the Spanish Crown, together with the huge new landholdings taken by those who were to become the leaders of the Argentine revolution, had already developed the cattle ranches into very profitable enterprises exporting abroad salted and jerked beef as well as hides and tallow. English and French importers who had traded their goods for gold and silver, draining the country of precious metals used for currency, now also turned exporters shipping the meat products back when the ships returned home.

The elimination of Spain from Argentina created a great power vacuum to be filled on the one hand by the leading ranchers controlling the latifundias on the coast and in the Province of Buenos Aires and, on the other hand, by the British merchants and other traders in the metropolis.[4] The leaders of Buenos Aires insisted that all trade go through the city port and that the imposts levied there go not for the benefit of the entire country but only for the metropolis itself.

The Federalist program of the interior provinces was expressed in 1813 in their "Instructions" to their eastern deputies:

1. Immediate declaration of independence;
2. Federation of states;
3. Each Province to have its own sovereignty and government;
4. A National Republican Government assuring autonomy to the confederated states;

---

[4] Mirón Burguín in *Aspectos Económicos del Federalismo Argentina* (1961) states that Buenos Aires raised the price of beef from $3.30 a head in 1809 to $9.60 in 1819. (Mentioned in Marcos Merchensky: *Las Corrientes Ideológicas en La História Argentina,* p. 64.)

5. The seat of national authority to be outside Buenos Aires;

6. The erection of Maldovado and Colonia as free ports.[5]

To develop the hinterland better the leaders of the port tried to plan not only in terms of cattle but also in terms of agriculture and wanted to bring in Europeans to colonize and farm the lands as was being done in the United States. But this was not to be. The big cattle men of the coastal regions, mobilizing their henchmen, the gauchos working on their big estates, knowing that agriculture would hamper free ranch grazing, staged a revolt with the aid of the West and overthrew the leaders of Buenos Aires with Rosas taking the place of Rivadavia. The lands Rivadavia wanted to rent on long term leases were now distributed to a fistful of Rosas' faithful who set up veritable land empires for themselves. More than 8½ million hectares were given to 538 proprietors each of whom immediately created a private army of his own owing allegiance only to himself.

All through the interior in similar fashion the big landowners became *caudillos*, forming their own private armies and creating in fact their own laws to suit themselves. Agriculture was by-passed in favor of cattle raising, to the great joy also of the British exporters of cattle, British ship owners, and British importers of finished goods needed by the port and ranch owners who favored free trade, with the result that British goods could completely undersell and defeat any competition arising within Argentina itself. Under Rosas the cattlemen of Entre Rios, Santa Fe, and Corrientes were brought into the *Associación de Mayo* headed by the big estates in Buenos Aires Province.

For a considerable number of years after its independence, then, Argentina remained simply a cattle-growing country having to import not only finished goods of all sorts from Europe but even its food and flour, except in the interior where a self-sufficient economy was maintained on the simplest and crudest basis.

Then came the change to shipping iced beef, a change in technology that led to a change in productive relations. Iced beef demanded better fed cattle than those simply feeding on the grass of the range. Such plants as alfalfa now had to be planted for fodder so that the beef could be well fed and have a better taste. Later big American and British companies would come to build huge refrigerators that would de-

[5] See Marcos Merchensky: *Las Corrientes Ideológicas en La História Argentina,* (1961) p. 66.

mand grain fed beef if Argentine animals were to compete with beef raised elsewhere.

At this later stage the big refrigerators would begin to dominate the cattle raisers. The cattle raisers would have to turn to cattle breeding and turn over these cattle to the cattle feeders who in turn would be affiliates of the large refrigeration companies. These feeders would have little of the trouble and risk taken by the cattle raisers and would pay them low prices. The internal market also would come to be dominated by the foreign owned refrigerator companies who would induce Perón to eliminate the independent action of Buenos Aires butchers while still later Frondizi would take on the job of liquidating the State-owned *Frigorífico Nacional*.

From Perón the private *frigoríficos* got more than 3 billion pesos in the ten years from 1946 to 1955, while in 1956 General Aramburu, as part of his coup d'etat, gave them another 2.7 billion.

As a result of all this hierarchy of control the cattle situation today stands about as follows: 81% of the cattle owners own only 15.5% of the cattle (mostly in small herds—35% having less than 10 head, 46% having from 10 to 100 head), 17% own 42.5% of the cattle (medium owners with herds from 100 to 1000 head), while 2% own 41% of the cattle.

With the freezers, true agriculture had to come into its own, the rancher making room for the big *estancia* owners who were producing corn, wheat, oats, barley, and other crops for human consumption as well as for cattle. Argentina developed into a tremendous granary exporting its grains and linseed to the entire world. These new economic agrarian leaders also wanted their place in the sun and their share of the government. A national Constitution was formed in 1853 to balance all these interests and the country was finally considered not as two Argentines but as one.

It is significant that even now, with the tremendous development of agriculture, Argentina failed to parallel the lines of development pursued in that other great "free" country, the United States. In the United States it was the colonist who first came with his family to settle in the country; in Argentina it was the *conquistador* adventurer who seized the Indian woman for his wife. In the United States it was the homesteader who cut down the forest and built his home and worked his farm, in Argentina it was the Spanish favorite nobleman who was granted the vast lands and it was the aristocratic American-born Spanish *criollo* who seized tremendous ranches for himself driving out all true homesteaders and farmers. In the United States the whole coast was settled at about the same time, in Argentina all immigration came through one single port taxing all entries for its own special benefit and centering all trade and imports-exports into its own hands to the detriment of the rest of the country.

In the United States there was no great standing British army but a colonial militia. In Argentina there was no colonial militia but only a specially privileged army not responsible to the people. And when the Spanish army was finally driven off, instead of a people's militia there arose large standing private armies surrounding the big provincial wealthy families taking matters in their own hands. After independence, the United States was relatively free of foreign interference, after independence in Argentina the vacuum left by Spain was quickly filled by the British who completely monopolized the export-import trade, the money and currency fields, the manufacture of needed finished goods, the shipping trade, commerce, etc. In the U.S., after independence, agriculture dominated the port, maintained the homestead, supplied the country with necessities, attracted vast numbers of educated handicraftsmen and mechanics from all over Europe; in Argentina, after independence, the port dominated the country, cattle raising dominated agriculture, the large *hacienda* and *estancia* owner made the small homestead impossible.

With the growing need for the better feeding of cattle Argentine leaders again began to consider the colonization of the land by Europeans. The first colonization attempts in the middle of the 19th century were made by the government under the leadership of the *Associación de Mayo*. The government induced Germans, Swiss, and other skilled agrarians to come in and gave them property, homes, and instruments of labor. By 1861, however, a total of only 1400 families and 7,600 individuals had been placed on 10,000 hectares of land. When the possibilities for enormous profits were seen, even this hesitant venture was soon terminated and from 1866 to 1872 sales of lands were made only of vast areas to wealthy speculators or to big enterprises who proceeded to the division of land into lots and then sold these lots to European colonists. Some 400,000 hectares of land were sold to about 50,000 settlers under this system until, with the arrival of the railroads and the great grants of land given to them, the price of land was raised so high as to prevent it being bought outright by private settlers. Colonization ended and gave way to the renting of land on short terms. The German and Swiss colonists were replaced by the Italian and Spanish immigrant. Foreign capitalists entering the scene with refrigerators and railroads, not only reinforced the big landlords but became big landlords themselves. As late as 1947 rent absorbed an average of 20%-25% of the total land return, sometimes reaching 45%.

At first agriculture had been carried on in Entre Rios, Santa Fé and Córdoba but with the advent of the freezers, it spread also to Buenos Aires Province where the renter had to leave the land growing with alfalfa when he was forced out so that the landlord not only received the rent but also the alfalfa and other forage crops. Under such conditions the renters, of course, would not take any care of the land. Soon there arose great erosion. The land became undercultivated, overgrazed, with no rotation, no good tools, or real intensive capital investment. We have already noted statistically the terrible results of such abuse of the land.

Fifteen proprietors, each with over 100,000 hectares, owned 2.8 million hectares in Buenos Aires Province alone; 1041 properties there had over 5000 hectares each for a total of 10,200,000 hectares, or about one-third of the total land in the entire province! In Patagonia the Menendez family is master of no less than 6.6 million hectares. Large corporations, mostly British, owned 26 million hectares in 1948, but these are now being surpassed by American interests, with the King Ranch having 224,000 hectares in Santa Fe and the Coney interests owning one million hectares in Mendoza. These trends are well evidenced in the following table:

Table 9[6]

ARGENTINA: PERCENT OF LAND CULTIVATED

	1914	1947
0-25 hectares	.6	.9
25-100 hectares	2.9	4.5
101-500 hectares	12.2	14.3
501-1,000 hectares	5.9	6.4
1,001-10,000 hectares	45.0	42.4
Over 10,000 hectares	33.4	31.5

[6] Leopoldo Portnoy: *La Realidad Argentina en El Siglo XX, Vol. II, Analisis Crítico de La Economía* (1961), p. 181.

Ninety percent of the agricultural workers have no access to the land and must be renters or day laborers. While 37% of the agrarians do own land, the great majority of this group have lands too small to be self-sufficient. In 1952 it was revealed that 5% of the land owners possessed 75% of the land, while 67% of the land owners worked only 5% of the land in lots of less than 100 hectares.

With the closing of the Pampas the immigrants had to go elsewhere. They left to engage in intensive farming, such as tobacco, cotton, maté, sugar, vines, rice, coffee, and other crops in the tropical regions in northern Argentina. From 1920 to 1957 such production as sugar and vines jumped 170% and the cultivated area from 923,000 hectares to 2,412,000 hectares. In the vineyard country the immigrants were rented bare lands and when their leases expired they had to turn over full grape lands as well as having paid the rent. On the sugar plantations the workers were paid in kind and not in money except at the refineries themselves. Only near the refineries were there very small parcels of peasant land.

The situation is well illustrated in Tucumán where there are 295 *latifundistas* with more than 5,000 *surcos* each, 2,709 medium producers with 500-5,000 *surcos* each, 12,975 small land holders with less than 500 *surcos* each and 100,000 peons and rural workers. (A *surco* is a piece of ground furrowed in the middle.) Naturally, some of the very large plantations are owned by the refineries themselves. The refineries control the sugar production as the refrigerator plants control the cattle raising.

The agricultural situation described above had decisive political and social consequences for Argentina. During the latter part of the 19th century and the first part of the 20th a great flood of European immigrants poured into the country, the figures showing that of the 6.6 million immigrants, 44% were Italian and 31% Spanish. The European groups that came were hungry for land but found this land already too dear, monopolized as it was by the big landholders known collectively as the Oligarchy. Instead of rooting the settlers on the land the Oligarchy converted them into peons. The foreigners learned to settle in the cities, as did many Argentinians driven off the countryside by the monopolists.

What kind of conditions these agrarian peons and workers found in Argentina is best illustrated by the statistics of birth, marriage, and death in comparing the city of Jujuy, the center of the sugar and vine fields, with Buenos Aires. It is well known that the poorer the social stratum the higher the birth rate, the lower the marriage rate, the higher the death rate. In 1958, the birth rate in Buenos Aires was 19.2 per thousand, in Jujuy it was 40.3 per thousand; the marriage rate in Buenos Aires was 8.1 per thousand while Formosa (a town similar to Jujuy) had 4 per thousand; Buenos Aires had a mortality rate of 8.5 per thousand, but Jujuy had a rate of 13.9 per thousand. In that year the average for child mortality throughout the country was 61 per thousand, in the federal capital of Buenos Aires it was 32.3 per thousand, while for Jujuy it was 131.0 per thousand. In Tucumán for each 18 children born alive, one was born dead, the statistical records showing 700 born dead to 13,000 born live. This alarming fact was accounted for by the fact that the women workers worked at factories or at the sewing machines in their homes, sometimes even to the very days preceding the child's birth, as well as to the bad conditions of diet and work.

Industry developed late in Argentina, thanks in part to the pressure of British imperialism and the policy of complete free trade adopted by the Argentine wealthy controlling Buenos Aires. But with the closing down of land settlement, with the sweep of immigrants from Europe (between 1880 and 1890, 850,000 immigrants entered the country, many of them skilled workers), with the challenge to the British by the Americans, and with the advent of two world wars and a major depression, Argentina had to develop its own manufactures and industrial power.

In 1895 there were 23,000 establishments with 55,000 horsepower producing food, clothing, toilet articles, construction materials, furniture, cleaning materials, etc. The majority were very small concerns employing in all about 170,000 workers, of whom 85% were foreigners. By 1914 this grew to 48,000 establishments with 410,000 persons and 84,000 horsepower. The plants now included freezers, refineries, public service works and other large installations. With World War I and the absence of consumers goods, manufactures such as textiles, shoes, and such received a big push forward so that in time Argentina could not only become self-sufficient in these items but actually think of exporting some of them.

Between the two World Wars a great deal of foreign capital came to Argentina, especially from the United States which incidentally concentrated a good part of its funds in the field of manufacture and fabrication. Such names as Armour, Goodyear, Firestone, Philips, General Electric, Johnson & Johnson, and later General Motors, Ford, Kaiser, Singer, and many others became quite well known. By 1935 foreign capital represented about 50% of the total invested in Argentine industry. Then came World War II and by 1948 there were 917,000 workers in 81,000 establishments with 1.7 million horsepower. United States investment alone came to over half a billion dollars, about 50% of which was in manufactures.

Foreign interests now control the energy, the refrigerators, the metallurgical, chemical, electrical industries, construction, exports and most important imports. They have mixed undertakings with the government as partner. They get government machinery and plants turned over to them. They sell patents and various perquisites and thus thoroughly penetrate all industry. Only 12% of their investments are in the form of money (7%) and machinery (5%). In return they get freedom from customs dues, charges, taxes, deposit guarantees, etc. They occupy a privileged position with tremendous advantages over all others.[7]

Very noteworthy is the concentration of Argentine industry. In 1954, 57.5% of the establishments with 66% of the workers producing 72% of the goods was concentrated in Buenos Aires Province, overwhelmingly in the city of Buenos Aires.

By this time the large companies had such a dominant position that there were 88 firms with over 1,000 workers each, in all producing 17.5% of the total products, and about two-tenths of one percent of all the firms had 300 or more workers producing about 34% of the total goods. A little more than 1% of the enterprises were producing more than 50% of the total goods.

The State, for military, political, economic, and social reasons, also began to take a hand in production. It built the furnaces of Zapla, a military steel works with Siemens Martin furnaces, a bronze foundry,

[7] For a long list of American firms operating in Argentina, see Marcelo Isacovich: Work cited. Such lists are given regularly in the periodical *The Review of the River Plate,* printed in Buenos Aires.

various explosive plants, a TNT unit, large machine shops for airplane production, motors for planes, automobiles, motorcycles, and tractors, a plant for naval stores, an electronic factory, and various laboratories. It built the Y.P.F. refineries, sugar refineries, warehouses and establishments of the DINIE complex taking in 20,000 workers and including metallurgical, electrical, chemical, and other works. Then there are electric factories like those in San Nicolás, Mar del Plata and central entities such as *Agua y Energía* (Water and Energy), gas plants, and railway shops. Besides, the government operates now the railroads, the coal mines, metal mines, the maritime and river fleet, telegraph, telephone and other communications systems, Argentine Airlines, and other public undertakings.

In 1948 such State undertakings embraced 529 enterprises with 82,000 workers and 12,000 employees. This total was further increased until 1954 when a reverse process was started while some of the plants were dismantled and sold to such capitalists as Kaiser Industries, and Fiat. With Frondizi, the whole trend became one of giving to international capitalism full opportunity to control completely the country's wealth and resources.

Thanks to this relative growth of industry the country has completely changed its position. In 1958, for example, of the total gross product produced in the country, 40.8% pertained to agriculture and 45.6% to industry, whereas only 23 years before the statistics showed that 51.5% pertained to agriculture and 36.5% to industry.

This growth of industry, however, is purely for domestic purposes and not for exports. So far as exports are concerned they are still almost entirely products of the field. In 1959, for example, 97.5% of the total exports came from the field, of which 52.5% were cattle products (wool 12%, leather 7%), 43% agriculture (grains, linseed, etc.), and 2% forest. These exports, however, as we have seen, were steadily diminishing per capita: in 1959 the per capita exports amounted to only 427 kilograms, whereas the 1924-28 average had showed 1,400 kilograms. On the other hand, of the total imports in 1958, 75.1% were represented by industrial products and 13.1% by fuel imports.

The present level of industrialization of the country may be evidenced by the following: In 1957 of a total population of about 20 million, of which about 25% was centered in Buenos Aires and vicinity, the totally active population of 7.7 million persons was classified as follows:

Table 10A
ARGENTINA: CLASS DISTRIBUTION OF GAINFULLY EMPLOYED POPULATION: 1957

Workers	3,000,000	39%
Employees	2,900,000	38
Middle Classes	1,800,000	23
Top controllers	30,000	

Table 10B
ARGENTINA: DISTRIBUTION OF EMPLOYED WAGE WORKERS
BY INDUSTRIAL SECTORS: 1957

Industry	1,250,000
Agriculture	970,000
Transport	600,000
Construction	150,000
Mining	30,000

Table 10C
ARGENTINA: DISTRIBUTION OF EMPLOYED SALARIED EMPLOYEES
BY INDUSTRIAL SECTORS: 1957

Public	1,000,000
Commerce	750,000
Industry	350,000
Domestic	350,000
Banks, etc.	450,000
Total	2,900,000

Table 10D
ARGENTINA: DISTRIBUTION OF THE MIDDLE CLASSES
BY ECONOMIC CATEGORIES: 1957

Farmers	800,000
Small & average merchant	500,000
Artisans & small enterp.	200,000
Professional	150,000
Others	150,000
Total	1,800,000

Table 10E
ARGENTINA: DISTRIBUTION OF GAINFULLY EMPLOYED POPULATION
BY INDUSTRIAL SECTORS: 1957

Agriculture and Cattle	1,800,000	23%
Manufacturing	1,750,000	23
Transportation	600,000	8
Public Functionaries	1,000,000	13
Domestic Service	350,000	4
Building Construction	100,000	3

How the country has changed from agricultural to industrial activity is also evidenced by the figures showing that the weight of agriculture in the total gross internal product fell from 25.9% in 1935 to 18% in 1955, while the weight of industry and construction rose from 16.8% to 28.5% in the same time (and that of government from 8.2% to 10.3%).

It must be again emphasized that the transformation of Argentina from an agricultural to an industrial country does not mean that there has been a per capita increase in production or in productivity. On the contrary, there has been a very slow growth in productivity and an actual regression in the accumulation of capital. For example, if we compare the average of the years 1925-29 with 1955 we find that while the rate of annual accumulation of capital was 1.8%, the rate of growth of the population was 2% and thus the rate of capital per person actually diminished .2%. This can be contrasted with the average year during the 1900-04 period as against the average year in the 1925-29 period when there was an average annual rate of capital accumulation of 4.7%, of population 3.4% and thus an increase in capital per person of 1.3%. In the thirty years from 1925 to 1955, while the gross product doubled, the number of jobs increased by about 50% so that the gross product per active person increased only 30% in 30 years or about 1% a year.

In part this result was due to a deliberate policy, a conspiracy on the part of the landholding Oligarchy and British interests to slow down and prevent the industrialization of Argentina up to then economically a British colony. The slow development of the steel industry is an illustration. No one seemed to want to develop a native Argentine steel industry apparently, as this would be against the interests of dominant imperialism that needed Argentina as its market. Finally, when the military insisted and the needs of the State demanded it a steel plant was started in San Nicolás. The plans, however, were placed under the technical control of a U.S. firm with the result that construction went on so slowly that a complete replanning was needed because the project no longer could meet the needs of the nation.

At the same time the steel monopolists charged Argentina such high prices that iron and steel consumption did not advance very far as seen by the following:

Table 11A
ARGENTINA: STEEL CONSUMPTION

Ave. Year	Tons	Kilograms per capita
1900-04	322,000	67
1915-19	251,000	30
1925-29	1,282,000	117
1930-34	732,000	59
1950-54	290,000	20
1956	1,255,000	64

The next table illustrates the same situation but in regard to petroleum production.

Table 11B
ARGENTINA: PETROLEUM PRODUCTION (INDEX 1950 EQUALS 100)

1939	79.3
1941	101.0
1944	103.3
1945	97.5
1946	88.7
1948	98.0
1950	100
1951	104.0

Under Perón some stimulation was given to the petroleum industry, but while he raised production to the index level of 130 in 1955 he also allowed the U.S. *Companía Argentina de Petróleo SA* of Delaware to enter the scene, giving it very large privileges in drilling lands previously discovered as oil bearing by the Y.P.F. state enterprise.

Argentina's decline in per capita production and in per capita investment can be markedly seen when comparing Argentina to other Latin American countries as in the following table:

Table 12
ARGENTINA: COMPARISON WITH LATIN AMERICAN COUNTRIES IN
PER CAPITA PRODUCTION AND PER CAPITA INVESTMENT

Country	annual rate of increase in per capita production 1950-1958	annual rate of growth in per capita investment 1945-1957
Venezuela	6.0	15.0
Brazil	4.4	5.0
Mexico	3.1	5.5
Peru	1.6	7.5
Colombia	1.5	4.5
Ecuador	1.5	5.5
Chile	.6	1.5
Cuba	− .3	9.5
Argentina	− .4	− 3.0

The change-over of Argentina to an industrial country could also be seen by the figures giving the distribution of capital in productive activities:

Table 13
ARGENTINA: VALUE OF PRODUCTION BY INDUSTRIAL SECTORS
(1950 PESOS MILLION)

Ave. of years	agro-cattle	manuf'g	min'g & const.	transp't	elec & comcat'n
1900-04	12,850	3,734	267	7,414	382
1925-29	29,281	15,235	1528	19,307	3458
1940-44	31,067	17,146	5282	24,271	5797
1955	34,068	28,287	7209	22,397	6925

In the period 1900-04 the ratio of agriculture to other productive industries stood at 28.8 to 26.5; in 1955 this had changed to 14.7 to 28.

There is no doubt that Argentina has steadily grown in production. As a matter of fact the gross internal product showed a growth of 85% in product value in the 25 years from 1935 to 1960. The per capita situation, however, is entirely different as can be seen in the ensuing figures:

Table 14
ARGENTINA: PER CAPITA PRODUCTION (1950 PESOS)

Ave. of Yrs.	1950 pesos
1935-39	2,953
1945-49	3,556
1950-54	3,508
1955-58	3,566
1959	3,331

Thus, compared to 20 years ago the per capita production has not really advanced at all and more recently has tended to decline.

We turn now to the foreign trade and balance of payments of Argentina.

From very early times imports were greater than exports thanks to the luxurious tastes of the ranchers and the Buenos Aires elite. Argentina, however, differs from most other Latin American countries in that it is principally an industrial country with a population almost entirely of European stock, including a large city proletariat, and thus can not be treated in the same manner as the others. In the course of time Argentina's import difficulties have steadily increased and have been met by: a) a loss of gold, b) increase in long and short term debts, and c) investment credits. (Because of U.S.-Argentine hostility, the Argentine Government had not received military and other grants as had other Latin American countries.)

The following table shows Argentina's balance of payments in terms of an annual average and in fixed 1950 million dollars:

Table 15A
ARGENTINA: BALANCE OF PAYMENTS (ANNUAL AVERAGES IN 1950 $ MILLION)

	1945-49	1950-54	1955-59	1960
Exports, Goods & Services	$1354	$962	$1160	$1270
Effects of Terms of Trade*	− 20	− 83	− 297	− 261*
Income Payments Sent Abroad		− 12	− 27	− 53
Net Foreign Financing		40	160	192
Imports, Goods & Services	− 1112	− 907	− 996	− 1148

* Represents losses to Argentina because of unfavorable terms of trade.

According to U.N. statistics, Argentina suffered a peak trade deficit of $496 million in 1961 alone. The drain continued in 1962 although reduced to $140 million, forcing Argentina in 1963 drastically to reduce imports, from 10.6 million tons in 1962 to 7.2 million in 1963.

The 1962 deficit was realized even though exports greatly increased in physical volume as compared with 1960, jumping from 9.4 million tons in 1960 to 11.9 million in 1962. This was due to the fact that the greater amount of exports brought a lesser total in money than the smaller amount of exports had brought in previously. For example, in 1960, 438,000 tons of meat were sold for $259.3 million while in 1962, 564,000 tons brought only $226.1 million. Again, 140,000 tons of wool were sold for $145.3 million in 1960 while 158,000 tons brought $144.1 million in 1962. Mining products exports which rocketed from 70,000 tons in 1960 to 991,000 tons in 1962, or an increase of 1,416% brought an increase in value of only 450% or about one-third as much as they would have brought in 1960. On the other hand, imports of manufactured tobacco goods which dropped from 2,000 tons to 1,000 tons yet cost four times as much in 1962 as in 1960. Similarly with textiles, paper, and other items which though sharply reduced in volume imported yet cost more for the smaller amount than for the larger.[8]

The balance of payments is given in Table 15 B below:

[8] Given in the periodical "Business Conditions in Argentina," issued by Ernest Tornquist & Co. Ltd., March, 1963.

Table 15B

ARGENTINA: BALANCE OF PAYMENTS ($ MILLION)*

	1955	1956	1957	1958
Imports	$1172.6	$1127.6	$1310.4	$1232.6
Exports	928.6	943.8	974.8	993.9
Bal. Trade	− 244.0	− 183.8	− 335.6	− 238.7
Net Bal. Serv.	2.5	52.7	32.9	− 20.6
BALANCE	− 241.5	− 131.1	− 302.7	− 259.3

	1959	1960	1961	1962
Imports	$ 993.0	$1249.3	$1460.3	$1350
Exports	1009.0	1079.2	964.1	1210
Bal. Trade	− 16.0	− 170.1	− 496.2	− 140
Net Bal. Serv.	− 5.0	− 34.2	− 88.5	− 200
BALANCE	11.0	− 204.3	− 584.7	− 340

* Source: Argentine Central Bank (printed in Bank of Boston periodical: "The Situation in Argentina," issue of January 28, 1963, except for 1962 figures which appeared in the issue of March 25, 1963.)

For the eight years, 1955 through 1962 the accumulated losses in the balance of trade amounted to close to $2 billion, the accumulated losses in the balance of payments to over $2 billion. For the five-year period from 1951 through 1955 the aggregate negative balance of payments on Argentina's current account totalled $702.1 million; for the period 1956 through 1960 the negative balance was $887.6 million; for 1961 the negative balance was $584.4 million.

These steady persistent negative balances for Argentina could only be remedied either by a flow of foreign capital that would cover the deficits for the time being or by a drain in the nation's gold supply, or by a combination of both methods.

Table 16 (page 123) gives the flow of long-term private investments over a long period of time and illustrates how this inflow was able to meet any negative balances of payments Argentina may have had during this period. The Table also gives the distribution of these investments and shows how the influence of the United Kingdom was reduced and the relative position of the United States improved.

Foreign capitalists and governments, however, not only lend and invest, they also draw out income payments and liquidate their loans and investments. In 1962, for example, over and above the negative trade balance of $140 million recorded there was also a net capital exodus of $160 million, making a total foreign deficit in payments of

Table 16

ARGENTINA: LONG-TERM PRIVATE FOREIGN INVESTMENTS ($ MILLION)

year	United Kingdom		United States		Other		Totals
	amount	%	amount	%	amount	%	
1900	$ 912	81.4					$ 912
1927	2002	57.6	$487	13.9	$984	28.5	3473
1934	1813	50.3	743	22.2	929	27.5	3485
1949	243	19.4	323	25.7	689	54.9	1255
1955	324	21.6	466	30.0	747	48.4	1537

Note: The great drop in long-term private foreign investments in Argentina between 1934 and 1949 can be attributed, first to the effect of the depression, later to the effects of World War II, when the British and European continental powers had to sell their investments and Americans withdrew because of hostility to Perón. The Argentine Government took this occasion to buy out as much foreign investment as it could.

$300 million. The total Argentine overseas indebtedness committed in 1962 and due to be paid from 1962 through 1968 was estimated at about $2.5 billion![9] In the meantime the gold supply which had fallen to $189.6 million in 1961 had shrunk to $52.2 million by March 1963, thus practically disappearing. (Source: *Banco Central de la Republica Argentina: Boletin Estadístico,* Vol. VI, No. 4, April 1963)

The tremendous loss of gold reserves in Argentina should be compared with the situation in other South American countries such as Uruguay which has a population of about 3 million persons, which is also suffering from inflation but had a gold supply in March 1962 of $180 million; or Venezuela with a population about one-third that of Argentina but with no inflation and with a gold reserve at that time of $398 million. Even Brazil with an inflation even more fantastic than that of Argentina had a gold reserve of $285 million.

The following table shows the rise in the Federal Internal Public Debt:

Table 17

ARGENTINA: FEDERAL INTERNAL PUBLIC DEBT (PESOS BILLIONS)*

1958	92	1960	111	1961	130	1962	162

* Source. Banco Central de la Republica Argentina

In addition to the debt in the table, the Province of Buenos Aires alone had another 40 billion peso debt!

Apropos the negative balances, galloping government indebtedness

[9] Given in periodical: "The Situation in Argentina," April 29, 1963, issued by the Bank of Boston in Argentina.

has been matched by galloping government printing presses turning out fiat money, and galloping inflation accompanied by a galloping cost of living. In 1943 the money in circulation amounted to 1,380 million pesos; in 1959 to about 173 *billion* pesos. Before the military coup d'état of 1930 the Argentine peso exchanged at 2.4 to the dollar; by the time of Perón it was 7.5 to the dollar; with his removal it fell to 18 to the dollar; by the time of Frondizi it was 82 to the dollar; toward the end of 1962 it was over 150 to the dollar.

It is clear that with such a development it is ridiculous to call Argentina (or for that matter Brazil, or Mexico) an "underdeveloped" country in the same sense as one would use the term for such countries as the Congo, or Nyasaland, or Burma, or Thailand. In regard to what is Argentina "underdeveloped"? In regard to its structure, its infrastructure, or its superstructure? In comparison with Canada, Australia, or New Zealand which are never called underdeveloped? Or in comparison with Spain or Portugal? And yet manufacturing in Argentina embraces 23% of the total labor force and over 28% of the total capital in production, just about the same ratios as in these other countries mentioned. Argentina is about 70% urban and has a capital and center with more than 5 million inhabitants, perhaps the second largest city in the entire Western Hemisphere, containing about 25% of the country's total population.

It is true, indeed, that the domination by the landed Oligarchy preventing the proper settling of the land, the flooding of the Argentine markets with foreign goods so as to make impossible the rise of a native industry and an all-rounded development, the control of all vital industrial processes by foreign capitalists who drained the resources of the country to the limit, all produced a distorted situation that can be seen clearly enough even when compared to that existing in "free" countries which also functioned as prime exporters in grain and meat.

Argentina can be considered "underdeveloped" only in the sense that its capital investment has not been allowed to grow as it should, thus dragging back per capita production and productivity. The reasons for this can be summarized as follows: First, the landholders did not invest their profits and gains in industry, but spent their surpluses, in the main, in riotous and luxurious living with expensive trips abroad for themselves and their families. This habit they still indulge in as can

Table 18
ARGENTINA COMPARED WITH CANADA, AUSTRALIA, AND
NEW ZEALAND IN SIGNIFICANT ITEMS. 1926

	Argentina	Canada	Australia	New Zealand
Vehicles per 1000 inhabitants	22	97	67	91
Railroad kilometers per 1000 inh.	3600	7100	7570	4050
Merchant Marine 1000 tons 1922	342	1416	-642-	
Electric Consumption kw per cap.	120	1558	383	354
Cotton spindles (1000)	3.8	122	3.7	
Total deposits per cap. 1933	301.60	645.70	788.03	780.40
Death rate per 1000 (1933)	26.8	9.9	9.9	8.0

be seen from the following item appearing in the *Buenos Aires Herald,*
July 10, 1962, in the midst of the present tense situation:

"The casinos in Mar del Plata took in $124,814,700 during the
week-end holidays. Gamblers left this enormous sum at the roulette
and baccarat tables from Saturday to Monday . . . At the Central the
movement of gambling chips on Sunday totalled $42,204,000, a new
one-day record . . . The influx of gamblers during the July 9 festivities
was so great that the cloak rooms were unable to cope with the situation. A number of bathrooms and toilets were commandeered for the
occasion but even these were not sufficient. For the first time in history
of local gambling, men were seen playing their chips clad in overcoats
and with their hats on." (Here the $ sign no doubt stands for peso.)

Second, the landed wealthy monopolized the land and did not allow
others to come to earn, and save, and make investments. Like dogs in
the manger, they refused to allow others to do what they could not do
themselves. On the other hand they repudiated the levy of any income
taxes on themselves but placed all the burden on the poor consumers
in the form of indirect sales taxes.

Third, through import and export taxes, charges, licenses, fees, surcharges, etc., the Oligarchy drained a good part of the wealth into government channels and then proceeded to loot the government, stealing
immense sums for themselves and forming a military machine that systematically milked the country.

Fourth, they paid out to foreign money lenders an immense portion
of the surplus product in the form of usurious interest charges.

Fifth, they did not encourage domestic industry but permitted industrialization by foreign firms which then exported vast sums in the form of dividends and profits sucked out of the nation's wealth and labor, leaving little in return.

The Oligarchy was not content merely to own the land, it had to control the government as well, although in Buenos Aires Province it was forced to share its control with the big money interests in the metropolis itself. At first the port of Buenos Aires took all the customs dues collected for its own use but then under the dictatorship of Rosas and his ranchmen it had to share these dues with the rest of the Province. From 1841 to 1850 approximately 90% of the income of the Provincial Government came from custom duties. In 1853 the formation of a national Constitution transformed the customs into a national affair no longer merely for the benefit of one city, or region.

The Provincial *caudillos,* or "chiefs" who with their armies laid down the law in the Provinces, once they became heads of the national government naturally formed national armies that would brook no interference from any one. The dictatorship of the Oligarchy meant in essence the dictatorship of the army. The State became the property of the army which soon showed its teeth whenever army leaders were thwarted or not made leading parts of the government. In the 19th century the army did not object to working at times under civilian politicians who served its purposes while it, in turn, served the interests of the Oligarchy as a class whose members the officers in the main were.

Government expenditures in Argentina represent not a small portion of the gross consumption of the country, and have steadily grown. In the period 1900-04 such expenditures averaged 16.3% of the gross internal national product, in 1950-54 they averaged 28.5% (of which 9% represented capital investment). Of this total the share allocated for local government expenses fell in 1954 to 20% whereas previously it had been considerably higher.

How much did the Oligarchy and its sons steal in the government through bribes and special gifts, or through outright robbery? It is impossible to tell but common knowledge is that such practices were considered most natural and normal and the amounts taken were huge and cumulatively fantastic. And now consider that such actions have been going on for one hundred and fifty years and that the amounts the "fleeing military dictators" have taken with them are only a small portion of the total loot!

The army also made sure, of course, that a good deal of the State's funds went to it in the normal course of operations. Traditionally, in Argentina the armed forces received 25%-30% of the total State funds and sometimes went to far higher levels. In 1956 Argentina's armed forces totalled in number almost as much as those of all the other Latin American republics put together save Mexico and Brazil, or as much as Mexico's and Brazil's combined. In 1948 the *New York Herald Tribune* reported the following relative pay for officers in Argentina and in the United States:

Table 19[10]
ARGENTINA: YEARLY PAY FOR ARMY OFFICERS, 1948

	U.S.	Argentina
Lieut. General	$8800	$11,250
Major General	8800	10,000
Brigadier General	6600	8,750
Colonel	4400	7,000
Major	3300	4,250
Captain	2760	3,250
First Lieutenant	2400	2,500

Oligarchy, government, and army made sure the wealthy were not taxed much in fact. The principal forms of taxation were customs duties, licenses and sales taxes passed on to the consumer. Direct taxes on land, on personal property, and on income were avoided or made relatively light, although laid regressively heavy on the poorer layers of the population. In 1959 the indirect taxes were estimated at 75 billion pesos. Of the 35 billion pesos levied in the form of income taxes only 16 billion were collected. In 1958 it was estimated that 10-15 billion pesos were cheated in export-import taxes, thanks to wholesale bribery and corruption. In 1962, at the very time the government with great difficulty was trying to get a loan of 5.7 billion pesos from the Inter-American Bank and National Mortgage Bank for houses, it was estimated that cigarette smuggling alone cost the State 5 billion pesos, 180 million packets of cigarettes being smuggled in annually!

Now we can see why Argentina was not allowed to develop its social capital, such as highways, schools, sanitation works, water systems, etc., and why its infrastructure suffered.

[10] Given in Robert J. Alexander: *The Perón Era* (1951).

Joining hands as partners to the Oligarchy and to the military in draining the country's surplus and keeping it "underdeveloped" were, and are, the foreign money lenders, investors, and imperialists. With their supplementary help the country has been sucked completely dry.

The British money lenders who were the first to come into the scene with the ejection of Spain were not ones to take small interest rates. The first loans made between 1822 and 1826 of 7 million pounds sterling were to be repaid by 21 million pounds and given under such conditions that the British could receive $36 million with a little additional outlay. From this favorable beginning the leaders could go on to bigger fields by expanding private loans in all directions until Argentina was literally mortgaged to the money lenders.

The British also early took control of the Argentine banking system and emitted paper notes authorized as medium of circulation. Here, too, was a source of great profits and drainage of the wealth of the country. To this must be added the fact that British traders insisted at the start on taking metal—gold and silver—for their goods so that soon the country became quite empty of metal currency and forced closer to the money lenders and bankers.

To money lending must be added investing. The British first came into the field with railroad development so needed for exports to Britain. A large part of the capital could be obtained by loans in Argentina itself and by tremendous grants of land given by the Argentine government gratis to the railroad company. By raising railroad rates, by favoring British imported goods, and by various other means a tremendous drainage of Argentine wealth into British hands took place.

Following the railroads came the investments in *frigeríficos* by both British and Americans. And then electric services, street cars, gas and water services, slaughter houses, huge import-export warehouses, and finally industrial investments by branch American and foreign concerns under conditions in which all the profits could be shipped out of the country while their operations remained free of the customary charges and fees levied on native firms. To this must be added control over shipping and food processing, over import-export markets under terms of trade damaging to Argentina, over patent rights, and over various financial charges which last alone in 1958 amounted to $34 million.

During the great depression in the 1930's when the cost of production of grain and linseed was much higher than the market prices, and farmers were ruined, the food processors and large warehousemen made big profits. The British railroads then took 40% to 60% of the total price obtained by farmers as transportation charges. All during the depression railroad charges were not at all reduced. The dividends of the National City Bank of Buenos Aires in 1931 amounted to 21.9%, and in the five years from 1928 through 1932 totalled 110%. While foreign firms could bring in their fuel and raw materials free, the Argentine people faced increased taxation from $770 million in 1931 to $886 million in 1932. With the Argentine military dictators illegally paying off in gold reserves the government debts to foreigners, the Internal Credit Bonds of Argentina fell from $90.64 to $39.10 from $100 par value.

The political history of Argentina up to relatively recently can be said to be a series of struggles among sections of large property holders as to how their differences were to be reconciled. The mass of people, both workers and rural toilers on the one hand, and small property elements such as small merchants, artisans, handicraftsmen, and such on the other hand, had very little to say. The first struggles were within the port of Buenos Aires between native merchants and British merchants who were also importers of European goods and had extensive British credits. Naturally, the British merchant importers won the day and Buenos Aires set itself up as a port separate from the rest of the country.

The rise of the cattle industry, however, forced the hinterland of the port, the Province of Buenos Aires, into the picture. It now became not so much the importer who counted as above all the exporter, or the exporter-importer. The whole Province of Buenos Aires was now considered superior to the rest of the country. Following the extension of cattle raising into Entre Rios and Corrientes with the need for forage and feed for cattle, Buenos Aires had to form a confederation by means of which these provinces fused their forces against the rest of the country as need arose. This also meant the opening up of the River Plate and other ports like Santa Fé.

The settled policy of all these coast and river provinces receiving their goods from abroad was to encourage imports, to orient themselves toward European culture and civilization and strongly to support free trade to the detriment of the interior centers of the country such as Córdoba, Mendoza, Tucumán, etc. A marked political change occurred with the development of agriculture. To the *ganaderos* and *rancheros* had to be added the *haciendas, estancias*, and *chacras;* that is, to the big ranch owners had to be added the big agricultural land-owners and farmers. Through the Constitution of 1853 the various practically independent provinces were brought under federal control and the merchants, bankers, exporters-importers, cattlemen and large landholders could all adjust their interests. No one else counted.

There were no homesteaders. There were only the big estates. The *gauchos* or cowboys who had roamed the country eating wild steer at will now were forced to prove they either owned land or were employed by one of the big landholders, or else they were conscripted into the army to fight against the Indians and rival Provincial cliques. In the metropolitan center of Buenos Aires the artisans and handicrafts-men were not strong enough to protest their lack of political say. Voting was done not by secret ballot, but openly, the rancher gathering together all his henchmen and peons and bringing them up to the polls to vote as he ordered. Following the Constitution of 1853 politics was the monopoly of a social class, the landholders now called the Oligarchy, in which perhaps no more than two hundred families exercised the controlling voice. This was the "National Organization."

Matters began to change drastically when agriculture became fully developed and railroads were introduced by the British. Now a wave of immigrants from Europe began to pour in. At first they went to the countryside seeking land, but as the land was under monopoly control these Europeans became peons and agricultural laborers. Some pioneered in other parts of the country, especially in the tropical north-west, or settled in the cities, especially Buenos Aires. This led to a two-fold result: First, with the tremendous development of the countryside the Oligarchy took on a comfortable liberal tinge; second, when the contradictions of world capitalism began to squeeze the money market and exports of Argentina the masses directly concerned began to protest their disfranchisement.

During the first part of this period, when the smug, self-satisfied Oligarchy was comfortably installed without challenge and had named its rule was comfortably installed without challenge and had named internal policy of concessions and accords so that there would be no sharp opposition in the political field and one government would give way gracefully to the other. The successive political leaders, Bartolomeo Mitre, Sarmiento, Avellaneda, Pelligrini, Luis Saenz Peña, and the others were all of the same social status.

The first shock came with the financial panic of 1890 when it seemed to the Argentine "Chicken Penny" Provincial Oligarchy that the "sky had fallen" on their heads. These conservatives quickly saw to it that the armed forces took over and ordinary methods were put aside during the emergency.

The second shock came with the formation of militant unions on the part of the immigrant workers raising the cry of the people for the right of free, universal, secret suffrage as in the United States and in Europe.[11] A so-called Radical Party was formed to push this demand. (The Radical Civic Union was born officially Nov. 17, 1892.) In 1912 Saenz Peña introduced a bill which soon became law realizing the principle of free and secret suffrage. In the very first election conducted under this law in 1916 the people turned out in great masses and swept the Radicals headed by Yrigoyen into power. This was to be the first and perhaps only honest national election ever to be held on Argentine soil.

In foreign policy the "Illustrious Liberals" Oligarchy tied themselves ever more closely to Great Britain and took the lead in Latin America in opposing rising American imperialism. Expressing great contempt for the slavery existing then in Brazil, Argentinians spread the same contempt for the same reasons to the North Americans. When the Monroe Doctrine was launched in the U.S. Argentina made it clear that this was a unilateral doctrine of which it was not at all a part. Argentina refused to oppose European interference on the ground that its own people came from Europe and looked to Europe for culture and enlightenment, for labor and for capital.[12]

Later on Argentina would decline to enter into an inter-American coalition proposed by the United States, making this point very clear at the first Pan-American Conference in 1889. Still later Argentina would call in the Germans to train its army in the Prussian manner and the Oligarchy would later develop strong attachments in favor of the Mussolini-Franco-Hitler Axis.

[11] See Sebastian Marotta: *El Movimiento Sindical Argentino,* Vol. I covering the period 1857-1907 (1960), Vol. II covering the period 1907-1920 (1961); Vols. III and IV in preparation.
[12] See Sergio Bagú: *La Realidad Argentina en El Siglo XX, Vol. III, Argentina en El Mundo* (1961).

In the first World War Argentina played a sort of Italian game; it was neutral at first and only during the last few months did it declare war against Germany. It did not play any active part in the League of Nations. In World War II it was neutral although its rulers favored the Axis powers and only at the very end changed their tune to follow the United States, and, in order to be able to enter the United Nations, declared war on the Axis Powers. In no case did Argentina fight Italy or Spain. In no case did Argentina really aid the United States.

The Radicalism headed by General Yrigoyen that swept into power in 1916 was composed of heterogeneous groups with vague oratorical phrases meaning very little to the mass of people. Radicalism did allow freedom of political expression, however, and soon Argentine Radicals had broken into a large number of groups stemming from the base trunk, the *Unión Cívica Radical*. There were Blue Radicals, White Radicals, Black Radicals, *Oficialista* Radicals, *Situacionista* Radicals, Intransigeant Radicals, Radicals of the People, Bloquist Radicals of San Juan, Lenconist Radicals in Mendoza, Antipersonalist Radicals, and the Unified Radicals. In the 1930's, following the seizure of power by the Conservatives there functioned Federalist Radicals, *Tradicionalista* Radicals, *Concurrencista* Radicals, the Reorganized National Committee, the Radicals of San Juan, Radicals of Santa Fé, and, in the 1940's before Perón, the Independent Radicals, and others. Today the Radicals have two principal groups, the *Unión Cívica Radical Intransigente* (UCRI) and the *Unión Cívica Radical del Pueblo* (UCRP).[13]

The victory of Radicalism over the Oligarchy was a sure sign that Argentina was becoming industrialized and urbanified. The immigrants streaming into the cities were acquainted with Socialism, Syndicalism, and Anarchism. They were forming militant trade unions and taking to the streets in strong demonstrations which the Oligarchy and its army did not quite know how to handle, but they were not strong enough to have any militant political spokesmen truly their own. So, for the time being, they followed in the wake of the lower middle classes into Radicalism.[14]

[13] See Alfredo Galletti: *La Realidad Argentina en El Siglo XX, Vol. I, La Política y Los Partidos* (1961).
[14] See Jorge Abelardo Ramos: *Revolución y Contrarrevolución en La Argentina* (1961 ed.)

According to the election laws, any party having a plurality of one-third or more of the votes received two-thirds of the seats in parliament; the party that came in second obtained one-third of the seats; all the other parties got nothing. This was conceived on the theory that there would thus be constituted a "strong" government with the old idea of the Oligarchy of minority rule still carried out. Thus one candidate in 1926 received 2,381 votes and took his seat while another with 63,350 votes could not become a deputy; and 47.5% of the votes were rewarded with 71% of the seats while 52.5% of the voters elected only 29% of the deputies. Of course there was no protest on the part of the "democratic" Radicals at such outrageous results even in "honest" elections.

During the period of Yrigoyen's presidencies—there were two lasting from 1916 to 1930 and broken up in between by the Presidency of the Radical Marcelo T. Alvear—the Radicals were in a veritable euphoria of optimism. The First World War had overthrown the old autocrats of Europe including the Kaiser whose Junker officers had played such a role in training the Argentine army. The Russian Revolution had erupted with tremendous repercussions all over the world. The War had made neutral Argentina prosperous and had resulted in the beginning of a native manufacturing industry of considerable standing. It looked as though the Radicals would be in power for a long time and there was no need to press for economic and social reforms. In fact, the temper of the workers was such that the Radicals considered it very advisable to take it easy, very easy. Bribery and election frauds regained their normal place. The new industrial bourgeoisie among the Radicals now began to make peaceful overtures to the Conservatives.

The 1916 elections gave a most rude blow to the Oligarchy and wealthy. Their *Unión Nacional* was shattered into fractions: *Modernos, Cívicos,* and *Autonomists Nacionales* forming one grouping, and *Gubernistas, Vacunes,* and *Progresistas* another. The *Unión Nacional* itself first turned into the Conservative Party, second into the National Concentration which would support the military coup d'etat that was to come, and then into the *Partidó Democrático Nacional* composed of fractions calling themselves Autonomists, Popular Concentration, Conservative, Democratic, Liberal, Provincial, and Union Provincial parties.

The Conservatives were observing events with fear and dread. The War had led to a terrible defeat for their kind all over the world. Their army was smarting from the defeats their mentors had received. The landed interests saw their friend, Great Britain, now yielding second place to the United States which was entering more and more into the Argentine scene with new methods, new industries, and new policies. So long as there was prosperity, with the workers contained by the Radicals and denied many concessions, matters were not so bad and the Conservatives could afford to bide their time.

But then came the great world depression starting in 1929-1930. The Oligarchy was greatly shocked to learn that England was talking of changing its policy of free trade and favoring the Commonwealth nations of Canada, Australia, and New Zealand in the purchase of meat and grain. So frightened was the Oligarchy by this turn of events that it was quite ready to make the most obsequious concessions in order to get at least some of the market, even to the extent of maintaining that England had a responsibility to Argentina since Argentina was only a colony of Great Britain.[15]

The peso, which had been rated at 2.4 to the dollar and during the post-World War I period of prosperity had been backed by a gold reserve equal to 71%, began to fall. Standard Oil, which had become the bitter enemy of Yrigoyen because of the latter's intransigeant support of the national petroleum organization, Y.P.F., took a leading position favoring a military coup d'etat.

The workers were talking of seizing power all over the world. The Socialists already had repeatedly obtained a majority of the seats in the Buenos Aires Council and as many as 24 members in the Chamber of Deputies. The Radicals, it was feared could no longer stem the masses of workers and toilers of the country. The Conservatives had absolutely no hope of winning back power so long as there were free, secret elections. Now there was a great fear of the unemployed who had already shown their teeth in the United States, in Germany, and throughout Europe. It was time for the army to act and seize power.

An unknown general by the name of Uriburu with a small group of 1,000 men marched on the practically senile Yrigoyen who consented to retire. The army, however, made the mistake in April 1931 of permitting new elections which when held resulted in a new big victory

[15] See Jorge Abelardo Ramos: Work cited.

for the Radicals. The army, in retaliation, annulled these elections and proceeded to hold new ones after first, however, barring the Radical leaders from running, placing many in jail, and disfranchising the Radical parties. To expose the farce of such elections, the Radical leaders then ordered their supporters to refrain from voting. At the elections the frauds committed by the conservative and army groups were positively fantastic so that they were able to dominate the election returns completely. Later, under the same dictatorial conditions, fraud and terror were lavishly employed to elect as President General A.P. Justo, to be followed later by Ortiz and Castillo who, in turn, was to be ousted by the Perón group in 1943.

The army rule of the Conservatives, lasting from 1930 to 1943, was marked by the steady drift of the wealthy rulers of Argentina toward fascism, phalangism, and nazism. The country was becoming further industrialized. The army greatly needed industrialization. The old landed Oligarchy now was willing to recognize that its greatest safety lay in giving a share of the power to the more modern industrial bourgeoisie and to army industrialists who believed in the new systems of autarchy and self sufficiency being practiced by the dictators in Europe. To the Oligarchy it was necessary to deal with the workers the way Franco, Hitler, and Mussolini were dealing with them.

During World War I, and also during the depression in the 30's, immigration from Europe had practically ceased. The progressive industrialization of the country had to be performed by native workers who were now brought in from the interior into the cities. (This process was to become extraordinarily accelerated during World War II.) The new growing industry did not need workers with as much skill as previously when the work had been performed by craftsmen in small shops. Shops of over 500 workers grew from 22% of the total to 29% of those employed in manufacturing during the period from 1930 to the time of Perón, while those shops with less than 10 workers fell steadily in importance.

So long as they were led by the Socialist Party, which had generally taken an extremely moderate position hardly different from that of the Radicals in many respects, the foreign workers had not generated much fear among the ruling groups. But now the Socialist Party had become split. In 1920 there had been formed a Communist Party, called at first the Internationalist Socialist Party, which was forced to taste the bitter dregs of police persecution. These communists formed the General Confederation of Labor in 1931, actively organized many strikes, and culminated their efforts with a big general strike in 1936. When the Spanish Civil War broke out, most enthusiastically supported by the Argentine masses who were strongly against Franco, the police began a severe persecution not only of communists but of thousands of trade unionists and ordinary democrats. By 1942 the number of union meetings fell to 67% of the number held in 1935, the attendance to 20%.

Just as the emergence of the depression in the 1930's gave the Conservatives their chance to establish their dictatorship, so the eruption of World War II gave them their chance to use their army for totalitarianism. The war also offered the Oligarchy a chance to break from the chains of the British market, since now Argentina could sell its exports in many places at very favorable terms. The country was now more industrial than agricultural, more urban than rural and it was time for the industrial bourgeoisie with its more modern methods to take over. The Argentine Army understood more clearly than ever that its power depended on the industrialization of the country more than on any single factor and that it was time to end the naive system of free trade and non-nationalization of industry that had retarded Argentine industrialization.

The chances of resistance to a military coup were lessened by the fact that at the moment the working class was split into two Confederations of Labor, a No. 1 in the hands of the Socialists and reformist trade unionists, a No. 2 in the hands of the communists and militants. Both of them had a leadership now thoroughly bureaucratized; they were fighting each other, and were mainly interested in the Italian and European immigrant sections while in the meantime the native Spanish workers from the interior had come to Buenos Aires in ever increasing numbers (300,000 of them were to come before the end of the war). The Radicals had by now lost all support from the mass of workers who concluded the Radicals had done little for them and had used them for ulterior purposes.

The totalitarians in Europe had shown the Argentine army how to mobilize and win over the workers for the cause of capitalist dictatorship. The democratic imperialist powers could do nothing to interfere since they were tied up in a bitter struggle for survival. The events of 1930 had given the Army a "mission" to act and it did so again in 1943 when it saw that the Conservative President Costillo was going to give way to Costas, a landholder favoring Great Britain and the United States in the War.

At first the Army moved in the old ways to which it was accustomed. On June 4th General Rawson marching from the Campo de Mayo barracks near Buenos Aires forced President Costillo to flee. A state of siege was proclaimed. Political parties were outlawed and those arrested sent to concentration camps. The General Confederation of Labor No. 2 was dissolved, the principal officers of General Confederation of Labor No. 1 were ousted and military officials substituted for them. All newspapers were censored and many closed down. With the support of the clergy, Catholic religious instruction was reintroduced in the public schools, a question supposedly settled as far back at 1884.

The army coup of June 4, 1943 had been carefully prepared by an officers club called *Grupo de Oficiales Unidos* whose leading spirit was Col. Juan Perón. Perón had taken an active part in the 1930 military coup under Uriburu, even writing a report on it. Then he had left the country for an extensive study of the fascist-nazi movement where he became convinced that the military could retain power only if they had popular support and this could be secured by the same mass demagogy used by Mussolini and Hitler. The trick, however, was to find the necessary nationalist coloration that would appeal specifically to Argentinians.

The old army policy in a coup d'état was to issue no program but merely to utter some vague generalities. This was the line at first pursued when the take-over was accomplished in 1943. The army officers issued a statement in which they called themselves the "faithful and jealous guardians of the honor and tradition of the country as well as of the well-being, the rights and liberties of the Argentine people." The officers emphasized that the armed forces were not taking over for their own material interests, in fact they were renouncing all emoluments. As he closed down all opposition political parties General Rawson could affirm that now all were only Argentinians and not party divisionists. Aping the aggressive nationalisms of Hitler and of Mussolini the United Officers Club did manage to hint that it was apparently the manifest destiny of Argentina to unite all Latin America, Chile, Uruguay, Bolivia, etc., into one large country whose heart and center would have to be Argentina.

None of this empty phrasemongering, however, found any warm reception among the masses. Soon General Rawson gave way to General Ramirez who, after being recognized by the United States, misguidedly decided to lift the state of siege in August, 1945 in preparation for elections to be held February, 1946. At once the most tremendous anti-military demonstration in the history of Argentina broke out as all the popular parties protested against the military seizure of power. Frightened, the Army immediately clapped down the state of siege again. Much violence now erupted. Many new persons were arrested. The bitter open resistance of the university students had to be physically broken. It was now clear that the Army, by itself, isolated from the masses, could not long endure in power.

Sensing this and believing all was lost, on October 9, 1945 General Avalos at Campo de Mayo staged a new revolt supposedly on behalf of the people. Perón, now recognized as the chief active organizer of the original coup, was arrested. The law concerning political parties was restored to its previous authority. All political prisoners were released. The universities were reopened. The Communist Party was made legal again. Avalos now called on the former opposition parties to cooperate with him until the elections were held when the army promised to step down.

But no! Avalos himself had taken power by a military coup, therefore the opposition refused its cooperation. Instead these Radicals and Socialists demanded that the government be turned over to the Supreme Court, claiming it was the only "legal" body left. But this very Supreme Court had always been controlled by the Oligarchy, had always hated the social reform movement sponsored by the masses, and at this very moment was plotting to declare certain pro-labor measures advocated by Perón as illegal. Whooping with joy, the industrial bourgeoisie now also refused to pay the workers for their new holidays coming due.

Aghast at the strange legalistic logic of the Radicals and, above all, at the stupidity and treachery of the Socialists, the workers poured into the streets of Buenos Aires in a wild demonstration of anger. They smashed the Socialist headquarters and forced the leaders to flee for their lives, they demanded the immediate release of Perón and called a most effective national general strike to realize this objective. The Army, not having been allowed to withdraw thanks to the decision of the opposition, simply stood by and allowed matters to take their course. Avalos freed Perón who mobilized all his forces to strike terror into the opposition. When the February elections were held, Perón, supported by the workers, won an enormous victory.

It now becomes necessary for us to trace the events leading to this astounding triumph by Perón. We have already noted that Perón had early realized the necessity of using the new methods first employed by the totalitarians of Europe, and when the military coup succeeded in 1943 he was given the post, created especially for him, of Secretary of Labor and Social Welfare. Acting as monitor over the trade unions he immediately immersed himself in the problem of winning over the workers.

As we have noted, the workers were now functioning in two main streams: one included the foreign born and children of former immigrants familiar with industrial life and, as the more skilled workers organized in craft or trade unions, following an old style bureaucratic leadership. The other stream was composed of newer, native, less-skilled workers who had arrived from the interior of the country and were working, in the main, for the larger, more modern companies. They were practically unorganized, naive, and provincial, imbued with pride in nationalism and in the army as its representative.

The strategy of Perón was relatively simple: Smash the Marxists and militant revolutionists, take over the other organizations from the opportunist and bureaucratic socialists and simple unionists, and build up new organizations with the native, naive, patriotic elements from the interior. In this Perón was only following what had been done by others, even by President F. D. Roosevelt in the U.S. when he liquidated the Communist Party by a deal with Stalin, won over the A.F. of L. and helped build up new C.I.O. unions through Government legislation and encouragement. The methods were different, the basic strategy the same.

The way to the worker's heart was through the stomach. If Perón could see to it that the workers obtained economic gains which they considered substantial, and if these gains were obtained only through Perón, the job would be more than half done. If, in addition, he made the workers feel important and he himself helped them build new and powerful labor unions with new leaders entirely devoted to him, the game was won.

Perón took over the negotiations of labor contracts. Where the trade union officials could be bribed or won over to follow his lead, he saw to it that the employers paid what the workers thought was a good deal. Where the union officials were reluctant to follow him the union got nowhere. Where the union called strikes, the strikes were broken.

All during the war years previous to Perón's coming to power, although Argentina was prosperous, the workers had not improved their relative position. Nor did they really improve their share in the first years after Perón took power. It was only when the social security legislation became truly effective that a marked change occurred. The following table tells the story:

Table 20

ARGENTINA: DISTRIBUTION OF NET NATIONAL INCOME

Year	Share of workers	year	share of workers
1939	46.3%	1946	45.2%
1940	46.0	1947	46.2
1941	45.3	1948	50.2
1942	43.1	1949	56.1
1943	44.1	1954	57.4
1944	44.8	1955	55.0
1945	45.9	(1959-1963	45.8-46.0%)

In the packing house industry which had hitherto been unorganized, Perón helped the workers build a new, strong, militant organization which became his and his alone. So he did with the sugar workers of Tucumán and Mendoza and other places. This great increase in unionism aided by Perón finally won over the entire General Confederation of Labor to Perón, with the dissidents (railroad, textile, and shoe unions) withdrawing. These dissidents were soon destroyed, except the railroad unions, which returned to the fold of the General Confederation of Labor in 1945.

In addition to advancing real wages during 1944-45, Perón introduced a strong social security system for the workers and moved Argentina from the backward lot of the Latin American workers in this field, to a very forward position comparable to what existed in Europe. For his rationalization Perón assumed the name of "Justicialism", a philosophy similar to that of Salazar in Portugal and of Franco in Spain, so heartily approved by the Vatican and the Catholic Church.

Justicialism, or system of social justice, was later embodied in Perón's new Constitution adopted in 1949. This Constitution declared the State must protect the rights of the workers, of the family, and of the aged. The rights of the worker included the right to:

work,
a fair reward,
acquire skill,
worthy working conditions,
preservation of health,
well-being,
social security,
protection of the family,
economic improvement,
defense of occupational interest (which right, while it included the right to form trade unions, apparently did not include the right to strike).

Protection of the family included the duty of the State to support marriage and family property, to give consideration and attention to mothers, to see that children received special favored treatment, including primary and advanced education even up to university training.

The rights of the aged listed were the right to:

assistance,
lodging,
sustenance,
clothing,
care of physical health,
care of moral health,
recreation,
work,
tranquility,
respect.

The Constitution also declared that private property had a social function and was subject to the obligations the law imposed for the common good. The State henceforth was to control the distribution and utilization of land. It also was the obligation of the State to control foreign trade, national resources, and public services.

Even before this Constitution was enacted, from the early days of

1944-45, Perón was advocating the basis for an advanced social security system. It was made very difficult to lay off or discharge any worker except for causes restrictively defined. Medical care was organized to treat the sick and injured. A very extended pension system was erected in which one could retire with pay at as early an age as 55. Workers were to receive an annual bonus at Christmas time equal to one month's pay. Each worker could enjoy from 10 to 15 days paid vacation and a considerable number of paid holidays. Perón was able to get an appropriation of a billion and a half pesos set aside for low-cost housing.

At this time Perón forced through certain corporate forms of legislation recognizing union contracts as part of the law of the land enforceable by State sanction. The Corporations formed under this law embraced all employer and employee organizations so that contracts could be enforced in the name of all. Perón established a minimum wage for each union and industry. He reduced the hours of work. He built up a structure of social tourism so that the workers could make good use of their vacation time and be under his guidance while away from work. He also formed a National Council of Social Security.

On the social front Perón's wife, Eva, became extraordinarily effective. She advocated and secured women suffrage. She drew the women into both political and charitable affairs, her charitable work earning her the Spanish Grand Cross of Isabella, Colombia's Cross of Boyacá, Peru's Grand Cross of the Order of the Sun, Mexico's Order of the Aztec Eagle, Netherland's Grand Cross of the Order of Orange Nassau, and Ecuador's Grand Cross of the Order of Merit.[16]

With all this work behind him, naturally when Perón was arrested by General Avalos who tried to return the nation again to the sterile Radicals mouthing abstract phrases but doing very little for the workers, there would arise a big protest movement. This protest was initiated not by the more sophisticated and skilled European and city workers but above all by the Argentine "hill-billies," the *cabezas negras* (black heads) who had moved into urban areas only recently and, working for large corporations, had great need for security, since they did not know when the war and their work would terminate. It is this section of the native population that poured into Buenos Aires from all sides, that took to the streets in huge mobs and forced Perón's

[16] See George I. Blanksten: *Perón's Argentina* (1952).

release. It made no difference to them that Perón really had done little against the Oligarchy except make speeches, that he was supported by ominous Nazi and Fascist organizations, that he favored the Axis powers as against the U.S. and England, that he was merely aping in Argentine style the totalitarian dictators of capitalist Europe, that this was only his method of building a more modern and efficient capitalism, that he had no use for democracy and that he and his generals were planning to steal more than half a billion dollars for themselves before they quit. A regular reign of terror was now started against Perón's opponents.

Supported by the Army, the Government, and the masses, Perón decided to go through with the elections to be held February 1946. To do this he got the organized labor movement, the General Confederation of Labor, to form a Peronist Labor Party which, however, after he had seen the great danger of teaching organized labor to have its own party, he later changed to a Peronist Party under the pretext that he had won over a section of the Radicals and wanted a renegade Radical Vice-President on the same ticket with him and thus had to bring the Radicals directly into the Party.

Perón had now placed his opponents in a desperate crisis. For the first time they realized their empty phrases were not enough and they, too, had to come out for some improvements for the workers and for the nation. The Intransigeant Radicals were thus forced to advocate nationalization of the sources of national energy, of public services, and of foreign and national monopolies which in private hands were obstructing the country's progress, for the protection of social and labor rights, for social security, for the right to organize and strike, for full education for the people, etc., etc., as well as for the right of "individual liberty." Allied with them were Socialists, Communists, and the Democratic Progressives united in a Democratic Union. These latter groups stressed Perón's anti-Soviet, anti-United States, and pro-nazi fascist views. But it was all too late. Perón counter-attacked with charges against the U.S. Ambassador, Braden, and emphasized Argentina's destiny to be freed from U.S. imperialism. To clinch matters he got the Army to declare a state of siege before the plebiscite was taken.

The result, as we have already noted, was a smashing victory for Peronism: Perón receiving 54% of the total vote, the entire Democratic Union 46%. The Socialists could not elect even one member to the Chamber of Deputies, the Radicals only a few, the Conservatives were wiped out. Even in Buenos Aires proper, the very stronghold of the Socialists, they came in only third.

Had Perón wanted to he could have continued his regime as a democrat, since he had won by means of the majority of votes. But this wily fox understood full well that he was the representative not of the workers who had voted for him but of the new modern bourgeoisie arising in Argentina and could not allow himself to be supported by a labor party or rely permanently on labor votes. He had granted the unions large authority, but only when they were officered by him. He had brought poor people into the government which had previously always been reserved for the wealthy, but only when these people took orders directly and solely from him. He had opened the road to university and other media for culture to large groups of the previously deprived, but only when such cultural media taught what he wanted them to teach. He had raised the standard of living of the masses somewhat and had promised them some security, but these matters could prove to be very illusory, inflation could reduce real wages to below what they were, pension funds could be looted, as indeed they were, etc. Perón was not satisfied with a political system where those that gave him power could take it away. He stuck to the principles of military and personal dictatorship, especially since he could not show his hand and develop a dictatorship of the industrial and modernized bourgeoisie.

Before the elections, officially neutral Argentina had begun to make the war pay off and with favorable terms of trade Argentina had considerable gold reserves and credits behind it. This continued for the first few years after Perón became President. Since, as we have seen, imports were hardly to be obtained, Perón decided to use the reserves to nationalize certain industries and buy out the imperialists as far as he could. He also made efforts to re-equip and modernize industry and realize a superior purchasing power for Argentine exports by centralizing all export sales of grain and meat, etc., in the hands of the government.

Thus Perón nationalized the Central Bank and Insurance, created a merchant fleet and a national civil aviation. He bought back the railroads and 17,000 adjoining properties, as well as the telephone companies and all means of transmission. He took over, with compensation to the private owners, all public services, gas, energy, local transport, running water, etc., as well as the port equipment and grain elevators that had been the monopoly of the imperialists.

To secure the maximum funds for his purposes and in order to pay off the foreign debt that was costing Argentina 2.5 million pesos a day Perón forced the sale of all exports to be made through the government. The producers were given a price they had expected, the government in its deals secured a much higher price, what with the scarcity of meat and grain during and immediately after the War, and Perón's government pocketed the difference which was such an enormous sum that Perón could not only pay off the foreign debt, transforming the country for the first time from a debtor to a creditor country, but could also re-equip the industries taken over, such as transport, ports, etc., and have considerable loot for himself and friends as well.

Thus Perón saw to it that there was something for everyone, including himself. The Oligarchy was not bothered much. Perón's fine phrases that there must be agricultural reform with the poor masses given the big estates were never implemented. In fact the neutralized Oligarchy received better prices for their agricultural exports than before. The industrial bourgeoisie was greatly stimulated and developed by the growth of industry and manufactures during the War and after and by the fact that imperialist competition had been somewhat removed. The intellectuals had been given fine managerial opportunities in the new national undertakings the government had sponsored. The students had been made to feel that the old curricula based on law and religious philosophy were outmoded and that it was better to go along with Perón favoring physics, chemistry and the natural sciences and techniques leading to better industrial strength. Perón showed them the place they would have with the development of heavy industry, steel, chemicals, etc., that was in the plans of the government. With the elimination of strikes the workers were given better real wages, Christmas bonuses, pensions, tourism, and job and social security. Prices were controlled, the cost of living advances were fought against, a campaign was made against speculators in money and in commodities. The role of the women was raised to great heights by Eva Perón.

Nor were the armed forces neglected, this great source of support for Perón. Their ranks increased from 45,000 men to 170,000. The pay to officers was greater than that in the U.S. The most modern and costly equipment was bought and new warships built. Under military aegis were started big metal shops, airplane plants, tank and automobile motor plants, etc., so that the military machine became a great industrial organon controlling a large number of jobs and having its pressure in many ventures.[17]

Strange as it may seem it was this very Army that was to overthrow Perón. Let us not forget that Perón had incurred the deadly enmity of American imperialism and that bourgeois Argentina could not withstand such enmity on the part of the greatest power in the world. Now that the exceptional war and post-war years were over and Argentina again had to sell her stuff at unfavorable terms of trade, again she had to come to imperialists, especially the U.S., for industrial help, again she was barred from selling her exports. American industrialists were penetrating Argentine industry more than ever and could not tolerate nationalized industry barring the way to their profits.

Nor could the U.S. forget the fact that Perón had favored the Axis Powers during the war and that he had risen to power by a campaign against U.S. imperialism. America had placed all Europe on rations immediately after the War, and through the Marshall Plan of Reconstruction in the next post-war period. At this juncture no European country could afford to favor Argentina over the U.S. The friends of Perón in Europe had been ground into the mud. The U.S. was making generous loans and grants to many countries, but none found its way to Argentina. The U.S. was giving away great military grants for the bolstering up and modernization of many armies, including those in South America, as in Brazil, Argentina's chief rival for Latin Amer-

---

[17] The following evaluation of Peronism is given by Rogelio Frigerio, a leading Radical supporting Frondizi: *"El peronismo es un fenómeno político y social de extraordinaria importancia y significación. Ni siquiera sus mas enconados enemigos aciertan a negarlo. Su gran contribución histórica fue la de promover a primer plano la conciencia de las masas trabajadores de la ciudad y del campo; unir en la lucha por sus reivindicaciones al proletariado industrial con los peones rurales, rescatando del olvido a grandes masas de trabajadores sumergidos; infundir sentido nacional al movimiento obrero liberándolo de los falsos planteos sectarios y anarquistas de sus viejos dirigentes; incorporar el sindicalismo nacional organizado a la conducción política y económica de la Nación, juntamente con la central empresaria, propósito que nunca se logró per entero, pero que señala una saludable tendencia en nuestro proceso de desarrollo nacional. Esta fue esencialmente la dinámica del justicialismo y la que lo sitúa con caracteres inequívocos en nuestra historia."* See Prologue in Marcos Merchensky: Work cited, pp. 13-14.

ican hegemony, but none was available for the Argentine Army. Training of the Argentine Army in modern weapons would have to be done by U.S. military missions, but none could come to Argentina except on U.S. terms of capitulation.

U.S. imperialism wanted: 1. Greater freedom for Standard Oil and private petroleum exploitations; 2. Greater say in the electrical industry and less for the State *Agua y Energía* entity; 3. Greater say in the great steel works at San Nicolás; 4. Dismantlement of some of the army's machine shops and turning over of the machinery there to Kaiser, American industrialist, for the construction of an automobile plant, and to Fiat Company, in which American interests were strong, for a tractor plant; 5. Purchase of military equipment only from the U.S. under the guidance of a military mission; 6. Cooperation of Argentina in the Organization of American States for use against the Soviet Union and in the United Nations; 7. Return to civil control of the government so that bourgeois interests subordinated to imperialism could play a direct role; 8. Return to the system of large scale loans from the U.S. and full protection of U.S. private investments; 9. Return to the system of private enterprise and the end of nationalization schemes.

Once the Army, as the executive committee of the bourgeoisie, decided to act, it was easy to find "issues." The church found an issue that Perón had tried to separate church and state and favored a divorce law to which it was opposed. The Army feared that the people's militia was a dangerous experiment. Sections of the industrial bourgeoisie declared that they needed U.S. partners in their development. The petty bourgeoisie complained that inflation was gaining and prices rising, including the cost of living. And, of course, there had always been the opposition of the sophisticated sections of the working class.

In anticipation that the Army would one day act against him, Perón had tried to free himself from its grip by attempting the organization of a popular militia where workers would have arms at their place of work and be trained to fight for him. Perhaps Perón would have fared better had he organized a special S.S. elite corps as Hitler had done. At any rate, the Army never gave him a chance to complete this dangerous instrument. Under General Aramburu the Army in Córdoba and the Navy in Mar del Plata combined to overthrow him in 1955.

Had Perón really been a workers' man he would have called on the trade union leaders and the people's militia to fight for him. This he refused to do, however for it would have opened up the road in Argentina to a real workers' revolution, the last thing Perón wanted. He was content to flee to Spain while the Peronists were outlawed.

The fact of the matter is that Perón had opened up a veritable Pandora's Box of precedents too dangerous to be long tolerated and which may be summed up as follows:

1. He had helped sponsor the first Labor Party, organized by the trade unions of the General Confederation of Labor. Were a Labor Party to become a permanent feature of Argentine politics it could eventually rule the country and, given the revolutionary nature of the Argentine workman and agricultural laborer, this could mean the end of the world for capitalism there.

2. He had nationalized not only public utilities and extraction industries but had also started on basic heavy industries favoring a government plan which could be reoriented by workers into a Soviet style affair. He had also centered all exports in government hands and fixed prices. He had raised the dangerous question of workers' control in the productive process and their security in society. Workers could now be induced to challenge the right of private profit and the efficacy of private ownership.

3. He had made ridiculous the pretensions of the old ruling groups and their intellectuals in the universities, and had taught even the most backward masses to have contempt for their ideas. This could never be undone.

4. He had raised the question of a people's militia that could form a dual power against the State and its regular army and become the military arm of a true people's revolution.

5. He had exposed the dangers of imperialism, especially that of the U.S., and had urged the unity of all Latin America to carry on this fight. Here was a definite area for an alliance with the Soviet Union.

After the military coup d'etat of 1955 the government abruptly changed its policies. Whereas previously there had existed control over foreign commerce through the *Instituto Argentino de Promoción del Intercambio* (IAPI), now all such control was removed. Whereas under Perón the export of grain was in State hands, now there were free exports as before, except for certain price supports. Instead of subsidies of consumption, there were free prices for articles of prime necessity. Instead of the nationalization of bank deposits there was the return of banks to private hands.

The Peronists received the same treatment by the Army that they had given others. The Peronist Party was made illegal, their meetings barred, and their newspapers suppressed. Their candidates could not run for office in the elections to be held in 1958. All the other parties now strove to get these Peronist votes for themselves, while the Peronist Party leaders ordered their people to cast blank ballots.

Since the Peronists had revised the 1853 Constitution by their own Constitution of 1949, another Constitutional Convention was called in 1957 for the revision of that Peronist Constitution. The following national parties appeared with candidates as delegates to that Constitutional Convention: *Unión Cívica Radical Intransigente* (UCRI), *Unión Cívica Radical del Pueblo* (UCRP) *Partido Democrática Cristiano, Partido Socialista, Partido Democrática.* In the elections the Radicals together received 45.4% of the votes cast (21.2% for UCRI and 24.2% for UCRP). The blank votes (Peronists) amounted to 24.3% of the total, while all the others together received 30.2%. Although the Conservatives appeared in a Federation of Center Parties, they did not make much of a showing.

Following the Constitutional Convention the elections for President were held in 1958. Since the Radicals had learned something from Peronism and indeed could not unscramble the eggs already scrambled, they came out for a program containing the following points:

1. Sovereignty of the people; republicanism and representative government;
2. Defense of agrarian production;
3. Nationalization of energy sources, public services;
4. Land as an instrument of labor and national wealth;
5. Protection of city and country labor: right to organize and strike, social security and similar measures;
6. Universal education, free and laic, completion of university reform;
7. Political independence and sovereignty.

The Democratica Progresista Party came out for:

1. Proportional elections;
2. Separation of church and state;
3. A ministerial parliament regime;
4. Partition of land to the toilers with long payment terms and the division of the latifundias;
5. Labor code enforcement;
6. University autonomy.

The Socialist Party had been badly hurt by Peronism, its locals and library having been burned and its leaders much persecuted. It had dropped some of its class struggle principles and had split into two wings. The Communists had two delegates to the Convention in 1957 but put forward no candidate of their own in 1958.

The *Partido Democrático Cristiano* was a party relatively newly created, taking after the models which had successfully participated in recent elections in Italy and in Germany. It integrated within its ranks the democratic catholics and was more conservative than the other groups. It was opposed both to individualism and to collectivism, to liberalism and totalitarianism, but declaimed on the basis of the Papal Encyclicals for the moralization of public life, for the improvement of the conditions of the proletariat and its responsibilities as citizens, for civic peace, and for secret and obligatory universal suffrage.

In the 1957 elections there also appeared some fractional parties, such as, on the "Left," the *Partido Laborista* and the *Partido de los Trabajadores,* branches of the Trotskyists, and the *Partido del Pueblo,* all of whom got a very tiny vote. On the extreme "Right" there was the *Partido Unión Federal,* while the conservative catholics had their *Democrático Conservador Popular.*

The principal candidate for President in the elections was Frondizi, representing the UCRI which differed from the UCRP in that it was in favor of allowing greater freedom to the Peronists as individuals and integrating them into national life once more (a policy called "integrationalism"). This policy became decisive because the Peronists now decided to throw their votes for the UCRI formula and the number of blanks greatly decreased from the percentage reported in 1957. The Communists also threw their votes for Frondizi who now appeared as a sort of girl for all. To the catholics Frondizi was the candidate who came out against the divorce law and for "free" religious education. To Communists he posed as an anti-imperialist. He also said he favored nationalization and industrialization.

Once elected, Frondizi met the demands of American imperialism, as we have already noted in this study. At the same time he felt the pressure of the Peronists and Communists who supported him. The pressure was generated by the following situation. The share of the working class in the total national income fell back in 1959 to 45.8% and has remained at about this level to the time of this writing. For a family of four (man, wife and 2 children under 14 years) the normal budget was estimated as 10,093 pesos a month, the minimum budget at 6,718 pesos, in October 1959. But the average pay at that same time was only 50% of the minimum budget. Thanks to a chronic and large housing shortage, rent alone in Buenos Aires was three-quarters of the wage paid the *skilled* worker (3,000 pesos). Many people had to take on two jobs. Added to this was the threat of unemployment. In the countryside the agricultural laborer received only half to two-thirds the average pay of the city ordinary workers. And these conditions prevail today.

On the one hand the economic and political crisis grew steadily worse and the intervention of the Army in preventing free elections became steadily more and more intolerable. On the other hand Frondizi could or would not prevent the Peronists from taking an active role again, although not under their own name but in the form of various fronts.

Thus, when the Provincial elections were held in March 1962 the Peronists were able to win an astounding victory and elected governors in most of the key Provinces where the vote was held. This undoubtedly would mean the return of Peronism on a national scale. As Frondizi refused to annul the elections, the Army removed Frondizi, placed him under arrest, and annulled the elections itself, posting its own key men in the various ruling offices in the Provinces.

The Army has also learned a lesson or two. It is no longer operating in "Caudillo" style, with one great leader taking over on a personalist basis. Now the "Junta" takes over collectively: the Army, Navy, and Air Force, all sharing responsibility in this nameless and faceless "Junta." This is the modern way, the staff way, underlying not the ambition of any given individual for power, but the ambition of the armed forces themselves to take and keep control as the executive

committee for the capitalist class as a whole, which class is too cowardly, congenitally too weak in the face of the proletariat, to do so
itself.

Furthermore, in Argentina the *Junta* repeatedly stresses the point
that it does not want the power and that it must have civilian technicians at the head of the government to run it for the army and the
capitalists. The Army wants to pose as "neutral," as merely defending
the country's honor, or the people's interests, or the moral code of
God, or some such very holy principle it says it believes in. The un-
popularity of the Army itself is so great that it can rule only behind the
skirts of civilians. Such civilian sycophants are not too hard to find. In
the case of Argentina one was found named José Maria Guido, who
agreed to act as President with Alsogaray as economic minister heading a full cabinet of other civilians. All of them represent nobody, so
far as the people are concerned, except a tiny handful of profit makers.

The extensive economic and political historical review we have just
completed may give us an idea of the climax toward which events
have been moving in 1962 and 1963. Now the crisis has entered a
double phase: that of raging inflation with a great increase in the cost
of living, seconded by an economic depression with large-scale unemployment where considerable numbers of toilers have no wages or
means of support at all. How long can such a situation endure?

Let us summarize the situation:

1. Per capita production and per capita exports have steadily fallen.
At fixed 1950 prices per capita production was 3,623 pesos in 1961
and only 3,424 pesos in 1962.

2. Business failures jumped from 2.8 billion pesos in 1961 to 13
billion pesos in 1962 and have continued to rise in 1963.

3. Many industrial establishments have closed down with a consequent great increase in unemployment. The index of the demand for
labor, given the level of March, 1962 as 100, fell by October, 1962 in
Buenos Aires to 62, in Rosario to 50. But even in March, 1962 the
employment index had been 25% under the previously established
base par. The number of *new* unemployed in 1962 was estimated at
over 360,000, not counting state and rural employees.[18] Total unemployment may be considered as being over one million persons, or

[18] See *Boletín Económico* issued by the *Federación Empleados de Comercio*,
No. 34 May, 1963.

perhaps 15% of the wage-salaried labor force. When the general strike was announced by the General Confederation of Labor in Buenos Aires at the end of July, 1962, it was openly stated that the warehouses were so filled with refrigerators and other appliances that the manufacturers of these items would welcome a general stoppage of production.

As for the extent of the economic depression, the index of manufacturing production in October 1962 stood at the same level as in 1959. The first four months of 1963 showed automobile and metallurgical industries down 38% from the level of 1962. The following table gives the motor vehicle production:

Table 21A[19]
ARGENTINA: MOTOR VEHICLE PRODUCTION
Units Produced (All Kinds)

1961	136,188
1962	56,359 (first five months)
1963	36,564 (first five months)

As a result of the depression the average per capita consumption dropped in 1962 13% below the level of 1961. The gross product fell 10% below the level of 1961 while the workers suffered a loss in real wages of 13%.

How the recession of the past few years is deepening into a fierce depression is revealed by the following table:

Table 21B
ARGENTINA: PRODUCTION IN GIVEN INDUSTRIES (INDEX LEVEL 1955 EQUALS 100)

	1959	1962 (first quarter)
Food and Drink	100	89
Textiles	72	62
Wood and Furniture	91	73
Leather and Products	71	53
Electrical Machinery & Apparatus	95	83

Source: U.N. *Boletín Económico de América Latina:* Vol. VII, No. 1 (October, 1962).

4. The purchasing power of the masses has been greatly reduced. Given 1958 as 100, the index for retail sales of food dropped to 90.1 by January 1961, to 78.8 by January 1962, and to 71.2 by January 1963.

[19] Given in *The Review of the River Plate,* Vol. CXXXIV, No. 3501, July 22, 1963.

5. The situation on the countryside even for those employed is far worse than that elsewhere. In 1960 a basic budget for a typical family of four persons (married couple with two children) was calculated in full detail at 120,000 pesos a year. Permanent rural workers, however, received an average wage under the law *Estatuto del Peón del Campo* of only 35,600 to 43,200 pesos a year, depending on the zone. These wages are fixed in permanent form by the State, including lodging, food, rest, vacations, payments for accidents, rules of discipline, etc. Under the Statute, payment in kind is permitted and food can be deducted from the meager wages paid. In addition, wages can be reduced up to 30% for workers over 60 years of age, or partially incapacitated. As stated, the pay is fixed by the State with no conditions set, so that the Minister of Labor has the power to act at his own sweet will to revise the wages. Thus wages have remained immobile since October 1961, despite the startling inflation in force since then and despite the vigorous protests of the *Federación Argentina de Sindicatos Agrarios*.

6. Given 1960 as 100, the cost of living index in Buenos Aires jumped to 184.7 by July, 1963 and is still rapidly going up.

7. In 1948 the average food consumption in Argentina amounted to 3,240 calories daily. Now the estimate is about 2,600 calories, or less than the 3,000 needed as a minimum for physical laborers. During the period 1935-39, the annual average direct milk consumption in Argentina was 1,360 million litres. The population then was around 13 million. Now the population is 21 million, but the annual direct consumption of milk is only 1,290 million litres.

The glut in meat in Argentina is one of the things that has helped stave off a revolution. For there seems to be no real hunger in Argentina such as exists in some other countries. One can still get meat relatively cheaply, a steak that would sell in a New York restaurant for $4.50 may be bought in Buenos Aires for the equivalent of 45 cents. The ratio of beef consumption per capita is higher in Argentina than in any other country in the world (note: pork, lamb and poultry statistics are entirely excluded), the annual per capita consumption of beef amounting to 40 kilograms in the U.S., 52 in New Zealand, 53 in Australia, and 72 in Uruguay, while Argentina at one time consumed 92 kilograms per capita but this fell to 85.1 kilograms during the 1952-1960 period and to 79.1 kilograms in 1961. Of course, these "average" figures do not tell how much the average worker eats. Argentina now consumes 85% of its meat products.

8. The Government, in its desperation, has looted the social security funds so that it can not pay its pensions and other social security payments on time. In July, 1962, the State pensioners were three months behind in their receipts of payments.

9. The Government has not been able to pay its state employees on time to whom they were owing, in July 1962, salaries to the amount of 6.3 billion pesos.

10. The Government has not been able to pay its railroad workers on time so that they must go a number of months without pay, with consequent great suffering and discontent.

11. The Government is not able to pay its suppliers, and by July 1962 owed more than 20 billion pesos to vendors and contractors to the Government.

12. The Government is not able to pay its debts on the municipal and provincial level, to the tune of 1.5 billion pesos.

13. The gold reserve of the nation has practically ceased to exist.

14. There is a steady continuing negative balance of trade and much greater negative balance of payments. In 1963 draconic measures were undertaken to end the negative balance of trade:

First, the volume of imports was drastically cut. In 1960 it amounted to 10.6 million tons; in 1962 to 7.2 million tons. The first four months of 1963 showed a drop of 33% in imports over the preceding year, but this was really due to the deepening business depression which did not allow Argentina to buy more. The main declines (50% or more) were in machinery, vehicles, iron and steel, normally about 90% of Argentina's imports, and badly needed for modernization and industrialization.

Second, to reduce the cost of necessary imports, the import tariffs and internal sales taxes were removed from such items as fertilizers. While this reduced the import prices on such items by 25%-35%, it also reduced the revenues of the government.

Previously, under the Decrees of Peñedo, the Guido Government, following in part the recommendations of the International Monetary Fund, had a) increased taxes by 20% on all imports, including those very necessary for Argentina to have, so that production costs went up instead of down; b) increased the price of petrol fuel up to 50%;

c) increased the sales tax up to 13%; and d) exacted 100% prior deposits for all imports.

Third, to push exports, tax refunds of 12% were given to exporters of nontraditional exports shipped after July 1, 1963.

Fourth, traditional exports were pushed, especially meat. In this respect the Government was forced to remove its 13% sales tax because Argentina was being undersold by Rumania and Yugoslavia. At the same time exports of linseed and linseed oil which had been $177 and $275 a ton respectively in January 1962, fell to $132 and $208 a ton respectively by 1963.

Fifth, a great effort was made to improve the sad situation in the petroleum industry. In 1961 petroleum imports had cost Argentina $108 million of its precious foreign currency. In 1962, this cost was reduced to $76 million, and further reduced in 1963. The following table shows the petroleum production and imports in cubic meters (exclusive of lubricants):

Table 21C[20]
ARGENTINA: PETROLEUM PRODUCTION AND IMPORTS IN MILLION
CUBIC METERS (ROUNDED TO NEAREST 100,000) 1958-1962

	Production	imports
1958	5.7	10.3
1960	10.2	5.6
1961	13.4	3.8
1962	15.5	2.9

Very recently a meeting in Rio de Janeiro of the Argentine-Brazilian Mixed Group on Industrial Cooperation decided that Y.P.F. of Argentina would sell Petrobras of Brazil one million tons of fuel oil. Argentine railways would buy in return $10-$15 million worth of freight cars. They also reached the conclusion that by common and complementary effort the two countries could manufacture steam engines, small turbines and safety and control valves, automobile engines, electrical products, etc. Thus imports from the U.S. or from Western Europe could be avoided. Chile is also interested in this new project, born of LAFTA initiative.

Sixth, the big drain of payments abroad through imported automobile parts is being stopped. Such parts cost $165 million in 1961 and the same in 1962. Now for 1964 automobiles are restricted to imports

[20] Given in *Business Conditions in Argentina:* No. 317, March, 1963.

amounting to only 10% of the total value of the vehicle. And the same principle will be applied elsewhere, it was announced.

15. The paper money currency in circulation in Argentina must now have reached the level of 200 billion pesos. Promissory notes easily have doubled over 1961.

16. The internal Federal debt perhaps is about at the same level of 200 billion pesos.

17. The total foreign debts of all kinds that Argentina is committed to pay in the next few years must be around $2.5 billion.

18. The budget for the term October 19, 1961 to September 30, 1962 showed total government expenses at 34.3 billion pesos, but this had to be increased by 12.9 billion pesos more to meet pressing obligations. The budgetary deficit for only part of the year 1962 was 50 billion pesos and this has rapidly increased.

In an effort to reduce the internal debt the Government has issued debt cancellation certificates to be used by creditors to pay taxes. Thus the Government has been forced into a system of *advanced* taxation, making future returns all the less.

19. While government debts are rapidly increasing the collections and income are drastically falling for the following immediate reasons: a) That part of the State income that came from tax on imports has fallen greatly because import volume has so diminished that despite the recent rise in the import tax of 20% the total is still considerably less than before; b) That part of the State income that came from sales taxes is down due to the fact that consumers are purchasing much less than before; c) The income from Posts and Telegraphs is down 50% because of the economic crisis while at the same time the railroad deficit is enormous. Furthermore, because of the general deficit of the government the plans for the improvement of the railroad system have had to be put aside so that the railroad deficits can only continue to increase.

20. In July, 1962, the Economic Minister, Alsogaray, declared that should the peso go to 150 to the dollar there would be a tremendous number of bankruptcies. It did pass that ratio. In order to check the speculation in foreign exchange the government closed down the cambios at one time and then issued regulations for them to open only for a few hours certain days of the week. These controls were not very effective.

21. At the same time the banks have been making enormous loans at very high rates of interest, one bank lending an amount six times its capital. Should these loans have to be called in or the lenders go bankrupt there must result a tremendous crash and panic.

22. Because of the galloping inflation, long term loans can not be made now for less than 40% to 50% interest, since by the time payment is due the value of the money paid has greatly fallen. This must lead to intense speculation and risks.

23. The government has desperately tried to secure new loans and negotiate old ones on better terms. When the International Monetary Fund and World Bank were approached in 1958 they laid down conditions which we have already given in a previous section of this study. Since the condition of limiting the government deficit by the end of 1959 had not been met, Argentina has not been able to secure this loan although it did meet some of the other conditions which we shall mention.

The government also launched a great patriotic July 9, 1962, internal loan. But with the Guido government resting entirely on the bayonets of the army and earning only the contempt of the people, there was not much of a popular subscription. In order to attract capital the government announced a policy of "whitewash" as it was called, herewith explained.

On July 27, 1962, the Secretary of the Treasury, Sr.Ayala, announced that capital which had previously not been legally declared for taxation might be legalized or "whitewashed" by officially declaring such capital before September 30th and paying on it a reduced tax ranging between 5% and 10%, but only on condition that said capital was invested in the recovery loan and not moved for at least three months.

Thus the tax evaders of the past were given a big benefit. Those who had pilfered the people and engaged in illegal activities under the Perón and other regimes could now come out of hiding. So could the smugglers and other criminals of that type. All was forgiven. If they declared their capital and left it in the loan fund for 3 months they need pay only 5% or 10% tax and evasion for the past five years, back to 1956, would be totally forgiven and that before 1956 entirely forgotten.

24. In regard to the agrarian question, the long trend reduction in

production and export of meat has been matched by a similar reduction in regard to grains. We have already noted the warning given by the International Monetary Fund. We need simply add here that the basic causes for this reduction in production is entirely owing to the antiquated methods and dog-in-the-manger monopolistic attitudes of the old wealthy families, the Oligarchy possessing the large estates. All the parties talk of the necessity of "agrarian reform," each interpreting this in a different manner, but no one actually doing anything about it.

The *Junta del Movimiento de Partidarios de la Reforma Agraria* has made the following demands on the government:

a.) To suspend evictions and rents so long as there is no constitutional government that can enforce a complete agrarian reform law so as to secure the stability of the agricultural producers;

b.) To finally carry out the agrarian laws now on the books without further amendments;

c.) To see that there is a full functioning of the Agrarian National Council established by law, and to deliver the land to be parcelled out to the 25,000 petitioners at present asking for it;

d.) To pass a real reform law to compel the *latifundistas* with lands not under production to rent these lands at prices at a maximum of 10% of the annual production, and in the interim to establish emergency measures accordingly;

e.) To take effective measures of price supports in line with the costs of production for great, medium, and small producers;

f.) Wage increases for the rural workers in line with the dearness in the cost of living to assure the sources of work; simultaneously there should be established large emergency subsidies for the unemployed;

g.) State support for the agrarian cooperatives, to promote settlement cooperatives for the exploitation of the land, the creation of machine stations and technical cooperatives which would permit to the small and medium producers the access to mechanization and modern technification;

h.) Adoption of a policy of relations with all nations, including the Soviet Union, to permit the winning of new markets, instead of bilateral tricky pacts now in vogue;

i.) The year 1962 was plagued with a great drought that ruined crops in many parts of the country. The Government should give full banking credits and a debt moratorium for producers lacking resources and affected by the drought, with priority to the producers least able to continue;

j.) Measures must be taken for the speedy normalization of the country constitutionally by means of the installation of a democratic government legally elected by the people without exclusions and which will permit the stability and progressive development of the Republic.

Newspapers currently speak repeatedly of the movement of the agrarian toilers seizing unoccupied and unused lands theoretically owned by the *latifundistas* and working these lands themselves until they are arrested en masse. The class struggle in the countryside is also building itself up to a climax.

What are the chances of restoring exports to their previous per capita levels, especially when the competitive market is becoming keener? What are the chances of reducing export prices when the methods of production are archaic and antiquated run by a ruling Oligarchy no one dares to touch? What are the chances of importing modern machinery and equipment to lower production costs in agriculture when there is a declining level of exports due to bad terms of trade and thus the capacity to import is constantly reduced? Here is a vicious circle from which Argentina can not escape without revolutionary methods.

Other reasons for high prices are: a) the very high level of profits insisted upon by manufacturing and industrial companies, especially those controlled by foreign interests who insist on a minimum net profit of 20% a year and often go up to 50%; b) the high financial charges when items are bought on the installment plan (In the case of automobiles—a car selling for $2,000 in the United States costs $8,000 in Argentina—the buyer must pay 40% down with interest charges at 2% a month); c) special licenses and import taxes. An illustration of the last item is in the case of the automobile industry that generally imports many of the parts needed for assembly. The taxes on such parts have been until recently 40% if the value of the parts amounts to only 25% of the value of the car, and then 200% to 400% if the parts go beyond this limit, up to a maximum of 55% of the value of the car which is the maximum limit of imports. Now no more than 10% of the value of the car will be able to be imported, apparently.

The trouble with the import tax is that it also has taxed machinery, parts, and equipment, and other items badly needed for the further industrialization of the country. These items should be allowed to come in free so that production costs could go down accordingly. We have already seen this had to be done in the case of fertilizers. Luxury imports, on the other hand, should be so heavily taxed as to make such imports impossible. But this would hurt the Oligarchy and wealthy. Again, instead of raising the price of petrol fuel which would thus allow Standard Oil the better to compete with the Argentine Y.P.F., it would have been far better to have prohibited the import of petrol fuel, greatly advanced Y.P.F. development, and kept the cost of fuel so badly needed by industry at the lowest possible level. We have already noted the tremendous and wasteful drain of money for petroleum imports, a very good part of which is used for individual and wasteful consumption.

The Frondizi deals with American oil companies for drilling new wells and with American drilling companies for drilling on behalf of Y.P.F. have proved very costly. These companies must be paid in U.S. currency which Argentina finds hard to get. Although in 1962 oil production increased about 15% and now suffices for about 85% of Argentina's crude oil requirements, a loud demand has been raised by Argentine nationalists for the complete cancellation, or at least renegotiation, of these expensive American contracts.

Of course, no real effort to throw the burden of taxation upon the wealthy through heavy and progressive income and real property taxes has been attempted. And, of course, no effort to compel disclosures of bank accounts abroad and compulsory repatriation of all such funds so that they could be used to stave off bankruptcy and promote industrial investments has been hinted at.

Most important of all, the drain of gold through imports could be drastically diminished and the balance of payment changed if the army budget were to be slashed so that imports of needless military equipment, latest style jet fighters and bombers, useless warships, etc., etc., were eliminated. The military budget runs from 30% to 50% of the total budget, although it should not need more than 8% at the most.

But of course the military dictatorship that has been in effect in Argentina since 1930 would never stand for that.

The general increase in the sales tax of 13%, like the increase in petroleum prices, was meant not only to cut down imports but also to help the government raise money. In this it was part of the general scheme by which electric rates were raised. In Buenos Aires recently one electric utility raised its rates 39% at one stroke, the other 52%. An ordinary family house that paid 400 pesos two years ago for electricity now has to pay 1,800 pesos. And this for very poor service, with low tension, often cut off, and constantly getting worse. All these measures have merely the result of cutting down consumption and raising the cost of living even faster and higher than before.

In regard to the increase in electric rates in Buenos Aires more might be involved than mere policy, perhaps rather a systematic looting of the treasury by foreign investors. British investors had originally owned CADE, the electric service company in Argentina. Its contract had come to an end in 1957 when it was supposed to be taken over by the State. At that time its property was evaluated at only $4 million for reimbursement. Instead of taking over the company, Alsogaray under Frondizi fused CADE with the government concern SEGBA guaranteeing CADE shareholders 8% return on their stock while the stock capital of SEGBA and CADE was fixed at $128 million. In the first two years of its operation under the new arrangement the State "redeemed" 2 billion pesos of private stock with the result that 800 million pesos were paid over to CADE owners. To this was to be added the 8% guaranty on 20 billion pesos, the value of the shares of stock of CADE within SEGBA, or another 1,600 million pesos, the total being now 3.6 billion pesos all to come out of consumers rates.

Perhaps the whole idea of raising rates, raising the cost of living and cutting down consumption, is part of a conspiracy to restrict production and to slow down Argentina's development as an industrial power. Especially stupid are the import taxes on items badly needed by Argentina's economy, export taxes that make exports from Argentina harder to sell abroad, consumer taxes that merely raise the cost of living and make the competition of foreign goods all the easier.

What might be considered instead are the following measures:

1. Redemption of all Argentine money held by wealthy in banks abroad. Prohibition of all exports of such foreign currencies or devises.

2. Substitution of a much heavier income tax, progressive not regressive, instead of the various excise, sales, and transaction taxes. Establishment and collection of excess profit taxes on profits not reinvested.

3. Confiscation of all savings over a given minimum and utilization of this capital for industrialization and modernization purposes, with limited returns to the owners of such confiscated savings.

4. Prohibition of all imports not absolutely needed except where such articles can be purchased at proper terms with exports not otherwise sold.

The rise in taxes and in public utility rates must be also considered in the light of the tremendous rise in the cost of living especially due to the inflation of the currency. In 1962 the cost of living rose about 60% so recognized by employers who when faced with new labor negotiations granted a general increase of 55% to meet the rise in the cost of living. Thus went overboard the demand of the International Monetary Fund for the freezing of wages.

The existence of growing unemployment, coupled with the tradition now well established in Argentina of no easy dismissals or lay-offs without cause, has made it very difficult to reduce the working force in the State apparatus, although they now work only a 5½ hour day, or on the railroads, as demanded by the International Monetary Fund.

To the rise in the cost of living, to the failure of paying workers promptly, and to the failure of State social security payments, should be added the low wage level of the Argentine workers, the average pay for the industrial worker being about $10 a week.

The failure to pay wages to the railroad workmen during 1962 and 1963 inevitably has led to very sharp action by the railroad workers union. It declared a two hour strike each shift for certain days of the week. The railroads were completely paralyzed during this period and all schedules disrupted at a cost estimated at 102 million pesos.

The astounding victory of the Peronists in the elections of March 18, 1962, leading to the new army coup d'état of March 29th and the arrest and removal of Frondizi coupled with the installation of the puppet President José Maria Guido, made it plain to the military that it was absolutely necessary to deal with the Peronists the way the Peronists had dealt with the others and to the politicians that old methods of elections had to go. There was only one hitch to the plan, namely the Peronists were solidly in control of the General Confederation of Labor and as such controlled the actions of the working class.

A new statute was proposed to govern elections and political parties. All parties would have to get official State recognition before newly established Electoral Courts. No party upholding the ideas of Perón or depending on "foreign" ideas could qualify for such recognition. Thus the Communists, the Peronists and others of the 60 odd political parties in Argentina were banned. There were also reinstated the 1956 decrees forbidding all Peronist propaganda, including Perón's songs and his picture.

Nor could the leaders of these parties be allowed to run for office. A list of proscriptions of about 500 Peronist candidates was drawn up, including leaders of the General Confederation of Labor, no matter what ticket they ran on. Furthermore, to prevent new Peróns from springing up, the law declared that no military or naval officer, whether on the active list or on the retired list for more than the past two years, could run for office, or even hold executive or advisory posts in labor unions in any manner.

The legislation on political parties also changed the terms of elections so that now the principle of proportional representation would govern. The Peronists had won 30% of the total votes in the capital city of Buenos Aires. Under the old rules this would have given them a very solid majority in the city and Provincial councils. So long as the wealthy thought they could control the situation when there were many parties, many of them representing the poor, and the workers were without much money to make effective campaigns, it was all right to have the minority party that was on top obtain two-thirds of the seats. Now, however, that the workers or Peronists undoubtedly formed the largest minority party, this would not do—not do at all. Now it was necessary to get proportional representation so that the government would not be a "strong" one and the leaders could be defeated by a combination of the others.

There is just one trouble with this legislation stuck on the bayonets of the military guarding their puppet Guido, and that is that it will not work. Times have changed. Argentina has become an industrial country at a time when the working class, now far better developed and politically mature than ever before, is historically making a very strong bid for power. It is too late in history for the military to tell a city of over 5 million people with industrial unions of close to 4 million members, who shall run for office and who shall not, what elections shall be allowed and what annulled, which parties are permitted to function and which are not, etc. The absurdity of this tiny handful of generals operating as a state within a state has become crystal clear to all. The days of military dictatorship are numbered in Argentina and can only become the prelude for popular revolution.

The older traditional party hacks also do not quite realize the new situation, such as those who control the Radicals, both Intransigeant and Popular (although the "integrationist" faction does want to work with the Peronists), the Christian Democrats, the Popular Conservatives, the Socialists, and the National Federation of Center Parties who are all accepting the army decrees as enforceable, even welcoming them, and are all striving to see who can get most of the Peronist votes.[21] The Communists, the Socialist Party of the People, and the Trotskyists, however, who do not see matters in the same light are willing to form a common front with the Peronists on a common program demanding that elections be free, secret, and universal, with every citizen treated like every other. This position is especially strong in the ranks of organized labor.

With the army take-over in 1955 and the consequent flight of Perón, all the unions were placed under army intervention, supervision, and control until Frondizi took office. Under Frondizi the trade unions were made free again but in the interim they had broken up into three factions: the Peronist faction with about 1.8 million adherents and calling themselves the "62" after the number of national unions affiliated to them (such as packing house, food, metallurgical, leather, textiles, and others formerly aided by Perón), the anti-Peronists with about 2 million adherents calling themselves the "32" for similar reasons (railroad, public utilities, printing, public service unions and others dominated more by skilled workers somewhat like our own A.F. of L. although often led by Socialists), and the MUCS, a group of unions controlled by the Communists.

After Frondizi took office the "62" allowed the MUCS to fuse with them while the "32" split into two factions, one calling itself the "Independents" and taking with it most of the strength of the former group. Because of the split the "32" became greatly reduced in size.

[21] See the collection of the views of the principal political leaders and publicists in *Las Izquierdas en El Proceso Político Argentino* edited by Carlos Strasser (1959).

After the army intervention was removed, in 1961 the General Confederation of Labor (C.G.T.) formed a Provisional Committee of 20 members, 10 for the "62" and 10 for the "Independents," the "32" now dropping out of the CGT organization.

By the middle of 1962 the C.G.T. was able to call a national general strike for two days and to put forward the following demands:

1. Collective labor agreements to be brought up-to-date so that wages and salaries could recover their former purchasing power;

2. Reduction of custom tariffs on raw materials necessary for industrial development;

3. Reduction of sales tax;

4. Control of costs and fixing of maximum prices for articles of prime necessity;

5. Credit policy to strengthen production;

6. Severe repressive measures against all speculation, graft, and contraband;

7. Full employment with guaranty of job security and ban on imports which the national industry of the country can produce;

8. Immediate payment of pensions; payment by State of sums owed to pension funds and strict control over employers' quotas.

These demands, of course, define not a simple trade union program but a political program and show that the C.G.T. is preparing to step out as a political organization fighting for power.

At this time the Peronist leaders went to Madrid for a conference with Perón himself. They returned with the following program enunciated by Framini, one of the Peronist leaders and backed up by the "62" group of trade unionists.

1. Nationalization of all banks and establishment of one state centralized banking system;

2. State control over foreign commerce;

3. Nationalization of key sectors of the national economy: steel, electricity, petroleum, refrigerators, etc.;

4. Complete prohibition of all imports competing with domestic production;

5. Prohibition of all capital exports, direct or indirect;

6. Repudiation of financial commitments made at the expense of the people;

7. Expropriation of the landholding Oligarchy without compensation;

8. Establishment of workers' control over production;

9. Abolition of commercial secrets and strict control over commercial corporations;

10. Program of planned production of all the forces of the nation for the interests of the nation, with established priorities and maximum and minimum targets.

How revolutionary all this sounds! And, indeed, it is a revolutionary program, except that on closer examination one sees that there is nothing said or proposed how this program is to be realized, or how the Peronists, who appear to be moving to the "left," are to take and hold power. Perón, sitting far away in Madrid, seems to have taken a lesson from Castro, but Castro, at least, was in the very thick of the fighting itself. And Perón, with his loot and women friends safely tucked away, surely does not intend a secret invasion of Argentina with a dozen friends to try to storm the Argentine fortress as did Castro in Cuba.

What the Peronist intellectuals who are trying to direct this movement want is a fusion with certain sections of the Radicals (the Integrationists) so that Labor will not be the dominant force and the same sort of deal that went through in 1945-46 will go through successfully again. But this is not to be. This time the labor movement is not going to take second place to a discredited Frondizi Radical movement. What is more, they do not intend to remain a personalist party believing in some great personal saviour, the "Hero" Perón, who could find no other haven than Franco's arch reactionary Madrid. Many Argentinians feel that the vicious Perón would assume a deadly revanchist policy if he should ever return, and they would fight him to the finish with every weapon in their command.

What is very necessary now is for the labor movement to take the lead in the political field, as a sign of the real maturity of the working class, and fight for a program similar to that of militant socialism elsewhere, but with the removal of the "intellectuals" from leadership and with the nomination for Presidency and for all other offices of the government of labor leaders themselves. The trade unions are already in politics up to their neck. It seems it is time they played their own working class politics and no longer remain clowns playing the game of crooks like Perón.

It is highly significant that Perón and Framini say not one word about the chief immediate enemy of the workers and of the people, namely the military, the executive arm of the Argentine wealthy as a whole. The stupid Peronists still speak of the "patriotic aspects" of the army, of how it can be won over or split. And in this they are followed by the wily Radicals. Both Radicals and Perón have enjoyed power only because of the bayonets of this army stabbing to death the freedom and rights of the people.

The Argentine Labor Party, should it arise, must make its first and sharpest attack against the military. The outrageous arrogance of the military in thinking it can tell everybody what to do and that it is really responsible to no one but itself, its steady and consistent dictatorial rule over the State, its excessive share of the budget for no reason whatever, its scandalous pay and privileges, corruption and venality, its waste of the country's resources, its general stupidity and ignorance, the slavery of its conscripts, etc., all must be denounced.

A revolutionary Labor Party must have absolutely no truck with the military but must declare open war against it. It must demand now the end of conscription and propagandize the ordinary soldier in every possible way to show him how he can free himself from slavery to his officers. Such a party must demand a reduction of the armed forces, the dismissal of all unnecessary generals, colonels, admirals, and such, as well as those who have expressed themselves against the will of the people. It must call for the cancellation of military contracts for additional armaments for this vicious group. It must advocate the organization of a people's militia similar to Cuba's to replace the old army which must be entirely destroyed. It should insist on the transference of all military funds to refill the depleted civilian funds that have been systematically looted.

A military force without the backing of the people would fall to the ground in Argentina. That would be the end of this "paper tiger" that fights no wars save those against its own people.

Naturally, a revolutionary program that calls for such things as workers' control over production cannot be accomplished without a fierce resistance from the rulers and their police dogs, the military. The demand will have to be reinforced by a general strike, the general strike by the occupation of the factories and places of production and by the arming of the workers. This is the course workers' revolutions have taken elsewhere, why is it to be supposed that it will not take place in Argentina?

For such action a militant, aggressive proletarian vanguard is needed, since it can be assumed in advance that all the Peronist "intellectuals" who want a return to their fat salaries and corruption will run away at the first breath of such actions. There is reason to believe that such a vanguard can be found. Argentine labor fighters are not unused to conspiratorial work and to persecution. There is the Castro experience to learn from, and also the experience of Yugoslavia, of China, and of Russia.

There is time to write a postscript dealing with the July 7, 1963, elections finally permitted to be held by the military after the following actions had occurred:

1. Repeated attempts by military officers and sections of the Right to stage revolts in order to prevent any elections being held at all. All these were put down under the leadership of General Ongania.

2. The communists were outlawed and prevented from participating in the elections. A Government decree ordered the Party disbanded and established severe penalties for its members, excluded party members from civil service, educational institutions, labor communities and professional associations. Communists could not vote or be elected.

3. Large numbers of Peronists and trade unionists were arrested before the elections. The terms of the elections were constantly changed in such fashion as to make it impossible for the Peronists to have any chance.

At first the Peronists formed a National and Popular Front with the Frondizi wing of the Intransigeant Radicals, but when, apparently under the inspiration of Perón himself, the Peronists were induced to put forward Dr. Lima, the head of a small conservative group, as the presidential candidate, both laborites and Intransigeant Radicals rebelled. A section of the Intransigeants then put forth their own candidate, Dr. Alende, against the Popular Radical Party candidate, Dr. Illía, and the conservative front candidate General Aramburu. The Christian Democratic Party had placed a Peronist, Raul Matera, as its candidate and joined the National and Popular Front, but when later Matera urged blank ballots be cast and withdrew from the race with the other Peronists, a substitute candidate made the run for the Christian Democrats independent of the Peronists.

As the Army and its puppet president Guido increased the pressure, the Peronists decided to cast blank ballots in protest.

4. The electoral laws were changed so that there would be no direct elections for President but only elections for a college of electors who would be entirely free to select whomever they wanted, or in case of deadlock, to throw the election for Congress to decide. Other provincial colleges of electors were also to be elected to choose provincial governors in the same way.

All the parties recognized the fact that something had to be done to appease the masses. The Frondizi oil contracts were strongly attacked and pledges made to review and abrogate them. Five of the eleven members of the Board of Directors of Y.P.F. resigned to protest against these contracts, thus placing the issue sharply in the forefront. All parties came out for a strong foreign policy independent of any foreign power and for stronger pursuit of strictly national interests. The Christian Democrats denounced both the oil contracts with U.S. firms and the agreement Frondizi had made with the International Monetary Fund. The various parties also stressed further development of natural resources, a matter which came to the surface when it was revealed that the Sierra Grande region in Patagonia had proven resources of at least 50 million tons of good quality iron ore.

The fact that the labor organizations submitted to Perón's tricks and supported Lima rather than a laborite, placed the social problem second to the national and permitted nationalists to take the lead. As a result large numbers of voters decided not to make the fight on such a negative basis as refusing to vote for any one and violating the instructions of their leaders, voted for the middle class candidate still acceptable to the Army, that is either for Illía or for Alende.

The results of the amateurish subservience of the labor leaders was a victory for electors favoring Illía. The July 7th 1963 vote was distributed as follows (85% of the 11 million eligible voters, or 9.44 million voting).[22]

Some conclusions can be drawn from these elections:

1. The Conservatives, beyond question are out of the running. General Aramburu, darling of the Army, was exposed as having no

[22] Reported in Chamber of Commerce of the United States of America in the Argentine Republic, issue of July, 1963.

UCRP (Popular Radicals)	25.7%
UCRI (Intransigeant Radicals)	16.8
Aramburu Group	14.6
Blank	17.8
Neo-Peronist	5.7
Conservative	5.4
Socialists	5.8
Christian Democrats	4.6
Others	1.9
In doubt	1.7

effective mass support. The agrarian landlords clearly must play second fiddle to the industrialists.

2. The present President represents a small minority of the electorate. The whole middle class movement supporting the Radicals, when once the temporary labor support is substracted, represents perhaps only about a third of the electorate. In any real election, were the elections free and the workers allowed to vote for their own candidates, the Radicals would be hopelessly defeated.

3. It is for this reason that the Army will retain its vigilance and never permit free elections for a truly independent labor movement. The only time the workers will be allowed to vote in Argentina is when they show themselves merely as coolies to the middle-class parties, who now have the support of the modernized industrial bourgeoisie and its intellectuals.

4. The big winner is the nationalist bourgeoisie. They will now dominate both the agrarians and labor, but they will have to rule not directly but indirectly, through their intellectuals and middle-class lawyers. The more radical of them will try to pursue a policy to free themselves from the most galling aspects of U.S. control, making deals both with Europe and with the Soviet Bloc where possible, but essentially they must rely on U.S. protection and support both internally and in foreign relations.

5. The Peronist movement is bankrupt as a personalist party. As a "Justicialist" Party (for social justice for the masses) its program and thunder are more and more being stolen by the middle-class Radicals and nationalists. Its future lies as a native labor organization battling along class lines. But here it is cursed with a muddled provincial leadership and degenerated communist and socialist factions which can be purged and renovated only in the course of the active struggles which lie inevitably ahead.

PART THREE

Imminent Explosion in Brazil

At the end of July, 1962, Brazil felt the shock of a paralyzing general strike followed by large-scale hunger riots in the suburbs around Rio de Janeiro that left many dead, hundreds wounded, and the stores of a wide area completely sacked with losses estimated at $3 million. A short time previously, Janio Quadros, refusing to yield to military and other pressures put upon him had resigned, leaving behind him a chaotic situation in which the armed forces had threatened to intervene to set up a military dictatorship. Only the sharp internal conflicts dividing the Army leaders staved off this coup d'etat and allowed, finally, the regularly elected vice-president "Jango" Goulart, to assume the presidency of the Republic.

Before the end of July the Brazilian monetary unit, the cruzeiro, had been rated at 400 to the dollar; by the middle of August one could procure 550 to the dollar; by the end of the year the cruzeiro was cited at around 800 to the dollar. It fell in 1963 to 1000 to the dollar. Following this falling of the cruzeiro in the markets of foreign exchange ran a galloping continuing inflation throughout the country. No one seemed to want to keep the money that was pouring out in such tremendous currents from the Brazilian Government printing presses. In pace with the ever-mounting inflation the cost of living climbed.

Of course Brazil can not be considered alone. As in the case of Argentina the crisis in Brazil must be viewed not merely within the framework of the general contradictions affecting all of Latin America, and for that matter the entire colonial and underdeveloped world. There exists a chronic crisis in all of Latin America forming a dynamic background to violent revolution in Cuba, to a revolutionary crisis in Argentina, to mounting tensions throughout all the rest of Latin America, all mutually inter-related. Above all we must be aware of the interplay of the unique economic, political, and social forces historically developed in Brazil and dominating its destiny. Brazil is in the throes of an extreme effort to rise from an agrarian colonial status to an independent position among the world's industrial powers. In all likelihood she will not be able to achieve this goal without a tremendous explosion that might blow up the entire Latin American colonial world.

Brazil is a country larger than continental United States, exclusive of Alaska, with a single coastline 4,600 miles long. The population now about 75 million is increasing at the rate of about 3% a year. In 1900 it was estimated at 18 million; in 1950 at 52 million; in 1962 at 74 million. At this rate of growth Brazil may well equal the United States in population by the end of the century. Even now both in area and in population Brazil is equal to all the rest of South America put together.

Although a vast portion of Brazil has yet to be explored and evaluated, what is already known shows the country to contain enormous natural resources and wealth in minerals, fauna, and flora—perhaps more than any other country in the world. Already exploited have been, among its minerals, gold, diamonds, titanium, beryllium, thorium, quartz crystals, zinc, coal, iron, manganese, chrome, mica, petroleum; among its indigenous flora, manioc, castor beans, rubber, bananas, rope plants, herb and drug plants, such as tonka beans and curare, and the almost infinite variety of woods found in its matchless tropical rain forests; and the vast number of its wild animals. The immense iron ore deposits found relatively recently are estimated at 65 billion tons, with only the surface scratched. Near the iron ore fields are great deposits of manganese.

In the sphere of production of specific cultivated field products Brazil stands in world rank as follows:

Table 1[1]

BRAZIL: RANK IN WORLD PRODUCTION IN SPECIFIED FIELD PRODUCTS, 1960

Commodity	World Rank
Bananas	1 (240 million stems)
Beans	1
Castor Beans	1
Coffee	1
Manioc	1
Rice	1 (exclusive of Asia)
Mules	1 (3.5 million)
Cacao	2 (410 million lbs.)
Horses	2 (7.6 million)
Corn	3 (275 million bushels)
Hogs	3 (46 million)
Cotton	4 (1.7 million bales)
Sugar	4 (3.6 million tons)
Cattle	5 (72 million)
Tobacco	5
Sheep	... (22 million)

Besides, Brazil produces derivative products such as hides, rum, molasses, alcohol, and similar items, as well as substantial amounts of oranges, peanuts, pineapples, potatoes, sisal, soybeans, babassú, wheat, etc.

Brazil was discovered by the Portuguese in 1500 and is the only country in Latin America to speak Portuguese. In the 16th century its colonization was stimulated by the production of sugar; in the 17th century by the opening of the mines; in the 18th century by cotton, tobacco, cattle, and hides; in the 19th century by coffee and cocoa. Up to the 19th century Brazil was dominated by Portugal; after Brazil's independence, by England; in the 20th century, by the United States.

Brazil was the last country in the Western Hemisphere to emancipate its slaves, the last to become a republic. Others had to engage in protracted warfare to achieve independence, not Brazil. The United States had to endure a bitter civil war before emancipating its slaves, not Brazil. Hence the idea, often expressed by writers, that the Brazilian is not a revolutionist but an inherent gradualist who loves compromise and ease.

From its very earliest days Brazil was dominated and enchained by the institution of slavery. Indeed, the Portuguese were the pioneers in plantation slavery, at least on a considerable commercial scale. Por-

[1] See William Lytle Schurz: *Brazil, the Infinite Country* (1961).

tugal was the only modern country in Europe to have slaves, the first Negro slaves being brought to Lisbon about 1442. Following the formation of the Lagos Company for the purpose of importing slaves from the Gold Coast, by 1450 the trade was well established.

This slave trade and slavery were the direct result of the rapid rise of mercantile capitalism among the Portuguese. Portugal had become an autonomous State as far back as 1140 and was thus precociously centralized before any other in Europe. Under the protection of a stable monarchy, the ships of Portuguese merchant capitalism could pioneer on the high seas. Already in the 13th century Portugal had factories in Flanders, Antwerp, and England. As she drove the Arabs from the southwestern part of the Iberian Peninsula, Portugal retained slavery in the Algarve region where the Arabs had cultivated sugar.

The venturesome Portuguese, early sailing down the coast of Africa, soon discovered the Cape Verde Islands to which they brought Negro slaves for the sugar plantations they established there. Without these slaves the not-too-wealthy Portuguese mercantile capitalists might never have been able to compete in sugar production with the Arabs of the Near East.

Possessing now its own extensive plantations Portugal developed into a primary producer and exporter of sugar. Originally the sugar trade had been only a secondary development of the spice trade with the Middle East in which Portugal was but the ancillary distributor for the Genoese who had seized the primary role in dealing with the Arabs in the Orient for spices. With the closing down of the former land routes by the Turkish invasion in the Near East and with the desire to seize the first position in the spice trade for themselves, the Portuguese energetically travelled down the coast of Africa to its tip and came up on the eastern side finally to deal with the Indies directly. Concentrating on this Eastern trade Portugal paid little attention to the West until Spain began to receive a flood of gold and silver from Mexico and Peru.

This made it imperative for Portugal to try for the same results in her own possessions in the Western Hemisphere. And while there was no gold or silver to be found on the coast of Brazil, the Eastern "bulge" of South America was not so far away from Europe that it could not become the base for sugar plantations, provided the cost of production was lowered by the widespread use of slavery. At first it was thought possible to enslave the indigenous population but these prospective victims having lived in a primitive communist stage of culture far removed from the rigors of slavery, proved to be inefficient and incapable of sustaining life under such conditions as slavery imposed. It was far better to import Negro slaves from the Cape Verde Islands or direct from Africa. In this endeavor the Portuguese were greatly aided by the Dutch who became their virtual partners and protectors. The Portuguese brought their first Negro slaves to Brazil from Lisbon; in 1538 the first shipment was made direct from Africa. The total number of slaves brought to Brazil has been estimated at about 5 million. Some of them were from the Ivory and Gold Coasts of Africa (Whydah) but most of them from Angola which the Portuguese controlled. It has been calculated that in the decade 1840-1850 alone over 368,000 Africans were imported into Brazil representing a price of over 40 million pounds sterling.[2]

From the Luanda region in Angola in 1591 a Portuguese official could write that Luanda was so thickly populated that slaves would last until the end of the world. He underestimated the Portuguese. A century later, what with internecine wars, excessive forced labor, slave raiding, and small pox, the population of Angola had been greatly reduced. The mortality rate on the vessels bringing the slaves over was so great that the ships were called *tumbeiros,* or undertakers.

Angola exported practically nothing besides Bantu slaves and elephants' tusks ("black and white ivory"). From Luanda alone 8,000 to 10,000 slaves were shipped out each year in the late 17th century so that the duties levied on the export of slaves in Angola furnished most of the money for the upkeep of the garrison, the salaries of the officials and the clergy, and the vast tribute to Lisbon. In the 18th century it was estimated in Bahía, Brazil, that 10,000 to 12,000 Negro slaves had been imported into this one city from one port of Africa alone (Whydah).

The power of the master brooked no limits. "Some planters 'for trifling offenses threw their slaves alive into furnaces or killed them in various barbarous and inhuman ways'."[3] One of the recognized forms of punishment of a slave was "to tie him to a cart and flog him. After being well flogged, he should be pricked with a sharp razor or knife,

[2] See C. H. Haring: *Empire in Brazil* (1958).
[3] C. R. Boxer: *The Golden Age of Brazil, 1695-1750* (1962), p. 8.

and the wounds rubbed with salt, lemon juice, and urine, after which he should be put in chains for some days."[3] According to the same source "Where the master was sadistically brutal, the slaves deserted, if they could, or committed suicide, and the females aborted themselves rather than rear children in such surroundings."[3]

The deluge of slaves over Brazil had a devastating effect on all economic and social relations. As in all slave communities, manual physical labor was considered beneath the dignity of a free man and this held true for the most miserable, ignorant, and poverty-stricken immigrants from Portugal. Such an immigrant would rather beg, steal, or die than work manually.

Under such conditions it was not only impossible to have any free labor but equally impossible to have independent farmers, or self-supporting peasants owning the land they tilled. Indeed, it was hardly possible for anyone to get possession of a small portion of land.

When the land was first settled in the Northeastern part of Brazil, or what is now Pernambuco, the King of Portugal divided the coastal part into large provincial areas called *capitanias* (about 50 leagues along the coast and stretching as far as possible inland). Some of these the Crown gave to *donatorios* who were instructed, however, not to keep it all for themselves but to divide the land into *sesmarias,* an area equal to that which one man should be able to cultivate properly. In this way all the new immigrants would be able to share equally. (In the cattle country, the *sesmaria* was defined by law to be equal to an area five miles long and about one mile wide). From the start, however, these instructions remained a dead letter. The original donees seized vast areas of land for themselves and although they could cultivate only a small fraction of their estates they would not let any one else develop the empty lands except on condition of bearing all the expense of doing so and paying an annual rent in addition. Thus both the policies of the original large landholders and the universal extension of slavery in Brazil prevented the rise of any free or independent class of workers and farmers.

In the northeast, where the sugar plantation system was functioning, the planters had no need for the Amerind except to seize the women as concubines and prostitutes. Here lived only the few completely dictatorial plantation owners and their slaves, with a few Euro-

[3] *Ibid.*

peans to serve them in other duties, as officials, soldiers, clergy, managers, or in some similarly needed capacity. As new immigrants arrived, often as deported undesirables, they had to shift for themselves elsewhere settling in other coastal regions, one important grouping going far south near the Plate River and the Uruguay River in the region which is now the State of São Paulo. The poor people there, eking out a miserable living, were unable to buy or maintain Negro slaves. Their hope was to enslave the Indians which they energetically proceeded to do with their raiding parties composed of *"bandeirantes."* Since, as was also the case in the northeast, very few of the immigrants had brought along any women folk, all of them had continuous relations with the Indian women whose men they either killed or enslaved. Here in the south, with the free pampas able to nourish innumerable cattle, the São Paulistas developed into the same sort of wild gauchos that existed on the pampas of Uruguay and Buenos Aires. Here, however, the men also became expert jungle and forest hunters and trappers.[4]

Since Negro slaves also were few the settlers had to work for themselves and began to develop the same sort of feeling of unbridled freedom of movement as did the Argentinians to the south of them. It was the São Paulistas who first penetrated deep into the interior of Brazil and discovered the great gold and diamond fields in the State of Minas Gerais.

Although the São Paulistas, having to hunt and trap in the forests, were greatly dependent on their Indian slaves who were also their guides, there was no let-up in the ill treatment bestowed upon the indigenes. There are recorded expeditions in which more than half the Indians who set out did not return, dying from sheer overwork and harsh treatment.

Besides being a dumping ground for undesirables from Portugal, Brazil also became a great source of attraction for the Portuguese clergy, particularly those adhering to the Jesuit Order. It should be kept in mind that during the 16th and 17th centuries Portugal was probably the most priest-ridden country in Christendom. Many Portuguese monks and clerics came to the new world simply seeking

[4] For a full discussion of slavery in the *gaucho* country, see Fernando Henrique Cardoso: *Capitalismo e Escravidão no Brasil Meridional* (1962); for a general analysis of slavery under capitalism, see Eric Williams: *Capitalism and Slavery* (1944).

better flesh pots. Wallowing with Negro prostitutes and Indian mistresses they soon forgot all they ever might have known of chastity, charity, and charisma. The frequent complaints of the misdemeanors of many of the colonial clergy did not alter the fact that as a body they were the most powerful and influential, being held in awesome regard by the majority of the laity.

What kind of avaricious men composed the clergy can be seen from the following schedule of fees charged by the clergy in Minas Gerais in 1716. (It should be kept in mind that one dram of gold was equal in exchange to half a pound sterling at that time when a robust Negro slave sold for 300 drams.)

For each person who communicated:	1 dram of gold
For each person who did not communicate	½ dram of gold
For a sung mass	16 drams of gold
For a burial service	4 drams of gold
For reading the marriage bans	3 drams of gold
For a sermon	20 drams of gold
For a baptism (apart from the offering)	1 dram of gold

Since there were less than 30 priests in Minas Gerais at the time it can be imagined what large sums were raked in by these few worthies.[5]

The Catholic Church, however, was indeed greatly interested in saving the souls of the native Indians found in Brazil and sent over many missionaries for this purpose, among them the Jesuits who took over the lead throughout the entire country. It was the Jesuits who decided that Indians must not be enslaved, who went out into the wilderness and gathered the Indians around them into special villages or *aldeas* where they were taught the catechism, were baptised and supposedly converted into Christians.

In return for protecting the Indians from slavery the Jesuits saw to it that they worked for the Church hard and loyally. Later, when Portugal tried to revive its leading role in the spice trade by foraging for rare drugs and spices in the Amazon region, it was the Indians working for the Jesuits who found and collected the mass of such herbs and plants for export abroad. The Indian women were farmed out for house service by the Jesuits to the plantations where they were kept for years returning with many bastard children clinging to them.

While the northern planters were willing to forego having Indian

[5] See C. R. Boxer: Work cited.

slaves since the natives were not much good in the cane fields, the miserable São Paulistas were furious at being deprived of their chance for Indian slavery and carried on open war against the Jesuits until that Order was driven out of the country in the 18th century and the *bandeirantes* raiders could again have free play.

Naturally there were many Indian rebellions, all of them suppressed. It is recorded how on one occasion a number of captive Indians were released one by one from a stockade and were then ridden down on horseback as if they were bulls in a bullfight, being killed with sword cuts amid much laughter and jeering.[6]

The Catholic Church which was so solicitous in the case of the Amerind was not at all so solicitous in the case of the Negro. The Indian savage had a soul, it seemed, but not the African—he was just a work animal. There was no Jesuit to protect the Negro, as such protection would have offended the Portuguese planter and ruler. The treatment of the mulatto, for example, was much worse than that given the *mamelucos* or *caboclos* (Brazilian terms for mixed Indian-Portuguese bastards). Mulattoes were often coupled with Negro slaves in legislation and were forbidden to carry weapons, to wear costly clothes, to hold official positions in church or state (although this last was sometimes ignored in practice). Free mulattoes were always in danger of being enslaved again.

As capitalist slave owners, the Brazilians could not afford to be kind. They found the best policy to be to work the slaves to death in seven years and deliberately starved them. The result was a frightful mortality rate, a tremendous slave runaway problem, and large-scale stubborn slave rebellions.

Because of the crushing overwork the male slaves were too exhausted to reproduce. The females, viciously abused as prostitutes, had little fecundity and high disease rates both for themselves and for their children. The promiscuous sexual relations born of Portuguese unbridled libido and Negro and Indian slavery produced a vast army of unwanted children who, if they lived to grow up, became criminals and vagrants living precariously on their wits and on the margin of society.

The runaway slave problem was a continuous and persistent one since the almost impenetrable forests were generally close at hand. Periodically, bushwhacking expeditions were formed to track down the

[6] C. R. Boxer: Work cited.

fugitive slaves. The free mulattoes were all made to join these expeditions guided by Indians and strengthened by militia. The Negro runaways holed up in various *quilimbos,* as their refuges were called, were hunted down like animals and annihilated. To prevent runaways, sometimes all the slaves in a region had their achilles tendons cut so that while they were able to hobble about enough to work, they could never run again.

The number of slave revolts in which no quarter was asked or given was enormous. As far back as the 17th century Negro slaves succeeded in forming a Negro State in the backlands of Northern Brazil known as the Republic of Palmares which resisted all efforts of the Government to destroy it for close to 70 years—1630-1697—and succumbed finally only to the ferocious force of the savage Paulistas sent against them. As late as the early 19th century there were eight slave revolts in the Province of Bahía alone, culminating in a most serious outbreak in 1835. Indeed, it was the resurgence of open rebellion by the slaves that accelerated the movement toward inevitable and total emancipation.

In these developments lie the germ of today's inherited problems so difficult to solve, particularly on the countryside. At first only the northeast portion of Brazil's coastline was settled in the form of sugar plantations. These became the economic mainstay of the colony bringing enough profit to the Crown for it to pay more attention to that region. Following the recognition of how the great abuses of those controlling the *capitanias* were hurting the Crown's interest in further development, the *capitania* control system was abolished and a Government General of Brazil was created in the middle of the 16th century with its center at San Salvador in Bahía.

Portugal, however, was destined to become annexed to the growing Spanish Empire from 1580 to 1640, with the result that it lost its partnership with the Dutch and its alliance with the English as long bitter warfare opened up between these last two countries and Spain. Given the defeat of the Spanish Armada in 1588 the Dutch were able to land in Brazil and with the aid of their plantation partners take over the best developed part of Brazil as rulers. The Dutch, however, were not able to hold their conquests long. They withdrew after Portugal again became an independent kingdom closely allied with England.

During the 16th and most of the 17th centuries Brazil grew very slowly for the simple reason that outside of the sugar plantations and some tobacco there was little the country could offer the merchant capitalists who alone could sponsor and support such enterprises. To hold the coast against foreigners Portugal did have to erect forts and supply soldiers. There was also some immigration in other parts of the country, and near Rio Grande do Sul, as we have mentioned some wretched colonists eked out a precarious living.

The whole situation changed, however, when the Paulistas in the latter part of the 17th century reported the discovery of gold and later of diamonds in the interior of the country, now known as the State of Minas Gerais. This was what Portugal had been interested in originally and now her dream was to be fulfilled. A large flood of miners and adventurers now poured into the country, coming to the mines in two main streams, one from the north through the São Francisco and other rivers that form such an ample network in the center of the country, and the other through the south by way of the Rio de Janeiro gateway. This ever-increasing flow of rough men dominated the scene, bruskly pushing aside the Paulistas' claims, not, however, without threatened mass armed conflict. In the end the Paulistas settled accounts by becoming the suppliers of the camps with food, materials, and prostitutes. They made more money that way than by mining. Now at last São Paulo could find a viable economic base for the development of cattle and hides and for becoming a self-dependent economic community.

Ridiculous as it seems, such was the influence of slavery throughout the land that the miners themselves would not mine but insisted on bringing along their slaves to work for them. In cases of placer mining the slaves would stand in the water all day shaking the placer to find the gold and then hand it over to the master, the so-called "miner." Where digging had to be done the slave did it. Slaves also cooked for the miner, set up his tent, cared for his mule, served his meals, washed his clothes, and served him in every way he demanded.

Even so, the development of gold and diamond mining brought something different to the slave than the frightful terror of his life on the stagnant isolated plantation. Slavery could not really long survive in the wilderness of the mountains where the living was rough and dangerous for all in the same way as under the stable plantation system with a large staff always at the master's command. It became more common for the miner who struck it rich to emancipate his slaves and to treat them as equal human beings. The open world of luck and chance was bound to affect the attitudes and psychology of the slave as well as of the master.

The process of extracting the precious metals and stones from the country was quite different in Brazil than it had been in Peru and Mexico where the Spanish officials with their regular armies engaged not in mining but in plunder in order to get their loot. Here it was strictly private enterprise that was getting results and the Crown had to become extremely vigilant to see that its share was sent to Portugal. Despite every precaution taken, especially around the diamond fields, smuggling and law evasion was the regular thing. The miner thought he could get away with it, and did, until he tried to bring the stuff to Portugal. There he was often caught and completely despoiled of what he had thought was his wealth and fortune. The ubiquitous lawlessness in Minas Gerais, Sao Paulo, Rio Grande do Sul, and Rio de Janeiro lent belief to the tradition that in Brazil everything went, provided you had the requisite strength and cunning.

The slow growth of Brazil as an agricultural and primary materials producing country continued all during the 18th century. Thanks mainly to slavery, Brazil in 300 years could attain only a population of somewhat over 3 million, a result achieved by the U.S. American colonies in half that time. The cities were small and few in number. The regions were all isolated one from the other. In the extreme North and in the South cattle raising produced meat and hides. Domestic leather goods were manufactured to fill all the needs for which in other places hardware would be used. In the Northeast there were the sugar mills and plantations, the tobacco and the cotton enterprises; in the interior were the mines; on the coast were a few ports and administrative centers. There were no roads of any importance. The best and sometimes the only way to travel in the interior was by means of the wonderful network of rivers that interlaced the country. On the coast one had to travel by ship.

The regional isolation helped maintain and develop the rule of the large planter and landowner so that his word was really law not only over his slaves but over the entire territory which he controlled with his private gunmen. Each of these regions had its own laws of growth, change, and decay. No region had the vision to see over the entire nation of Brazil as a whole. The country was too vast, the distances too large, the environment too wild, the effort too great for the idle and decadent planter to attempt to control the whole. He was content to dominate simply his own part and remain the absolute master there.

This was the reason why the Brazilian planter was satisfied to let the Portuguese Crown handle all foreign relations for him. Brazil was a colony. Its surplus wealth was drained off by the Crown as far as possible. It was supposed to produce primary materials for export and receive finished goods from the metropolitan country. It could deal only with Portuguese ships and merchants unless special permission was granted to others.

But in the present instance the metropolitan country was a little Portugal, a frog that was trying to puff itself up to look like a cow. What with its dominions in Africa and Asia as well as in South America, it had bitten off far more than it could chew. It was swallowed up by Spain and when Spain had to disgorge its meal, it was served up to Holland and eventually to England. Thus Portugal had to make special treaties with England, favoring English goods over all others. It was these English goods that Portugal had to export to Brazil and it was to England that the wealth sucked out of Brazil eventually went. Portugal could be considered merely a convenient conduit for the redistribution of the profits taken out of the colonies.

Thus it was that when the French Revolution represented by Napoleon burst upon the European scene the Portuguese monarch, unlike the Spanish, did not stay but, taking England's advice, fled to his possessions in the Western Hemisphere, to Brazil. Since the English navy transported and protected the Portuguese court, English economy naturally was given a free hand in Brazil. English goods now could come in directly and without dues. England not only became the manufacturer for Brazil but her importer and exporter as well. This suited the planter also.

Naturally the regional plantation owners did not dream of breaking away from the Portuguese Crown supported as it was by the might of the British armed forces. How could they break away? Their gunmen were no match for the regular Portuguese Army reinforced by hired mercenaries from Europe. The local planters had no concept of how to rule such a vast country. They were terribly afraid of their slaves and afraid that independence would lead to massive slave insurrections. For generations they had been used to the indolent libidinous life and backwardness of the plantation. They were not the ones to look for toil and trouble.

Following the defeat of Napoleon, the Congress of Vienna agreed to elevate Brazil from a colony to part of a joint kingdom with Portugal on equal terms. When the exiled king of Portugal decided to leave Brazil and return home, however, the Brazilian wealthy cliques refused to play second fiddle to Lisbon. They repudiated Portugal but insisted that the son of the king stay to rule them. Thus on September 7, 1822 Brazil became an independent country with the heir to the Portuguese throne as its "Emperor." Bahía was made the first capital, later Rio de Janeiro. A Constitution was adopted by the Emperor in 1824.

The Constitution of 1824 gave practically complete authority to the Emperor. He controlled the two houses of the legislature established. Senators took office for life. The Emperor had the power to control the local governments. Suffrage was limited only to the upper cliques and their agents. Republican sentiment was suppressed.

The rule of Emperor Dom Pedro did not last very long. With the departure of the Portuguese Army there had been substituted an army of Irish and German mercenaries who were not always inspired by discipline. The regional plantation *caudilhos* naturally did not want a centralized government which would limit their power; nor did they like the new Portuguese immigrants who tried to play the part of noble aristocrats; nor did they feel that the great expense of the Emperor's court was always warranted. Furthermore, in all free America no kingdom had survived. At any rate, in 1831 Dom Pedro was overthrown, being forced to abdicate in favor of his son Pedro II and to leave Brazil to take over the throne in Portugal itself upon the death of his father, the king.

Dom Pedro II did not become ruler immediately as he was too young. A regency in power in the interim period had to deal with rebellions in Pernambuco and Alagoas from 1831 to 1835, in Ceará in 1832, in Maranhão in 1831-32 followed later by a bloody civil war, 1838-1840, in Bahía 1832-35 coinciding with a Negro insurrection and again later in 1837-38, in Minas Gerais in 1833, in Mato Grosso in 1834. Repeatedly the mercenary soldiers of the Crown mutinied.

Pará in the north (1835-1840) and Rio Grande do Sul in the south (1835-1845) tried to secede and failed.

These events made clear that Brazil was too vast, too wild, too torn by regional rivalries to be governed in absolutist fashion from some artificial center. In 1834 some constitutional reforms were enacted by which the provinces were given autonomous elected legislative assemblies with extended political powers. The Council of State that had tried to dominate the provinces was suppressed although the provincial governors still remained appointed from the Throne. The entailing of estates was finally abolished.

The compromises embodied in the new constitutional reforms were effective. By this time with coffee becoming a prime export, it was absolutely necessary to achieve some national stability. Under the regency railroads and steam navigation had been started from Rio. Brazil under British guidance was beginning to enter the 19th century economic currents affecting the world markets then being established. In 1841 Pedro II was crowned.

As could be expected in a slave-holding regime, Brazil was no country for democracy, honest elections, or separation of powers. Under the new Emperor the old Council of State was restored, all ministers of government were selected by the Emperor, the provincial assemblies were deprived of many of their powers, the judicial functions were turned over to the police, the lower house elected by the various localities was in turn manipulated by the center. Elections dictated by the Emperor were farcical. Fraud and corruption were rampant. The two parties alternating for office simply put on a punch-and-judy show, the Conservatives remaining in office till 1844, the Liberals till 1848, the Conservatives again till the early 1860's. The result was revolt in Minas Gerais and in São Paulo and the already mentioned secession in Rio Grande do Sul. A last flare-up occurred in Pernambuco. All were suppressed. Under the Emperor war was declared against Argentina to keep Uruguay neutral (1851-1852) and also conducted against Paraguay (1865-1870).

In the meantime the fact that it was being taken in hand by a power no other than Britain, the most advanced economic nation in the world, was bound to have a tremendous effect on Brazil. From the time Britain entered the scene as the protector of the Brazilian Crown she had made it clear Brazil's slave trade must go. That slave trade could not have existed for one moment without British protection and Britain was pledged to its abolition. Slavery was not for industrial Britain nor for her clients since it took vast areas out of the commercial market. Slaves could not buy goods. It was to the interests of the British to expand that market, not to contract it.

Because of slavery, Europeans were refusing to enter Brazil, the German Government actually prohibiting such emigration. Because of the slave trade, foreign capital could not be induced to invest in Brazil, not in agriculture, nor in commerce nor industry. The institution of slavery was becoming as impossible in Brazil as it was in the United States.

Finally, in 1850, the slave trade was abolished. In 1871, following the entrance of a new party upon the scene boldly proclaiming itself a Republican Party, it was decreed that all slaves should be freed on birth. In 1888 all slaves were freed without indemnification. But by that time Brazil was ready to overthrow her Emperor and become a Republic.

The acute agrarian problems which Brazil must solve as among its most pressing tasks at the present time stem directly from the historic circumstances we have described. Despite the fact that Brazil is rapidly developing into an industrial society the majority of its population is still rural with most of its active working force still engaged in agriculture, cattle raising, and related activities.

In 1950 there existed 60 estates each with an area superior to 100,-000 hectares, or 1,000 square kilometers. These big establishments were not being economically used but only held for speculation. For that year the census recorded about 37 million persons living in the countryside, but of these about 11 million lived on only 20 million hectares, or about 2 hectares to a person. This relative overpopulation must be contrasted with the great underdevelopment of land in Brazil which underworks 90% of its available 232 million hectares.

Brazil is so vast that in 1960 only 27.2% of the total area was being economically worked at all. At the same time, of the area given over to cattle-raising only 9% of the establishments possessed 200 hectares or over so that they occupied 75% of the land, 6% of the establishments with 100-200 hectares each occupied 8% of the land, while

85% of the cattle ranchers had less than 100 hectares each and occupied only 17% of the total land available.

Table 2 gives the 1950 census distribution of the 11 million economically active persons working in agriculture and cattle-raising:

Table 2[7]
BRAZIL: PERSONS WORKING IN AGRICULTURE AND CATTLE-RAISING
(ROUNDED TO NEAREST THOUSAND), 1950

Employees	3,729,000	33.9%	
Family Workers	3,957,000	36.0	(non-remunerative)
Parceiros	1,246,000	11.3	(share-croppers)
Manager-Owners	2,065,000	18.8	
Totals	10,997,000	100.0	

So then, of Brazil's rural population which embraced about 70%
of the total number of people in 1950, about 81% were landless and
only 19% owners. Of the owners, only 150,000 of them owned 75%
of the land. The very large number of family workers and the so-called
partners classified in the Table hide the fact that about 18% of the
rural population live in a state of nature, that is, outside the capitalist
market system, getting food, clothes, and shelter as they can but having no money to buy anything with or anything to sell, not even labor
power.

Although the rural economically active population was about 63%-
65% of the general economically active population, they brought in
only 18% or less of the national income. This low yield was due primarily to the persistence by the large landholding Oligarchy in rejecting
any change in their archaic methods of production, in recklessly erod-
ing the land, in wastefully burning the woods and forests, in working
the land to exhaustion without rotation of crops, in forcing subsidies
for vast overproduction of such crops as coffee while at the same time
producing so little food necessary for the people that Brazil actually
has had to import wheat and flour.

As one writer put it dealing with the Amazon region of Brazil: "The
ruling class of the region is resistant to new ideas and techniques. It
has failed to accept the full implications of the Industrial Revolution
and of the utilization of modern scientific discoveries. It has refused
to recognize that the conquest of the Amazonia is no longer a job for
the machete. For the most part, its economic doctrines belong to the

[7] Nelson Werneck Sodré: *Formação Histórica de Brasil* (1962), p. 354.

sixteenth century. If the economy of the region is still 'colonial' it is the fault of its leaders."[8] It has been estimated that were Brazil to use U.S. methods she could produce the same amount of field products as now with one-tenth of her present agricultural labor force.

During the period when the Amazon region was stimulated by the great need for natural rubber concomitant with the growth of the automobile industry in the U.S., the Oligarchy could solve the problem only by the old methods of slavery in the form of hiring workers to collect the rubber in the wild jungles, keeping them heavily in debt and refusing them their freedom until they died. The situation of these rubber workers has been poignantly described as follows:

"So long as he remained a debtor, escape was difficult. His employer guarded the entrance to the river and the forest behind him was pathless and full of hidden terrors. The authority of the state was against him, and there were agreements between the lords of the rivers that had the force of the fugitive slave laws of our ante-bellum South. So it was safest in the long run just to fall into one's hammock when night came and accept whatever fate each day might bring." "The *Seringuero* was the victim of a system of labor which Euclides da Cunha called the most criminal yet conceived by the shameless egotism of men."[9]

Of the 20 million people in the northeastern region of the country, about 70% are tied to agricultural and cattle-raising production. Of the 4.7 million economically active persons in this field about 750,000 could be classified as owner-managers of which only 2% disposed of about 48% of the lands in haciendas of more than 500 hectares, while 35% of the enterprises had less than 35 hectares each. The average income of this region is the lowest in the continent and does not attain one-third of the income of the south-center of the country, which in turn is far inferior to that in the cities of the south. The problem is so serious that the new economic minister of Brazil under Goulart has just created a specific project for this region with the help of the Alliance for Progress.

Two American firms dominate the area that produces cotton: SANBRA and Anderson Clayton. They deal only with the *latifundarios* and not with the actual producers (sharecroppers). The *latifundarios*

[8] William Lytle Schurz: Work cited, p. 69.
[9] William Lytle Schurz: Work cited, p. 59.

rent out lands to the sharecroppers for production and dictate the prices as they like, regardless of the market prices set by the trade. Then the *latifundarios* deal with the American firms. In this way the controlling Oligarchy is supported and maintained by the Americans. So backward is the cotton production in this region that in São Paulo, where cotton is also grown, there is three times the productivity that exists in the Northeast.

Sugar is also grown in the northeast and again to favor the Oligarchy the Brazilian Government has aided the out-of-date sugar refineries forcing purchase of their sugar and subsidizing them even though their production is markedly inefficient and costly because of their backward methods. To use up their sugar the Government has also founded the Institute of Sugar and of Alcohol. The U.S. has recently favored these sugar planters by increasing its sugar quota from Brazil. With its more modern methods of production São Paulo here too has seized the center of the stage, jumping its sugar cultivation from 500,000 hectares in 1950 to 1,340,000 hectares in 1960. São Paulo, with 28% of the area cultivated in sugar, now produces 35% of the sugar cane.[10]

Remnants of slavery, looking like remnants of feudalism, still persist in the northeast. There still exists the *cambão,* or system of forced labor, like the corvee in feudal France. Under this system the peon is given a free hectare of land to live on in return for which he must give four days work a week free to the landowner. The hectare is worth 10,000 cruzeiros (or, say, about $16). Even if the peon were paid only 100 cruzeiros a day (say 16 cents), this would still amount to 21,000 cruzeiros at the end of the year or about twice the value of the land he is allowed to work free but which still belongs to the landlord. Naturally, the children of the peon are also forced to work with him free. It is no wonder that militant peasant leagues under communist influence have now been formed who threaten armed revolution.

The northeast region has become a relative wasteland, a hole into which the U.S. and Brazilian Governments can pour unlimited amounts of money all going into the pockets of the Oligarchy. In 1939 the share of the Northeast region in the total national gross product was 30%,

[10] See Caio Prado Juniór: *"A Crise em Marcha"* in *Revista Brasiliense,* No. 42 *julho-agosto* 1962.

now it is 11%; in 1920 its industrial activity was over 24% of the total, now it is less than 17%. The territorial per capita income is six times less than the average in the rest of the country. Naturally, there is an enormous emigration from that region, 100,000 poverty stricken refugees fleeing to the southern cities and regions of São Paulo and Rio de Janeiro each year. In desperation the Brazilian Government has formed its special entity SUDENE, *Superintendencia do Desenvolvimento do Nordeste,* but it will do nothing to root out the chief cause of the evil, the avaricious, archaic rule of the descendants of the former slave owners.

In the far more modern coffee growing regions of the south the rule of the Oligarchy creates other problems just as desperate. Here a relatively small number of owners, each with 500 hectares or more, control 62% of the land while 22.2% of the 2.6 million establishments have an area of less than 4 hectares, with the smaller farmers being constantly squeezed out. Since coffee is considered such an important export, the big coffee growers occupy a very special position with the Government. These growers are generously aided with Government and bank credits, with special warehousing and transportation facilities, and with large subsidies.

The coffee situation may be described as follows: First, there is a chronic world-wide overproduction of this product in proportion to the market. The world consumption is about 41 million sacks of 60 kilos each, the world production about 72 million sacks. Formerly Brazil produced the overwhelming share of the world's production; now she has fierce competition from Colombia, Ecuador, Central America, Ethiopia and Madagascar, so that she has been reduced to a minor share of the world total. Her product is in considerable part shipped to the U.S. whose per capita consumption has steadily shrunk (13% in the ten year period 1948-1957). The tables on page 192 illustrate the situation.

To protect herself Brazil has been in the forefront to organize a world-wide coffee institute, composed of both producers and consumers such as the United States, in order to secure some stability of prices and to fix quotas for each major producer. Such an effort can have a very ephemeral success at best. Why should buyers subsidize the sellers and lose money? Why should Africa with a favored position in Europe give way to Latin America? Why should countries with

Table 3A[11]

U.S. IMPORTS OF GREEN COFFEES (ROUNDED TO NEAREST 1000)
(1000 -60 KG BAGS)

	1963*	1962*	Difference
Total	9,705	10,338	633
Brazil	3,347	3,928	581
Colombia	1,353	1,425	72

* Figures for first five months of each year.
As can be seen from the above table the shrinkage in U.S. Coffee imports as a whole during this period was surpassed by the shrinkage in imports from Latin America.

Table 3B[12]

BRAZIL: RELATION OF BRAZIL'S TOTAL EXPORTS TO HER TOTAL COFFEE EXPORTS
AND TO HER TOTAL EXPORTS TO U.S. (MILLION CRUZEIROS)

Year	Total Exports	Coffee Exports	Exports to U.S.
1956	1,482.0	1,029.7	734.3
1957	1,391.6	845.5	659.1
1958	1,242.9	687.5	534.4

Note: Coffee exports were about 66% of total exports in 1956 but about 50% in 1958; U.S. share of total Brazil's exports were about 50% in 1956 but about 42% in 1958.

more efficient methods help support those with poorer methods? The whole idea is opposed to the principles of GATT to which most countries give at least lip service.

Brazil sells about 15 to 20 million bags of coffee. Her recent coffee harvests were as follows:

1961/62	32-34 million bags
1962/63	25-27 million bags
1963/64	38-42 million bags (estimate)*

*(Because of a recent frost this last estimate has been reduced to 23 million bags)

Faced with these surpluses the Brazilian Government has adopted the simple policy of buying the entire crop at fixed prices, selling what it could, and storing or burning the rest. During the 1930's it burned 78 million bags, or the equivalent of five full years of exports!

In June, 1959, there were 24.6 million bags of coffee in the Government warehouses when the Government decided to buy the 1959/60 harvest. This raised the total to around 45-50 million sacks at which

[11] Given in *Conjuntura Economica:* Vol. X, No. 8, August, 1963.
[12] Nelson Werneck Sodré: Work cited.

level it has remained since then. This purchase by the State did not help matters any. In fact, it increased coffee production by about 40% (as can be seen by the 1963/64 estimate for it takes 5 years before the first harvest from new trees can be collected). Already the Government has burned some 7 million bags, with the stocks still remaining at 52 million bags and big harvests yet to come.

To meet this situation the Brazilian Government decided to tear up coffee trees. From the beginning of this coffee reduction program in June 1962 to the end of the year 207 million coffee trees valued at 275 billion cruzeiros were torn up. By February 1963 the total uprooted had reached 381 million trees. About 26% of the freed area was to be planted with corn, 10% with rice, and 6% with beans, or a total of 42% devoted to food products. In São Paulo peanuts and castor were to be the big replacing crops.[13]

The cost of this entire program to the people of Brazil is simply incalculable. The direct purchases by the Government have amounted to as much as 17% of Brazil's entire capital savings! Then there are the costs of warehousing. In March, 1962, warehousing costs were $16.5 million with an estimate of another $9.6 million needed soon.

These policies of the Brazilian Government favoring the coffee growing set are carried out at the expense of all the people of Brazil who are the victims of a raging inflation greatly exacerbated by such subsidies. Prices zoom higher. When the Government raised its coffee subsidies for the 1959/60 harvest, for example, the cost of living began to rise at a pace of 4% a month.

Since the large coffee exporters receive hard dollars for their coffee, the monetary inflation, so extreme and uncontrolled in Brazil, has the result that although the country may suffer from want of adequate purchasing power abroad due to the fall of the cruzeiro on the foreign exchanges, the coffee growers and exporters profit all the more since they can now change their dollars on far better terms than before. Perhaps it was precisely because the coffee Oligarchy has had so much influence that the Brazilian Government in the past has continued to allow inflation to soar to such heights and Brazilian money to fall so low without any serious effort to curtail the process.

[13] Figures given in *Conjuntura Economica,* Vol. X, No. 5, May, 1963. It is interesting to note that the price of this magazine which was 80 cruzeiros in June, 1963 had to jump to 300 cruzeiros in July, 1963.

Because, due to the fall of the cruzeiro, exporters could get better prices than others, there was an income transfer in favor of exporters in the order of 30% of value of exports. The Federal Government used to realize 42% of its Budget revenue out of the differences in exchanges. But when the exporters were favored this government revenue eventually dropped to zero at the same time as Government investments increased government deficits immensely. Coincidentally dollar prices dropped so that while exports increased 28% in volume they increased only 3% in value in 1961 as compared to 1953. All this led to a drop in Brazil's capacity to import and as the Government Report stated: "All indications are that the regaining of the importing capacity by Brazil will only take place as a result of the industrialization of the country which will then be able to join the most dynamic currents of international trade."[14]

We turn, finally, to the situation in the cattle-raising industry. The following table lists the big landowners among the cattle growers:

Table 4[15]
BRAZIL: SOME LARGE LANDOWNERS

	thousand hectares
Brazilian Land Cattle Packing Company	881 in Cáceres
	1,000 in Corumbá
	800 in Três Lagoas
	200 in Campo Grande
Brazilian Meat Company	311 in Três Lagoas
	5 in Aquidauna
Fomento Agricola Argentino Sul-Americano	26 in Pôrto Murtinho
Fazenda Francesa	242 in Miranda
	173 in Corumbá
Miranda Estancia Company	220 in Miranda
Agua Limpa Syndicate	180 in Três Lagoas
Sun American Belge S. A.	117 in Corumbá
Barranco Grande S. A.	550 in Corumbá
Emprêsa Mate Laranjeira	170 in Bela Vista
	300 in Ponta Porã
	21 in Pôrto Murtinho
	1,044 in Ponta Porã

So, while nine million agrarian workers have no land, these few companies have over 6 million hectares.

So now we have the structural arrangements of Brazil's field pro-

[14] Official Brazilian Government Report on its Three Year Plan, printed in *Brazilian Bulletin,* Vol. XIX, No. 433, May 15, 1963.
[15] Rui Facó: *Brasil, Seculo XX* (1960), pp. 154-155.

duction in its principal aspects: cotton, sugar, coffee, and cattle. A small number of large landlords, mainly the descendants of the slave holding plantation owners of the past who completely dominate the picture, export enormous profits and rents, demand special favors, use the most backward methods, hinder the progress of the country, and reject any concept of social responsibility.

It must not be conceived that the total number of farm establishments has decreased in an absolute sense—the great growth of Brazil's population forbade that—but only in a relative sense. Actually, the total area cultivated grew from 175 million hectares in 1920 to 197.7 million hectares in 1940, to 233.7 million hectares in 1950 (or 18% in the 1940-1950 period). The area cultivated during the 1920-1950 period rose from 6 to 19 million hectares, still only about 2% of Brazil's total 1 billion hectares; the number of farm establishments grew from 648,000 to 2,063,000; the number of bovines increased from 34 to 47 million head; the number of agricultural machines and instruments jumped 500%. The general rate of increase, however, was about 2.5% annually during the 1939-1956 period, far below the rate of industrial growth.

Furthermore it would be a great mistake to imagine that the great landed estates were not substantially profiting at the expense of the whole nation. From 1950 through 1960 the price index in the agricultural sector except coffee grew from 100 to 734 while the index for the national product as a whole grew from 100 to 540. Real income in the agricultural sector advanced by 86%. This means that there was a transfer to the agricultural sector of part of the benefits accruing from the increase of urban productivity. In fact it can be said that 50% of the agricultural increase in real income was due precisely to this transfer. The other 50% in the increase in real income in the agricultural sector was due in equal proportions to the fact that more toilers were put to work and there was greater productivity per person (but not per hectare).

As an official report stated: "In per capita terms, real income in the agricultural sector has grown by 5% yearly, a rate far above that recorded for the population as a whole. However, there is no indication that the living conditions of rural labor have improved at the same rate. Hence the most plausible conclusion is that the main portion of this income increase has been absorbed by the landowners and by medium and high income level businessmen."

Although in the 1940-1950 period the total acreage had increased by 18%, the number of farms grew only 6.4%. This shift was accompanied by a great expansion of pasture lands increasing by 22% in area and climbing from 44.5% of the total area to 46%. Agriculture, with its numerous workers, was being pushed out. At the same time herds increased from 32 million in 1940 to 45 million in 1950, to 74 million in 1960.

The prevailing favoritism for cattle-raising as against agriculture and within agriculture for coffee growing has coincided with a false policy adopted in regard to the need for expansion of food crops such as wheat and corn. These are foods which should be consumed on the average ten times as much in Brazil as they actually are and yet the domestically produced wheat has steadily fallen from 855,000 tons in 1956 to 580,000 tons in 1957, to 500,000 tons in 1959. This domestic decline in wheat production is in part owing to poor Government policy as well as to the heavy import costs of such things as insecticides, machinery, etc. A harvester which in 1956 could have been bought with 500 sacks of wheat, in 1959 cost 3,218 sacks (to which had to be added also port costs, custom taxes, etc.) Despite its extraordinary low wheat consumption Brazil has been forced to use its precious foreign exchange to import $100 to $150 million worth of wheat annually.

Between 1940 and 1950 many workers in agriculture and in cattle-raising and the extractive industries shifted to become workers in the transformation industries and in services. Previously, from 1920 to 1940, while agricultural labor had grown 18% industrial labor had increased 166% (although starting from a lower base). In 1940, 80% of the workers were in agriculture and 10% in transformation; in 1950, 72.6% were in agriculture and 15% in transformation. Since then the shift has been much accelerated. Between 1950 and 1960 the mass of rural workers grew 17.5%, that of urban workers 70%.

The masters of the land who have been in political control of Brazil practically from its very first days are not going to allow the State to tax their property without a real fight. Taxes on imports, on exports, on sales, on transactions, on licenses, on this, that, or the other thing paid by other groups, yes; taxes on real estate and on property, no!

A recent study shows that the ratio of indirect (sales, etc.) taxes to direct (property, income) taxes in Brazil was almost 3 to 1, or, in other words, all the direct taxes equalled only 25% of the whole!

As a U.S. Congressional Report stated: "Brazil's system of taxation is exceedingly complex. In the past the vast bulk of the Government revenues has come from indirect taxes, with income taxes on corporations and individuals constituting less than one-fourth of total tax receipts. Although taxes on individual incomes are progressive and rise to a maximum of 50 percent for the highest bracket, the fact that such a large proportion of the Government's revenue comes from indirect taxes would indicate that the tax system, as a whole, is not very progressive." (Recently, however, the Government has raised these direct taxes—See Table I-23B in Part I above.)

Table 5, below, shows the land taxes imposed by the various Brazilian States as percentage of their individual total State taxes:

Table 5[16]

LAND TAX IMPOSED BY BRAZILIAN STATES IN % OF TOTAL STATE TAXES 1951

State	Percent	State	Percent
Amazonas	.3%	Maranhão	.9%
Pará	.2	Piaui	3.5
Rio Grande do Norte	1.4	Ceará	1.4
Pernambuco	.5	Paraíba	2.1
Bahía	3.0	Alagoas	2.4
Minas Gerais	10.4	Sergipe	2.5
Rio de Janeiro	5.8	Paraná	3.1
São Paulo	4.9	Santa Catarina	3.8
Rio Grande do Sul	2.3	Mato Grosso	3.3
		Goiás	5.8

The emancipation of the slaves did not end the terrible conditions that existed on the countryside but only brought them into sharper public relief. The population still suffers from low life expectancy, high mortality rates generally and especially for children, insufficient food, low standards of living, large-scale prostitution, and low national income.

In the northeast region of Brazil the average span of life is 27 years, in the cities of Natal and Recife only slightly better—36.2 years and 37.7 years respectively. In all Brazil life expectancy averages 45 years for men, 50 years for women. In the most advanced cities of São

[16] Nelson Werneck Sodré: Work cited, pp. 406, 407.

Paulo it is 57.6 years. (In the United States as a whole it is 67 years for men and 74 years for women.) Over all Brazil 20% of all children born die before attaining one year of age, and 50% before reaching five years.

In the city of Recife, in the Casa Amarela quarter, more than 500 children die of every 1,000 born. (Rate in the U.S.: 105 per 100,000 births.) In Amazonia, in the municipality of Eirunepe, for each 1,000 children born, 800 die before the first year of life. In Guata, coal city in Santa Catarina in the south, of 200 children that survived the first year of life, only 30 lived in the second. But highest honors (!) should go to Pará where in the municipality of Breves, until recently, there did not survive one single child of all those born! Were Buchenwald and Dachau any worse?[17]

Table 6 below gives the infantile mortality rates in various Latin American countries and in important and typical cities both in Brazil and elsewhere. The table speaks for itself:

Table 6[18]
INFANTILE MORTALITY RATES PER 1,000

Copenhagen	30	Peru	121.6
United States	46.6	Mexico	127.5
Detroit	51	Ecuador	152
Canada	63.4	Brazil	217.2
Barcelona	69	São Paulo	126
Argentina	84.3	Belo Horizonte	153.7
Rome	75	Porto Alegre	223.1
Tokyo	103	Recife	285.8
Guatemala	104.7	Natal	343.2

From 1950 to 1958 an average of 140,000 children died annually from gastritis. Tuberculosis kills more than 100,000 persons each year. In many States there are no tuberculosis hospitals at all, so deaths are 92 per 1,000 cases there, as compared to 5 in Scandinavia. In Brazil 23 million persons are sick with hookworm; goiter is endemic with 18.5 million cases. Endemic also are liver fluke (a parasitic worm) disease and Chagas disease (a special form of trypanosomiasis). Ulcers affect more than one million, trachoma about the same number, bubos (swelling of the groin) about 600,000, leprosy 740,000. The people of Brazil are sick, sick of malnutrition, sick of poverty, sick of curable

[17] Franklin de Oliveira: *Revolução e Contra-Revolução no Brasil* (1962), p. 106.
[18] Franklin de Oliveira: Work cited, p. 114.

diseases. But what can be expected in a countryside where even sanitary drinking water facilities or ordinary toilets are often lacking?

In all Brazil there are only 120 child hospitals or 2.14 beds for each 1,000 inhabitants (in the northeast only .9), where the normal would be 7 beds. Nine hundred municipalities do not have a single doctor. Over-all there is an average of but one doctor to each 2,428 inhabitants. In the northeast and in the north 78% to 80% of all the municipalities have no general hospital aid at all (in Pará, 91.4%; in Maranhão, 93.3%; in Piauí, 93.4%).

The average per capita consumption is only 2,350 calories a day in Brazil when others in more advanced countries average 3,000 to 3,500 calories. Table 7 shows comparative standing of Brazil in daily per capita milk consumption.

Table 7A[19]
AVERAGE DAILY PER CAPITA MILK CONSUMPTION IN GRAMS

Switzerland	1,024.8	France	134
Sweden	832.8	Brazil	20
U.S.	420		

Brazil, however, is rapidly becoming industrialized and ranks with the more developed Latin American countries with which it should be compared. Table 7B below makes this comparison:

Table 7B[20]
GIVEN COUNTRIES: GENERAL RATE OF MORTALITY PER 1000 PERSONS, 1960

Mexico	12.7
Chile	12.5
Brazil	17 (1951-59 average)
Argentina	8.7
United States	9.4*
Canada	8.1

* U.S. figures distorted because of Negro discrimination.

As for bread consumption, or wheat, while the average annual per capita consumption in such countries as Russia is 200 kilos, in Brazil it is 36 kilos and in Northeast Brazil 10 kilos or as little as in India.

Because of the terrible death rate among the youth the percentage of the population over 40 years of age is relatively very small, only 16%. The 1950 census showed 52.3% of the population was 19 years of age

[19] Franklin de Oliveira: Work cited, p. 115.
[20] Given in *Conselho Nacional de Estatistica: Revista Brasileira de Estatistica,* Vol. XXIII, No. 91/92 *julho/decembro de* 1962.

or younger; (in the United States the median age was 30 years); only 4% was over 60 years old. It is no wonder that Euclides da Cunha could write: *"O verdadeiro Brasil nos aterra."* ("The true Brazil frightens us.")

The situation in Brazil illustrates that which exists generally in Latin America where 100 million persons lack water in sufficient quantity and good quality, where 50 million Indians live in utter degradation, where 70% of the population is ill, where 50% are analphabet, where 15 million children have no school at all and where 50% of those who go to school leave at the end of the first year.

Once the slave trade was ended in 1850 a stream of European immigrants began to come to Brazil, at first a trickle but then in larger and larger numbers, especially after the decree of 1871 when newborn slaves were freed. The newcomers averaged around 9,500 a year at first, then 15,000, and by 1870 were beginning to make their influence increasingly felt. At the same time railroads were being constructed and operated, steam navigation was in full swing, factories were being built, a cable to Europe laid, credit banks, insurance companies, mining companies, foreign capital investments all began to put in an appearance.

Between 1891 and 1900 the stream of immigrants turned into a mighty river averaging 112,500 a year. From 1900 to 1930 there entered 3,425,000 immigrants making a total of 4.8 million that had come to Brazil from its start. Of this grand total 1.5 million originated from Italy, approximately the same number from Portugal, more than half a million from Spain, more than a quarter of a million from Germany and about the same number from Japan. Later large groups were to arrive from the Near and Middle East: Arabs, Armenians, Lebanese, Egyptians, and others.

The European immigrants generally did not favor the monarchy, nor could they tolerate slavery. They were for democracy, an extended suffrage, federal decentralization, electoral reform, an elected senate, and for all the other modern demands that workers and middle class elements all over the world were clamoring for and obtaining. In Brazil they voiced these demands through a newly formed Republican Party. Even in 1881 when the electorate law was "liberalized," only 1% of the population could vote.

By 1888 the pressure had become too powerful for the old Brazilian Oligarchy to withstand. As soon as slavery was finally abolished it was decided to remove the Emperor as well and the following year an arranged military coup d'etat overthrew the Government and sent the Emperor into exile in Europe. This turnover was not brought about, however, by means of mass revolution. It was maneuvered in conjunction with the Army by the wealthy bourgeois elements, beneficiaries of the new forces developing within Brazil, who wanted to thrust aside some of the old obstacles standing in the way of progress. The revolutionary movement, therefore, although breaking sharply with its traditional, political past, was in most places actually a conservative one.

It was left to the Republic really to launch the nation upon its modern era of economic enterprise. A new Constitution was adopted and a protective tariff policy inaugurated that strongly taxed imported articles. Between 1890 and 1895 some 450 industrial enterprises were founded with a total investment of 200 million cruzeiros (a considerable sum in those days). In 1889 the number of wage workers had reached 55,000; by the time of the end of World War I it was close to 300,000.

The new Constitution of 1891 put into effect most of the general principles advocated by the Republican Party including the principle of federalism, the separation of church and state, an elected senate, and a checks-and-balances system modeled after the governmental set-up in the United States. The Constitution, however, was not to be respected for long. The first political experience of the Republic was to be the military dictatorship of Deodoro Fonseca which, upon the breaking out of the rebellions in Rio Grande do Sul in 1893, gave way to the military dictatorship of Floriano Peixotto. In 1896-1897 a bloody struggle of agrarians in the Canudos region of Bahía had to be put down[21] and in 1912-1915 a similar sort of revolt in southern Brazil, in Contestado.

Basically, these outbreaks were manifestations of the very uneven development in the various regions of Brazil. Up to this point the general rule of the Oligarchy had not been challenged, the struggle being confined to what aliquot share should go to what regional group. The

[21] For the terrible struggle in Canudos, see Euclides da Cunha: *Rebellion in the Backlands,* translation by Samuel Putnam (1944).

new industrial bourgeois layers were still closely linked with the old planters, while foreign investment had not as yet become so decisive. Until 1930 Brazil was governed by what was to all intents and purposes an Oligarchy, the so-called Republican Party. This was composed of a number of State political machines, each controlled by local family or allied economic interests.

The founding of the Communist Party of Brazil in March, 1922, was a sign not so much of a working class come of age as of desperate student and petty bourgeois elements who could only violently react to the stifling atmosphere carried over from the old days of slavery. Unlike Argentina, Brazil as yet, except for some of the immigrants, had no hard core of militant city workers tested in struggle. The Communist Party therefore made as its first chore the organization of a Workers and Peasants Bloc under which name it ran for office and elected representatives to the Municipal Council of Rio de Janeiro. The communists were soon driven underground coming out of illegality only 23 years later, in 1945, only again to be driven down in 1947. In 1924 a communist putsch headed by Carlos Luis Prestes developed into a long guerilla war lasting till 1926 and becoming as famous in Brazil as was Mao tse-tung's famous long march to the interior of China against Chiang kai-shek.

The period of the 1920's after World War I was one in which the rising modern layers of the capitalist class were bound to begin to challenge the older groups for more power and control. First of all there was a rising proletariat demanding certain rights which agrarian controlled legislatures found it difficult to understand. Sharp struggles, therefore, were being engendered between the growing cities and the stagnant countryside and between the industrial capitalists and their workmen. Second, there was the strenuous effort on the part of the industrialists to prevent the planters from shoving all the taxes onto the shoulders of others and from ignoring the problems of industry. Third, there was the insistent clamor to be heard on the part of the new middle classes rapidly increasing in importance. Finally, among the ruling elements in Brazil was the rivalry between the coffee group of São Paulo and the mining-metal groups of Minas Gerais. To climax matters the Minas Gerais groups armed themselves and by means of a military coup d'état in 1930 made Getulio Vargas President of Brazil.

The Vargas coup d'état coincided with the Uriburu coup d'état in

Argentina, both motivated by a great fear that the severe economic depression causing worldwide radicalization of the masses would affect the workers and toilers at home. In the case of Argentina there existed a hard core of militant anarcho-syndicalists and a socialist trade union leadership. Although such politically mature leadership did not exist among the workers in Brazil, the political ruling group had become painfully aware of the weakness of its central Federal authority. This was evidenced by the very ease with which Vargas overthrew his regularly elected opponent, Washington Luís; it had been illustrated also by Prestes' famous guerilla war. It was to be further borne out by the São Paulo uprising in 1932, by the revolt of the Liberation Alliance in 1934, and by the Integralist putsch in 1938.

Perhaps at the start the advent of the Vargas regime could have appeared as just another routine military coup d'etat. But it developed into somehting far different. Vargas, like Perón in Argentina to whom he showed the way, leading the nation full-flush into modernity, marked a fundamental turn of the country's evolution from which there could be no retreat. Unlike his predecessors, Vargas had to deal with a world-wide depression that cast Brazilian export prices into an abyss and stimulated an aggressive radicalism of the masses. He also faced a world-wide struggle between fascism and communism that had its counterpart in Brazil, and a World War in which Brazil had to play an active role. It is instructive to see how many pages Perón, coming to power 15 years later in Argentina, took out of Vargas' book.

Vargas was the first of the Latin American dictators to realize that to have the military on one's side in a social crisis was not enough; it was also necessary to have the masses. One of the first things he did on taking power was to create the Ministry of Labor, Industry, and Commerce which he used as a most effective weapon.

First of all, he enacted some badly needed social legislation which was bound to bring him the affection of the backward masses of Brazil. He put through such measures, unheard of up to this time in South and Central America, as limiting the workday to 8 hours, with overtime pay over that limit, and the work week to six days. Previously the workday had been 14, 16, or even 20 hours a day and the seven day work week was the rule. Children under 14 years of age were no longer permitted to work in industry. Women were to get the same pay as men for the same work. Pregnant women were not allowed to work four weeks before birth and four weeks after. A minimum wage was set bearing at least some relation to the established cost of living. Each employee, if employed a full year, was allowed a paid annual vacation of two weeks. Vargas made discharge, except for proven due course, difficult. He established retirement and pension institutes for public employees whose benefits were later extended to all Federal employees and to bank and commercial workers. Hospitals and clinics were added where workers and their families could get free treatment and medicine. For this both employers and workers contributed, as well as the Government.

At the same time Vargas completely reorganized the trade union movement. In 1927 the communists had organized a trade union congress that had decided to create in the various States regional federations in order to found a General Confederation of Labor as in other countries. Vargas used the occasion of the outbreak of various strikes to dissolve the United Trade Union Confederation and the National Federation of Maritime workers. Trade union meetings could be held now only with the permission and in the presence of the police. Vargas also dissolved the National Liberation Alliance and about 600 local unions. Instead of these he introduced a form of industrial syndicalism along the lines of Portuguese corporativism enforced by dictator Salazar and blessed by the Catholic Church. His unions were industrial: one industry, one union; and the machinery for collective bargaining was enforced by the sanction of the State itself. The right to strike was denied as anti-social. The direct connection between Mussolini-Salazar to Vargas and then to Franco-Perón was clear and unmistakeable.

To enforce his labor laws Vargas caused regional labor offices to be set up in every State of Brazil. Special Juntas were organized to decide labor disputes which bodies later, in 1939, were to be developed into regular labor courts.

Vargas also reorganized his Ministry of Education and Health with which he launched an extensive struggle against malaria. He also reformed the country's educational system in the course of which he overthrew the old separation of church and state and made religious instruction compulsory. As for the school system, elementary education was woefully weak. On the basis of the 1950 census reports, of about 36.5 million persons over 9 years of age there were nearly 19 million illiterates varying from 80% in Alagoas to 35% in Rio Grande do Sul, São Paulo, and Santa Catarina. In the backlands the illiteracy was almost total.

Following the lead of President F. D. Roosevelt, Vargas spent considerable effort to aid the agrarian wealthy by such projects as extensive irrigation, purchase of excess coffee surpluses to burn them, establishment of coffee, sugar, and alcohol institutes, stimulation of rubber plantations, etc. He was an advocate of industrial and agricultural protection.

Vargas had come to power in 1930 by virtue of the armed forces of Minas Gerais who were resentful of the favoritism shown to the coffee growers and who felt that the São Paulistas had held the presidency too much and too long. One of the first military actions Vargas had to undertake was the defeat of the São Paulo revolt which occurred. This was to make the coffee gentlemen understand that they could not run the country all by themselves for their own local benefit but had to share power with others in a truly national government.

On the other hand, the deepening of the depression and the rise of fascism in Europe had the result of moving the masses in Brazil to the left. An insurrectionary movement which broke out in Rio Grande do Norte, Pernambuco, and Rio de Janeiro, headed by the National Liberation Alliance with its slogans of Peace, Land, and Freedom, also had to be put down in 1934, but only after Vargas had decided he now had enough strength to turn democrat and run for office. Standing on his image as the "father of the poor" Vargas was triumphantly "elected" President. (The whole electorate amounted to about 1.5 million persons out of a population of around 55 million!)

Vargas' struggle with the "Left" had made him the darling of the "Right," the German and Italian colonists in Brazil who had been busy building up their specialized Brazilian forces known as the "Integralists" and who fervently believed that with the advent of World War II Vargas would take Brazil into the Nazi-Fascist camp. This was not to be, however. The power of the United States was too great to permit it.

In 1937 Vargas, not wishing to stand again for election, accomplished a new coup d'etat on the eve of elections and pronounced himself the head of his *Estado Novo,* or "New State." The 1934 Constitution was revoked and the Vargas dictatorship officially established.

All political parties were dissolved; the autonomy of the various States was abolished and their flags burned. The Axis organizations were firmly repressed, and when they revolted, their attempt to take power was thoroughly smashed. Vargas then threw himself on the side of the U.S., offered valuable bases to the Allies during the war, and even sent some fighting forces to join in the battle. The rumba displaced the tango in the U.S. dance halls.

During the war, when articles needed by Brazil were scarce, Vargas made a strenuous effort to accelerate the industrialization of the country. When petroleum was discovered in 1939 he would not permit private exploitation but insisted "Petroleum is ours," a slogan that has run ever since in Brazil's politics. During this dictatorial period of Vargas, 1937 to 1945, national industry literally leaped ahead in both volume and quality. Textile production expanded, the meat industry grew by 50%, paper and cellulose industries were installed, rubber production was pushed, and the great steel works at Volta Redonda started. By the time of the end of Vargas' rule the working class had grown from about 400,000 to about a million and a half.

With the end of the War it was evident that a one-man dictatorship based on fascist models had to be terminated and much-needed general elections held. Brazil was rapidly coming of age; vast new industrial, political, and social problems were calling for solutions that no single man could properly handle. While the value of a strong central government had been amply proved, yet it was also a fact that the various regions or States had developed at very different rates and had fluctuating national importance. All these matters could be threshed out only in a collective parliament in which each section of the bourgeoisie could be fully represented rather than through the biased mind of a single dictator. On this matter the decision was short and sweet—as Vargas would not consent to hold elections, the Army moved in in 1945 and Vargas was out—to be replaced by Dutra.

On taking over the government in order to hold elections for a new Constitutional Convention, the Army opened the prisons and freed all political prisoners, including the communists. The delegates to this Convention then in 1946 adopted the Constitution still in force which embodied many of the innovations Vargas had introduced, especially his labor and social codes.

The new Constitution enunciated such principles as:

1. The use of property is conditioned on its effects on social welfare;

2. The family is indivisible, entitled to financial aid;

3. Every one has a right to education (and 10% of the Federal budget is specified to be allocated for this purpose but is never carried out. In 1956 the percentage allocated was but 3.8% and in 1957 it was 5.3%);

4. The law must promote a just distribution of property;

5. Opportunity must be opened equally for all;

6. The law should restrain all forms of abuse of economic power, such as private domination of national markets, elimination of competition, arbitrary increase of profits, etc.;

7. Trade unions may intervene in the economic sphere or monopolize specified activities, etc.

Under this Constitution a syndicate tax of one day's pay a month has been levied on all workers and employees, while employers are taxed according to the size of their business capital. Regional minimum pay, the 8 hour day and the 6 day week, overtime payments, prohibition of work of children under 14, special protection for women, rest periods in industry, safety regulations, medical care, job security, pensions, paid vacations, and profit sharing have all been enacted into legislation. Every worker carries a labor card serving as identification and employment record—an excellent weapon for blacklisting and discrimination.

How much these measures are enforced is another matter. What is certain is that the unions are closely controlled by the political regime in power, since their funds are practically entirely obtained through the government.

On the whole the relations between the central government and that of the various States are modeled after the system in the United States, with some significant differences:

1. The President is elected for a five-year term and can not immediately succeed himself. He can initiate laws.

2. Three Senators from each State and Federal District are elected for eight-year terms; Deputies for four-year terms.

3. States are given very considerable autonomy so that they can distinctly affect inter-state commerce. For example, automobiles are produced practically only in the State of São Paulo which sets a heavy tax on each sale so that the people of all the other States must pay

enormous sums to São Paulo. This only follows the general line pursued so avariciously in Brazil where each group tries hard to use the government for special sources of wealth for itself.

4. There is, however, a right of intervention by the Federal Government over each State, when the central government so decides. A state of siege may also be proclaimed in an emergency in which all constitutional guarantees and rights may be held in abeyance.

5. Literate Brazilians over 18 years of age and able to speak Portuguese are qualified voters. This bars half the eligible population and presents a tremendous handicap to the workers and toilers everywhere but especially in the countryside. Thus the so-called democracy is a fake which only stimulates the people to take matters into their own hands by direct and violent action.

The 1946 Constitution restored the separation of church and state but the Catholic Church controls in fact one-third of all secondary schools. Here religious instruction is compulsory.

Removed as President, Vargas seeing many of his basic policies affirmed, continued his career by forming a Labor Party, as Perón was doing in Argentina, and running for the Brazilian Senate to which he was elected. In 1950 he ran for President and was elected, making the Brazilian Labor Party the most important political organization and a vehicle for all sorts of politicians to get office. The backwardness of the Brazilian workers due to their late start—thanks to the long duration of slavery,—their discrimination at the ballot box, their lack of independent organizations, the open manipulation by bourgeois elements of both their unions and their political groups, make it practically impossible for the workers to act on their own except spasmodically in emergencies. Naturally, following Vargas, all the other presidents ride the same way—Kuibichek, Quadros, and Goulart.

President once again, Vargas now pressed his industrialization policy. Favoring State control as an economic instrument he had to run afoul of foreign interests, particularly those represented by U.S. investors. This led to new pressures against him from all sides. Feeling himself abandoned, in a dramatic gesture he committed suicide in 1954 leaving, however, a political testament for his followers, a testament to which all his successors have given ardent lip service.

A description of the growth of industry in Brazil involves three aspects: First, a generalized aspect showing advance of gross national product, of income, of size of establishment, of the nature, character and dynamics of the economic structure; second, the special aspect of the growth of nationalization and state capital; third, the extent and depth of the penetration of foreign investment and the acute problems that have arisen therewith.

In a speech made by the Brazilian Ambassador to the United States, Roberto Campos, and printed in the January 1, 1963 issue of *Brazilian Business* it was stated that the annual rate of general economic growth in Brazil during the decade 1950-1960 had been about 6% a year and that had been accelerated to around 7% from 1960 on. Production had become so diversified that about 50% of Brazilian capital needs had been met by domestic production with no need for more imports. The Ambassador stressed that from 1957 to 1961 no other Latin American country, except Brazil, had met even the average target of 2.5% annual growth modestly set up by the Punte del Este Conference and the Alliance for Progress.

Between 1920 and 1957 while the general Brazilian population rose about 100%, the number of industrial establishments rose from 13,000 to 100,000, with the rate even greater in such basic industries as electrical energy, steel, cement, electrical materials, chemical products, petroleum, etc. From 1939 to 1956 the industrial weight of the production of means of production, or capital goods, rose from 20% of the total to 33%.

In 1939 industry furnished 13% of the national income, now it furnishes about 20% of which the São Paulo and Rio de Janeiro complexes are responsible for 70%. Between 1940 and 1956 while field labor grew by 68% the transformation industries, transforming primary materials into finished or semi-finished goods, advanced 357%, the means of production sector advancing 1132%, or over five times as fast as the means of consumption sector.

Between 1921 and 1955 Brazil's coast trade commerce quintupled; railroad transport rose from 19 million to 39 million tons; air transport leaped from 63,000 passengers in 1938 to 3.5 million in 1956. Thanks to industrialization the national income more than doubled in real terms from 1940 to 1955 while in per capita it grew 50%, although without equable distribution. The fact is the gains in real income are almost entirely concentrated in the hands of the middle and wealthy classes. While the masses are still spending their entire wages for the bare necessities of life, the rising middle and wealthy classes are increasing their expenditures on luxury and status items so that consumption in non-essentials grows much more rapidly than consumption of basically essential goods, and automobile sales rise far faster than those of food.

The concentration of industry in the hands of large establishments could already be clearly seen by 1950 as the following table shows:

Table 8
BRAZIL: 1950: DISTRIBUTION OF EMPLOYMENT IN MANUFACTURING
INDUSTRIES (IN %)

1-4 persons	13%
5-49	27
50-250	23
Over 250	37

Capital concentration and centralization can also be seen by the fact that in 1951 only 1% of the establishments took 65% of the profits, which ratio rose to 68% in 1959. Of the 66 large concerns, only 34 were in the hands of Brazilians. In 1961 the capital of these 66 top concerns amounted to 301.9 billion cruzeiros, or 46% of the capital of all 6,818 corporations operating in Brazil.

The discovery of petroleum in 1939 immediately set off a great battle as to who should control this industry. With the slogan "The petroleum is ours" Vargas organized a national entity known as Petrobras for the further discovery and exploitation of that liquid gold. Petroleum production soon began to leap forward. In 1945 production equalled 79,000 barrels, in 1950—339,000 barrels, in 1955—2,012,-000 barrels, in 1959—23,590,000 barrels. This was still not enough to cover more than 28% of Brazil's needs but production was pushed even higher, to an estimated 37 million barrels in 1960 with the hope that at such a pace Brazil might soon become self-sufficient.

The great American oil interests could never forgive Vargas for not allowing them to get concessions for the oil fields or for refining oil. They supposedly were responsible for some of the tensions that finally led Vargas to suicide with a warning to the people to defend themselves from foreign pressures. The Americans were successful under Kuibichek in at least getting the rights of distribution and sales in Brazil and in raising gasoline prices. Today Standard Oil is one of the great companies earning millions through the exploitation of such rights. Vargas charged them with pushing gasoline consumption to the detriment of the State railroads and vehemently defended Petrobras from attacks leveled against that entity as inefficient by countering these attacks were malicious and stemmed from foreign oil interests. Kuibichek, who ran on a platform to carry out Vargas' program, claimed that the opposition had tried to prevent elections after Vargas' suicide but had failed in this conspiracy. Nevertheless, the oil companies were successful in obtaining further concessions.

Vargas had also promoted the development of hydro-electric energy through the State controlled entity Electrobras. Here again he charged the foreign firms with pushing petroleum instead of electrical production as a source for energy and trying to take over Electrobras for their own purposes. And here again electrical energy production went rapidly forward. In 1953 the total energy so produced amounted to 10.3 billion kilowatt hours; by 1959 this had risen to 21.5 billion. With the construction of the new dams planned in the 1962-1966 period making the São Francisco River navigable for 1100 miles and also entraining a great flood control and irrigation program, it is estimated that some new 9 million kilowatts of energy will be added.

As in the case of petroleum the battle over electrical energy production and especially over its distribution and sale did not cease to rage not only under Vargas but also under his successors, Kuibichek, Quadros, and Goulart. It was the British who first installed the electrical street car system in Rio de Janeiro and in São Paulo and also the electrical utility system there. How this competition between State and private foreign enterprise has become involved can be seen by the following table:

Table 9[22]
BRAZIL: DISPOSITION OF ELECTRICAL ENERGY (IN 1,000 KILOWATTS)

Companies	1952	1960
Light (Rio de Janeiro and São Paulo)	959	1,923
Bond and Share	263	520
Hydroelectric of São Francisco	2	202 (State owned, Distribution by Light & by Bond and Share)
CEMIG	13	288 (Mixed Co.: State & Private)
State Electric Energy Commission	33	220 (Rio Grande do Sul)
Others	705	1,140 (1958)

[22] Rui Facó: Work cited, p. 250.

Under Vargas the State also went into the steel production business and at the time of his removal by the military after World War II the great plant of Volta Redonda was just beginning operations. By 1958 the Government *Companhía Siderúgica Nacional* was producing annually about 2 million tons of pig iron, steel ingots, rails, and other rolled products. And now a new COSIPA Works, a mixed Government company in São Paulo will have 2 million tons capacity. The Federal Government is also planning jointly with the State of Santa Catarina to have a new steel mill of 500,000 tons annually.

In the meantime a large number of foreign companies are also entering the steel business. At Vitoria USIMINAS, the largest steel mill in Latin America, has been built with an eventual 2 million ton steel capacity in which Japanese capital is involved. The Japanese are also setting up shipyards and now ships of 10,000 tons to 45,000 ton supertankers are being built at such shipyards. At Ferro a German-U.S. group is building iron ore and steel shipment facilities with their own rail line to the port. The Belgo Mineir Company is increasing its steel production from 500,000 tons to 1.3 million tons, to make it about the same as at Volta Redonda.

According to recent U.S. Department of Commerce reports made by its representative at Rio de Janeiro, the 1961 Brazilian production of steel ingots rose 9% from 2.2 million metric tons to 2.4 million, with the *Companhía Siderúrgica Nacional* accounting for 47% of the ingot production and 87% of the flat products. Thanks to this domestic advance, imports of steel fell from $93 million in 1960 to $69 million in 1961.

In 1937 Brazilian exports of steel amounted to 3.5 million tons selling for $50 million and making Brazil the fourth steel exporter in the world. Six million tons of iron are currently being shipped out yearly. A contract has been negotiated with Italy for 7 million tons of iron. To speed the shipments the *Companhía do Rio Doce* is greatly enlarging its plants and docks at Vitoria. Recently signed has been a pact with Japan to supply 10 million tons of iron ore each year for 10 years.

Brazil has had a phenomenal growth in the automobile industry, now actually occupying ninth place in world automobile production, following the U.S., West Germany, the United Kingdom, France, Japan, Italy, Canada, and Australia. Since 1957 more than 650,000 cars have been manufactured, the rate at one period surpassing 200,-000 a year. In 1961 the breakdown by companies was as shown in the table:

Table 10

BRAZIL: AUTOMOBILE PRODUCTION BY COMPANIES 1961

Name	Auto Production
Volkswagen	47,340 (passenger cars)
Willys-Overland	42,599 (Jeeps, etc.)
Ford Motor	14,031 (trucks)
General Motors	13,689 (trucks)
Vemag	10,919 (passenger cars; Brazilian plus German capital)
Mercedes-Benz	6,999 (trucks)
Simca	5,901 (passenger cars)
FNM	2,678 (passenger cars; Brazilian plus Italian capital—Feb 1963)
International	1,024 (trucks)
Scania Vabis	489 (trucks)
Toyoto	5 (Japanese Jeeps)
Total	145,674

What is very important to note in the automobile statistics is that the cars are assembled from parts made almost entirely within the country, the "nationalization," as it is called, being almost 100%. So well are the metal fabrication shops advanced that large-scale exports are actually being contemplated. Only recently Brazil agreed to ship $35 million worth of cars to Mexico. In October, 1962, Brazil shipped 120 completely equipped railroad freight cars to Uruguay. The tractor output for October, 1962, was a record 1,019. In 1960 the automobile industry employed about 120,000 persons and 90,000 more in auto parts production in about 1,200 factories.

In 1960 Brazil's production of metal household appliances was recorded as given in Table 11.

Following the lead of Vargas the Government has gone heavily into State owned industries. It has operated mines, the petroleum industry, hydro-electric plants, chemical plants *(Companhía Nacional de Al-calís),* key sectors of the pharmaceutical industry, the largest steel mill, an automobile factory *(Fábrica Nacional de Motores),* rubber plantations (now given up), most of the railroads, the bulk of the merchant marine, and the Bank of Brazil. It also operates mixed Government-private companies and promotion agencies for coffee, sugar, wheat, alcohol, maté, salt, *pinho* (pinewoods), etc., for specific

Table 11
BRAZIL'S HOUSEHOLD APPLIANCE OUTPUT 1960

Electric ranges	600,000
Electric irons	600,000
Radios	400,000
Electric fans	400,000
Electric blenders	350,000
Sewing machines	322,000
Refrigerators	320,000
Washing machines	250,000
Television sets	150,000
Vacuum cleaners	80,000
Sew. machine motors	60,000
Electric heaters	70,000
Electric mixers	50,000
Electric shavers	35,000
Air conditioners	10,000
etc., etc.	

regions. It controls foreign commerce and exchange; it fixes prices and wage scales. In the 1958 budget, to take an example, 18% of the outgo went for economic and social development, 25% went for the railroads, marine transportation and highways, 16% went for agriculture, education, and health, and 25% went for the armed forces. (Of the 24% of the budget which went for the Federal payroll, more than 50% went to the military.)

In the fierce struggle that has ensued between State controlled and private industry, dominated by foreign capital, a great hue and cry has been raised concerning the inefficiency of Government operations, especially on the railroads and in the merchant marine, as well as in such entities as Petrobras and Electrobras, and the absence of civil service standards in administration of Government offices. Thus the situation here is about the same as has been commented upon in the part on Argentina.

There is no question but that some of the criticism is well taken, although on the railroads at least the situation is not nearly so bad as in Argentina. In Brazil the Federal Government owns 78% of the railroad mileage and directly operates 67% of the system. One defect is that the system has two gauges: metric and standard, leading to some extra costs and inconvenience in shipping and travelling. In 1959 a new *Rede Ferroviaria Federal* (RFFSA), or Federal Railroad Network, was formed with a capital of 60 billion cruzeiros to administer, maintain, improve, and extend the railroads. Four hundred diesel en-

gines have been ordered since 1957. In 1959, 56.2% of the locomotives on Government lines were diesel, 25.5% were electric, and only
18.3% were steam.

The railroads, however, do not pay their own way because, it is
claimed, of inefficiency in operations, featherbedding, insufficient labor
effort, etc. The daily deficit of the Rio de Janeiro suburban lines of
the Central and Leopoldina railroads amounted to 20 million cruzeiros
a day in 1962. In 1961 the expenses totaled more than 7 times the
receipts on these Government lines.

There is no doubt that the two government ship lines are poorly
run. They ran a deficit in 1958 of 2.5 billion cruzeiros. Port conditions
are generally poor and river conditions often absolutely intolerable.

In the operations within the Federal administration itself, of course
nepotism and favoritism are rampant as must be expected in such a
corrupt and venal political system run by former slave holder families
who have always thought of government as private poaching pre-
serves to be personally possessed by their progeny. So long as the burden was on the Brazilian people there might be little quarrel among
the politicos. But now that the weight of the inefficiency, sloth, and red
tape falls upon modern business, especially upon the foreign investor,
it can no longer be tolerated.

It has been said that one of the reasons President Kuibichek was
so anxious to move the Federal Capital from Guanabara, or Rio de
Janeiro, to Brasilia was to use the occasion to make the most drastic
reduction in the government work force so as to be able to establish
some sort of efficient apparatus based on principles of civil service
which had been pressed so hard on him by foreign experts of credit
and loan agencies.

The outstanding dynamic factor in Brazil's industrialization has
been the pressure of foreign investments. The scope of these investments has not been easy to determine with any great degree of exact-
ness since they are both public and private. They may be in the form
of loans and credits, both long-term and short-term, and may be direct
investments or indirect as in the case of the portfolio type. Furthermore, the fluctuations in such investments may be considerable from
year to year and may shift from one country to another.

In the 19th century the great foreign investor that dominated the scene in Brazil was England. Then England was the manufacturer for Brazil, her importer and her exporter and became her first investor in transportation and in public services. In those days, too, the world division of labor was relatively stable. The cocoa butter, palm wax, coffee, cocoa, or other products England bought in Brazil were not countered by products made in England. At the peak of her investment prowess in 1930 England must have invested in Brazilian economic affairs the equivalent of about $1.2 billion. But the blows of two world wars were very costly to Britain and in the course of the 20th century for this and other reasons she had to give up more than 60% in value of her Brazilian investments so that now she has perhaps around $400 million still remaining. The U.S. took over the leadership Britain lost.

The leadership of the United States, however, was of quite a different sort. Investments centered on manufacturing enterprises rather than on other aspects of the private economy. They have been backed up by extensive public grants, loans, and credits. The Americans not only industrialized the country but began to control the very heart of it, building around themselves a great nexus of supporting companies that could oppose hostile action by the State such as would be involved in national expropriation or even national planning. Unlike England, the United States could also go into direct competition with Brazil and did so, finding substitutes for her previous imports from Brazil of natural rubber, cocoa butter, palm wax, etc., and thus throwing these Brazilian industries into depression and confusion. The United States masters could also block Brazil's commerce with others, for example her trade with Russia and Asia, or her wheat-coffee trade agreements with Argentina, etc. Finally, she could demand special treatment, as she did, as a war partner when Brazil sold 32,000 tons of radio-active thorium for about 30 cruzeiros a kilo while Portugal was charging 900 cruzeiros for tungsten (wolfram) per kilo.

From 1929 to 1946 U.S. capital doubled in Brazil and doubled again in the next six years. It multiplied six times from 1929 to 1956, or from around $200 million to around $1.2 billion. If loans are counted, the total went to around $2 billion.

In 1940 direct North American investments in Brazil were $240 million, by 1956 they were $1,209 million. In 1955 the direct U.S. investments in Brazil were estimated at $1,107 million broken down in principal categories as $188 million in petroleum, $563 million in manufacturing, $158 million in public utilities, and $137 million in trade. By 1959 these direct investments had reached a general total of $1,304 million with $701 million in manufacturing, $181 million in public utilities, and $171 million in trade. It is most important to note that this growth was not at all due to foreign capital imports but mainly due to internal growth of the original investments.

The following table gives the distribution of foreign investments in Brazil by principal countries of origin.

Table 12

DISTRIBUTION OF FOREIGN INVESTMENTS IN BRAZIL BY PRINCIPAL COUNTRIES OF ORIGIN 1958 TO 1962 ($ MILLION)

	$ million	%
United States	$219.6	43.0 %
West Germany	102.6	20.1
Switzerland	37.6	7.35
France	24.2	4.74
Canada	22.4	4.38
Others	104.8	20.43
Totals	$511.2	100 %

Note: Of this total, $379 million, or 74.2%, went into basic industries of which $235 million in automobiles and $44 million in chemicals while still other amounts went into heavy machinery, tractors, metal, ship building, smelting, cement, and such. Of the total 76.4% went to São Paulo with other good portions to Rio de Janeiro and Minas Gerais.

In a recent report made to Congress it was estimated that up to December, 1960, there were 200 German firms in Brazil with direct investments of about $160 million, Italy coming next with $70 million, and Japan with $45 million. (These figures, however, have already changed drastically upward.)

In addition to the U.S. direct private investments of, say, $1.2 billion as of December, 1960, there must also be included the large loans for economic development and balance of payments assistance of $1,345 million extended through the Ex-Import Bank (for Volta Redonda steel works, for railroad rolling stock, harbor improvements, etc.), the $175 million economic development loans from the sale of U.S. agricultural commodities under U.S. Law 480, and the International World Bank loan of $255 million.

There is now no known mineral in Brazil not tied up with foreign investments. The manganese of Amapá was delivered over to Bethlehem Steel, that of Urucum in Minas Gerais to U.S. Steel. Amapá will be exhausted in 30 years, the Minas Gerais findings in 40 years, but the royalties paid to Brazil are considered very low. One company was able to sell its mine product to the U.S. Government at 600 cruzeiros per kilo while it paid 60 cruzeiros for the stuff at the mouth of the mine.

North American investors now control the coffee, cotton, wheat and hybrid corn distribution, the meat freezers, the eucalyptus plantations, the paper and cellulose industries, the iron and manganese mining, electrical energy and petroleum distribution, such public services as city transports, light, telephone and international telegraph communications, a good section of the automobile industry, the private pharmaceutical industry, rubber manufacturing, cement, shoes, films, and even toys. The U.S. controls the coffee markets and the imports and exports of most goods.

The subject of foreign investments, credits, loans, and aids must also be considered with reference to the general foreign commercial relations of Brazil, including such matters as exports, imports, terms of trade, balance of trade and payments, etc. The table below gives the pertinent data to be considered:

Table 13

BRAZIL: POPULATION, EXPORTS, IMPORTS, AND CAPACITY TO IMPORT, ETC.
(INDEX LEVEL BASED ON 1937 AS 100)

Year	Population (millions)	Exports Quantity	Price Index Exports	Price Index Imports	Terms of Trade	Capacity to import	Imports Quantity	% imp. to avail. goods
1929	34.5	76.8	99	51	194	149	130.1	44.0%
1932	36	62	81	61	133	82	46.6	21.5
1937		100	100	100	100	100	100	
1940	41	103.1	94	122	77	79	76.7	24.3
1946	46.5	134.6	266	215	124	167	114	27.2
1949	49	117.0	350	270	130	152	145.6	28.6

The reader is recommended to turn to the notes pertaining to the similar tables (Tables 1-4A, 1-4B, and II-3) in the parts dealing with Latin America as a whole and with Argentina so as to get the full meaning of the terms, dates, and figures.

If we compare the above table with its counterparts pertaining to Argentina and to Latin America as a whole we can see that Brazil has occupied an exceptional and fortunate position in that

a) in the period before the Great Depression the index levels of her export prices were so far above those of her imports that her terms of trade were fantastically advantageous, enabling her capacity to import greatly to exceed her actual imports;
b) this situation actually continued during the very depths of the depression;
c) and although the terms of trade finally went against Brazil by the time of the opening of World War II, her current imports were still beneath her capacity to import because her exports had by then jumped so high as to overcome the lows of the depression and greatly to supersede the quantity exported before the depression;
d) these exports shot upward during the war under increasingly favorable terms of trade;
e) and this continued into the immediate post-war period.

. From the above analysis we can see how, under the control of its Oligarchy, Brazil missed the bus of industrialization. With terms of trade very favorable during the depression years, this was the time when vast imports of machinery and producers goods should have been made from industrial countries. Instead, the table shows that the amount imported in 1932 was not even 60% of what Brazil easily could have imported, if 1937 is taken as the base year for an index, since the percentage of actual imports to the total available goods in the country sank to about half of what it had been before the war.

Perhaps instead of modernizing the country the Oligarchy simply squandered its excess profits by conspicuous consumption in Europe and abroad, as the Brazilians had the reputation for doing. At any rate, the Brazilian writers and publicists who complain bitterly about the later adverse terms of trade and low export prices Brazil had to meet never seem to mention this long favorable period so foolishly thrown away by the Brazilian wealthy. Instead, the writers do what Ambassador Campos in the speech cited above did, namely, take the year 1953 as a base, when the terms of trade were very favorable to Brazil as a result of the Korean War, and denounce imperialism for not maintaining these advantageous terms forever, thus "stealing" $6 billion through lower terms of trade. This last figure was obtained by calculating from the base that Latin American exports increased in volume 30% from 1953 to 1960 (other than oil), while prices rose only 4%, and that in 1961 the prices of coffee and of cocoa were equal to only 60%, the price of bananas 85%, and those of cotton and wool 80% of what they were in 1953, while U.S. prices rose 10% at the same time.

What sort of imports were made by the ruling Oligarchy during this favorable period for Brazilian economy can be seen by the following table which shows how it was precisely in the most backward regions of Brazil, where the money obtained by wealthy planters would be spent not on economic advancement but on wasteful consumption at home and abroad, where the greatest ratio of imports to exports was steadily expanding:

Table 14[23]

PHYSICAL VOLUME OF EXPORTS AND IMPORTS FOR CERTAIN STATES OF BRAZIL
(INDEX LEVEL 1938/39 EQUALS 100)

	1950		1956	
	Exports	Imports	Exports	Imports
Amazonas	70	162	65	782
Pará	41	240	91	404
Ceará	50	144	21	693
Rio Gr. do Norte	32	685	43	1197
Pernambuco	57	231	41	242
Bahía	107	371	111	324

Certainly, the great fall in prices after the Korean War, especially following the world-wide recession of 1957, greatly affected Brazil. How prices have fallen can be seen from the U.S. figures relating to the cost of Brazilian vegetable imports to the U.S.: In 1959 the cost was $504 million; in 1960—$463 million; in 1961—$440 million.

The next table shows that if we use 1956 as a base, the average annual loss due to adverse terms of trade has been equal to almost the total value of Brazil's annual exports!

Table 15[24]

BRAZIL: VOLUME AND VALUE OF EXPORTS; UNIT VALUE PER TON;
TOTAL LOSSES SINCE 1956

Year	Volume Exports (1000 Tons)	Value ($ million)	Unit Value ($ ton)	Total Loss $ Mill. reference 1956
1956	5,751	$1,482	$258	
1957	7,713	1,392	180	$ 597 Mill.
1958	8,297	1,243	150	897
1959	9,884	1,282	130	1,268
1960	10,608	1,269	120	1,567
			Total	$4,329 Millions

[23] Sergio Magalhães: *Problemas do Desenvolvimento Económico* (1960), p. 132.

[24] Hilton Diniz: *"A 'Alianca para O Progresso' e A Realidade Nacional"* in *Revista Brasilense*, No. 42 (1962).

Thus an increase of 84% in the volume of exports between 1956 and 1960 brought an actual 14% decrease in total receipts because unit prices fell 53% in that same period. At the same time import costs rose.

The picture is made more detailed in the following table dealing with coffee exports only. Here it is shown that while the same volume of coffee was sold the income received during the five-year period 1953-1960 was 30% less at the end of the period than at the start.

Table 16[24]

BRAZIL: VOLUME AND VALUE OF COFFEE EXPORTS

Year	1,000 sacks	U.S. $ Million
1956	16,805	1,030
1957	14,319	846
1958	12,882	688
1959	17,436	733
1960	16,608	713

Perhaps the chief reason for the failure to import more industrial goods during Brazil's favorable foreign trade periods could be traced additionally to the fact that Brazil was essentially importing not goods but foreign capital, which capital was exporting the surpluses earned that might otherwise have been used for modernization and improvement. This is shown by the following table which correlates the deficit in the balance of payments, the remittance of profits abroad, the entrance of private foreign capital and the reinvestment of this capital:

Table 17[25]

BRAZIL: CORRELATION BETWEEN DEFICIT OF BALANCE OF PAYMENTS, REMITTANCE OF GAINS ABROAD, ENTRANCE OF PRIVATE FOREIGN CAPITAL, AND REINVESTMENT OF THAT CAPITAL

($ MILLION)

Year	Deficit	Remittance of Gains	Reinvestments	Entrance of Private Foreign Capital
1947	$182	$ 41	$19	$ 36
1948	24	66	42	25
1949	74	65	39	5
1951	291	92	67	4
1952	643	40	85	9
1954	203	104	40	11
1955	116	119	36	43
1957	204	100		143
	Surplus			
1950	52	76	36	3
1953	16	129	38	22
1956	166	143	50	89

[24] *Ibid.*
[25] Sergio Magalhães: Work cited, p. 19.

Table 16 (Continued)

Total Accumulated Deficit	$1,503 Million
Total Admitted Remittance of Gains	975 "
Total Known Reinvestments	452 "
Total Entrance of Private Capital	390 "

Total Remittance of Money Sent Abroad under Rubric of "Private Gifts" not in above table was $114 Million.

The table below shows Brazil's balance of trade in the decade 1950-1960:

Table 18
BRAZIL: BALANCE OF TRADE: $ MILLION

	1950	1953	1957	1958	1959	1960
Exports	$1347	$1539	$1392	$1243	$1282	$1269
Imports	1098	1319	1488	1353	1374	1462
Balance	249	220	− 96	− 110	− 92	− 193

Between 1951 and 1960 while world international trade increased 100%, that of Brazil fell 20% in terms of current dollars, from $1,541 million to $1,260 million. In December, 1960, Brazil had foreign financial commitments totaling $2,654 million, or an amount equal to two years' total exports.

As has been already noted, during the world depression in the 1930's after Vargas had assumed power, he adopted the policy of protecting domestic manufactures as a means of restricting imports. During the war and immediate post-war years imports were hard to obtain since the industrial countries were all at war or, after the war, were economically exhausted and needed all their strength for rehabilitation. Foreign investments, however, in the form of money or of capital goods, were not considered imports and are not figured in foreign trade tables.

At first imports were restricted by a system of licenses to do business in Brazil. In 1951 Vargas opened the gates for imports of industrial equipment and of raw and semi-processed industrial materials without any discrimination as to whether they were needed in each instance or not, or whether they would hinder or develop domestic industry. When a sharp disequilibrium became noticed in balance of payments, the Government reverted to drastic and indiscriminate restrictions, but in 1953 also partially freed foreign exchange, creating official and free market parallel rates of exchange. The free market was fed by the sale of foreign exchange stemming from exports. Imports, however, remained licensed at official rates. This system was to stimulate exports and the entrance of foreign capital, since such capital was allowed at that time free remittances of interests, dividends, etc.

In October, 1953, came Instruction 70 issued by SUMOC *(Superintendencia da Moeda e do Crédito)* to be administered by CEXIM *(Carteira de Exportação e Importação)*. All exports and imports were now to pass at the official rate, the free rate being confined only to merely financial deals, entrance and outflow of capital, etc. The previous ability, given as a favor to some, to sell foreign money at the free rates of goods exported now was substituted by subsidies. As for imports, they were subject to licenses conditioned by previous holdings of promises of sales of exchange offered in the exchange auctions. This Instruction 70 lasted till 1961 when it was substituted by the free market.

Before this, the 1948 rule of licenses for imports was subject to review by CEXIM as to the essentiality of such imports, but the 1953 Instruction replaced this with the auction system, and thus free exchange was furthered. Besides, the change in system seemed necessary because of the rampant favoritism and corruption prevailing in CEXIM. Under the previous system the beneficiary of a license had the right to pay imports at the official rate of 18.50 cruzeiros to the U.S. dollar instead of the free rate of more than twice as much, thus making an enormous profit.

In doing business with Brazil, foreign capitalists demanded guarantees in coming into the country, guarantees to remain, and guarantees to leave. They received many favors. In 1955, under Kuibichek, the way was opened further. Instruction 113 of SUMOC was issued authorizing CACEX *(Carteiro do Comercio Exteriór) do Banco do Brasil* to issue import licenses without any exchange cover (that is, without the previous exchange auctions) for industrial equipment corresponding to that classified as foreign investments. Practically, this meant bringing in foreign equipment without any exchange expense even of items which could be procured domestically, while, on the other hand, domestic firms were obliged to obtain import licenses to get the same stuff from abroad and paid double. This gave a tremendous advantage to the foreign firms and forced many native firms either to merge with the foreigners or go out of business, as has happened in the automobile parts and in the drug industries.

What kind of profits were made can be seen in the case of the Ford Company which in 1958 on its invested capital of 500,000 cruzeiros made a profit of almost 25 million cruzeiros (5000%), and a profit of 4,681% the following year; while General Motors earned 3000% profit.

The following table illustrates the sort of financial returns received by foreign capital investment:

Table 19A[26]
REMITMENTS OF FOREIGN CAPITAL BY BRAZIL (MILLION CRUZEIROS)

	1954	1958
Rents	Cr. 78	Cr. 200
Commissions	222	1,925
Stock Dividends	1,217	3,299
Profits	1,583	4,141
Royalties	838	2,972
Technical Services	266	1,673
Other	391	3,473
Totals	4,594	17,682

These returns were distributed in 1958 as follows:

Table 19B[26]
DISTRIBUTION OF 1958 FOREIGN CAPITAL REMITMENTS BY
PRINCIPAL COUNTRIES (%) 1958

U.S.	56.1%
Great Britain	8.7
Switzerland	7.2
Canada	5.1
France	4.5
Panama	2.6
Others	15.8

Notes: The United States received 47.2% of the stock dividends, 50.3% of the royalties, 60% of the technical services, 75% of the profits; not counting hidden U.S. interests in the totals given for Panama, Canada, Switzerland, and even France.

The above trend was accelerated with the rise of the automobile industry in 1959.

The next table gives some further pertinent data on foreign investments.

[26] Nelson Werneck Sodré: Work cited, p. 379. The author wrongly gives *"dolares"* instead of *"cruzeiros."*

Table 20A[27]

BRAZIL: FOREIGN INVESTMENTS, REINVESTMENTS, LOANS, AND FINANCING
($ MILLION)

Year	Entered	Left	Difference
1955	$ 103	$ 209	$106
1956	270	398	128
1957	349	490	141
1958	373	823	450
Total	$1095	$1920	$825

More detailed is Table 20B following:

Table 20B[28]

BRAZIL: FOREIGN CAPITAL BALANCES ($ MILLION)

	1947-53 (7 years)		1954-60 (7 years)		Total 1947-61 (15 years)	
	aggregate	annual	aggregate	annual	aggregate	annual
A. Risk Capital						
Entries	$ 105	$ 15	$ 608	$ 87	$ 831	$ 55
Remittances of profit	− 328	− 47	− 235	− 34	− 594	− 39
BALANCE	− 223	− 32	373	53	237	16
B. Loan Capital						
Entries	1341	192	3047	435	5262	350
Amortization	− 529	− 76	− 1921	− 274	− 3014	− 201
Interest	− 158	− 23	− 467	− 67	− 732	− 46

Source: SUMOC*

* SUMOC now makes a fantastic and egregious error in its calculations which we must note. It adds together the items "Interest" and "Amortization of Loan Capital" in order to get a so-called balance. Actually, the interest is a separate item. Only the item "Amortization" should be subtracted from the "Loan Capital Entries" to get a "Balance." If you lend me $100 and I pay you $10 in interest and also return $50 of the principal, I still owe you not $40 but $50! Thus the true balances should be as follows and not as given by SUMOC:

Table 20B (continued)

LOAN BALANCE	$ 812	$116	$1126	$161	$2248	$149
Total Balance	589	84	1499	214	2485	165
C. Profits Remit & Reinvested						
Remitted	328	47	235	34	594	40
Reinvested	326	46	215	31	559	38
TOTAL	$ 654	$ 93	$ 450	$ 65	$1153	$ 78

[27] The Same: p. 409.
[28] *Brazilian-American Survey,* No. 20, 1963: Article by Herculano Borges Da Fonseca: "Legal Regime for Foreign Capital."

The totals collected under the headings remittances of profits, amortization of capital and interest payments, enormous as they were, were still not enough for foreign capital. They had to bleed Brazil in other ways as well. Under the heading of "International Travel" the amounts supposedly spent by foreign investors amounted in 15 years to the enormous total of $311 million, in recent years, actually more than the total of profit remittance—the profit remittances during the period 1956-1961 totalling $195 million while the "International Travel" expenses amounted to $232 million. Then there were "royalty" payments which during the period 1954-1961 averaged $15 million a year; and also the "technical assistance payments" which averaged another $17 million a year; and the "private gifts" we have already mentioned.

The fact is that on September 30, 1962, Brazil's foreign debt reached a total of about $3 billion in all currencies, value of principal and interest carried out by official and private entities.

At the present time, as part of the aggressive nationalism under Goulart, a new regulation regarding the remittance of profits has been approved. All capital entering the country must be registered with SUMOC whether in the form of investments, money, or goods, as well as the repatriation of capital or capital remittances of profits, dividends, interests, amortizations, royalties, payments for technical assistance, etc. The registration of the capital will be in the money of the country of origin. All deposits abroad must be declared on penalty of being considered illegal with criminal action taken against the offending parties. Foreign capital is defined as goods, machinery, and equipment entering Brazil without initial expense of foreign exchange, destined for the production of goods or services, as well as reserves introduced for economic activities. Foreign capital will be treated equally with national capital. SUMOC is given the power to control cambio operations. Foreign banks of countries placing restrictions on Brazilian banks can not have more than 30% of the voting stock in national banks. The annual return of profits sent abroad can not surpass 10% of the value of registered investments. If more is sent it will be considered as repatriation of capital not more than 20% of which can be sent out in any one year. Profits above this limit will be considered as supplementary capital and will not have the right of remittance of future profits.[29]

Cheating in regard to payments for international travel, donations, royalties, patents, payments for second-hand goods imported, etc., is now supposed to be carefully guarded against with harsh penalties provided for offenders. For those foreign investors engaged in activities of lesser national interest, the income tax on profits and dividends is increased by 20% and duties on imports of machinery and equipment can be raised 30%.

As a result of this legislation, at least in part, apparently, new foreign investments which were $266 million in 1961 dropped to $62 million in 1962, and to only $5 million for the first half of 1963![30]

The liquid outgo from Brazil from 1939 to 1952 amounted to a total of around $1 billion or $70 million a year. In the period from 1939 to 1952 long-term foreign investments in Brazil amounted to $97.1 million but the remittance of income amounted to $806.9 million in that time while the repatriation of foreign investments amounted to $83.8 million. A Brazil-U.S. Mixed Commission showed in a report that in the years 1939-1952 the value of the returns transferred abroad was 60 times greater than the liquid ingress of capital. Between 1955 and 1958 foreign investments totalled $1,095 million but remittances totalled $2,020 million. Between 1939 and 1955 the effective ingress of capital was $173 million but sent out as income return was $1,112 million. From 1940 to 1955 foreign investment grew from $240 million to $1,107 million or about five times, but the profits sent out were seven times greater.

This same result was also true for all Latin America, which received in 1959 a total of $37 million from the U.S. while the U.S. received $734 million from all Latin America: $593 million from direct investments, $70 million from portfolio investments, and $71 million from Government loans and credits.

In 1950, besides their direct investments, U.S. capitalists controlled others so that while their direct investments had grown to $4.7 billion as a result of the enormous profits they had accumulated during the years; they also controlled some $2.7 billion dollars in other fields or

[29] The text of the law is given in *Brazilian Bulletin:* Vol. XIX, No. 434, June 1, 1963.
[30] See *Conjuntura Economica* Vol. X, No. 7, July, 1963.

firms, or a total of $7.4 billion of which 36% was invested elsewhere than in their own company. In 1956 it was estimated that the total resources administered by American capital were $600 million (32%) coming from the U.S.; $600 million (32%) formed in Brazil; and $675 million (36%) of Brazilian capital administered by Americans.

It must not be imagined that all the foreign firms were actually needed by Brazil or in any way advanced her world position or strength. In 1958, out of the 1477 total foreign firms controlled over 50% by foreign capital, only 394, or 27%, were in primary branches of industry such as electricity or steel and 7 firms were in agriculture. On the other hand, 867 firms, or 59%, were in services of various kinds while 209, or 15%, were in secondary branches. There were also 96 firms not included in the total where foreign capital controlled less than 50%. The question arises whether most of these firms could not be taken over by Brazilians or not allowed to function at all without the slightest loss to the Brazilian economic structure.

In February, 1960, short-term loans which had to be paid to foreign creditors amounted to $1,008 million, while other loans made for specific financings for equipment, etc., loans made by one government to another, private national loans, and private foreign loans amounted to another $1,464 million, for a total of close to $2.5 billion. Of these, 71% were due the United States.

Generally the loans made for five years or less are at 6% to 8% interest on onerous economic and political conditions. The Ex-Import Bank, for example, has demanded Brazil increase taxes, reduce public expenses, freeze wages, and enforce rigorous restriction of credits, if the loans were to continue. The taxes that would be increased, however, would be the sales taxes already heavy on the backs of the general public, the reduction of public expenses would be at the expense not of the Army, or of the subsidies to the wealthy, but of education and social benefits; the freezing of wages would be at the deadly cost of the workers already suffering the lowest per capita income in the developed countries of South America, far below the average in Argentina, Chile, Mexico, Venezuela, Trinidad, and others; the rigorous restriction of credits would be to the detriment of the domestic firm, not the foreign. The compulsory purchase of U.S. goods, one of the conditions of such loans, and its compulsory shipment in expensive U.S. ships, another condition often imposed, would help throttle further the economy of the nation. As an example, Brazil had to buy freight cars from the U.S. although its own shops had lay-offs and could readily have accomplished the work.

As can be seen, foreign capital is capable of such adaptation as to be able to dominate the very centers of the economic structure and take over the economy of the nation. American businessmen come in not merely to import or export or sell goods or services. They now build factories and increase their investments. They sell stock to nationals and employ influential Brazilians. They place many Brazilians on their Boards of Directors and in leading positions. They influence the growing market of investors through their investment houses. Changing their seats to Brazil the foreign corporations transform themselves into domestic corporations so as to compete for certain contracts otherwise barred to them.

The advantages of having foreign capitalists invest in a backward country are that such investors build up and train a competent and efficient work force and bring in new techniques by which the country uses its own natural resources instead of producing merely for export and then depending on imports for survival. They also allow scarce foreign credits to be saved.

To Brazilians the great disadvantages are: First, that the foreign capital tends to devour the native capital, putting the latter under its control and domination. Second, the growth of the foreign capital brings with it a greater export of the gains of such capital. It also orients the economy of Brazil to that of the mother country of the imported capital, in this case, the U.S. Exercising control over Brazil's own legitimate national policy, foreign capital may distort the economy of Brazil into unbalanced forms. Thus Brazil can conceivably become another Canada where U.S. firms follow not Canadian policies but those of the U.S. in case of conflict (as witness the issue of exports to China where the U.S. bars certain exports Canada does not).

Let us turn to a more detailed study of this type of situation. The modern U.S. manufacturer in South America often does a highly constructive job, at least in a technical and economic sense. He builds solid, enduring plants containing modern machinery and equipment; he brings with him the best engineering techniques; and organizes his enterprise with the best administrative procedures. His personnel relations practices are generally very enlightened, his native employees receiving the same treatment as Americans in the U.S.A. and sometimes even better. He pays far better than average wages, establishes far better than average working conditions, really educates and trains the work force to standards equal to those found anywhere. And, generally, the people working for such Americans are the last to support the slogan: "Yanquis Go Home!"

The writer recently spent considerable time visiting two such plants: the *Industrias Kaiser de Argentina* (IKA) plant near Córdoba, Argentina, and the *Willys-Overland do Brasil* (WOB) plant near São Paulo, Brazil. These two companies may serve as good examples of the American businessman's modern methods of operation and the image he gives to the people there.

Both IKA and WOB have adopted the policy to make the company as completely as possible free from open U.S. tutelage or domination. Of the working force of 9,300 employees in IKA, only 35 or so are from the United States, and that includes all employees, from top executive down. WOB has gone even farther in that it now has 48,000 Brazilian stockholders who are part of the ownership, while IKA has 20,000 Argentinian stockholders.

Both American companies have had a truly remarkable growth since they first started in 1955 and 1956. By 1961 IKA had produced a cumulative total of over 150,000 automobiles and had developed a national network of over 250 sales agencies and a large constellation of supporting parts manufacturing companies. Similarly with WOB, which in April 1962 had beat all other automobile factories in Brazil with a production of close to 5,000 cars that month and supplied a national network of about 400 sales agencies. In both cases the product is almost 100% "nationalized," that is, manufactured entirely within the country.

The average pay at IKA attained a mark of about $140 a month, whereas the average factory pay in Argentina was about $55. In Brazil, while the minimum pay in 1962 for industrial workers was 13,000 cruzeiros a month, the average pay for semi-skilled workers at WOB was about 35,000 cruzeiros a month. In both cases must be added another 75% for auxiliary and benefit payments. Because of the galloping inflation in both countries wage contracts are opened periodically for pay increases to meet the rise in the cost of living. At WOB the contract was opened up four times in the year ending February, 1962, in order to grant pay raises totalling 48%.

At WOB all minor employees, office boys, and apprentices are entitled to complete their secondary education at Company expense, providing their grades and attendance do not fall below average. Furthermore, courses in shop mathematics, blueprint reading, drafting, hydraulics, etc., have been given to about 1,500 employees. Thirty-five boys, mostly sons of WOB employees, attend a two-year apprenticeship course for electricians, maintenance mechanics, and tool and die makers. During the week the big space available for the recreation and sports clubs is used as class rooms, where 250 children attend first and second grades. There are also courses for the alphabetization of adults.

One of the entities of IKA has constructed an Institute, housed in a spectacular aluminum building where some 200 students, 15 to 18 years of age, can be trained in physics, science, and mechanics in a three-year course in which the boys are paid 1,000 pesos a month the first year, 2,000 pesos the second, and 3,000 pesos the third (at that time the peso was about 125 to the U.S. dollar in the free exchange market). In addition, about 1,200 adults have already been trained in within-industry courses given at the plant.

Both IKA and WOB have a full complement of sports and recreational clubs for the members (shooting, judo, chess, football, darts, basketball, gymnasium, bowling, photography, automobile, dramatics, sewing, etc.). These clubs have about 3,500 members. Both IKA and WOB issue fine house organs monthly.

IKA has given much to charity and community services, in one year alone the Catholic Church benefiting to the tune of about $250,-000. WOB spends a very large amount on special benefits for its employees. On the equivalent of Christmas Day, 17,500 gifts to the children of employees were handed out. The Company sponsors a country club and furnishes free transportation from the public bus lines to this club. The facilities include a children's playground, tennis courts, basketball courts, swimming pool, library, ballroom, and a restaurant capable of serving 300 persons. WOB employees can also get discounts at São Paulo theaters.

At both company plants excellent cafeterias are provided, although at WOB the meals are really splendid and served at one-third actual cost. One could not buy these meals in the city for less than 15-20 times what the employees pay for them. At WOB about 8,500 meals are served a day, or 135,000 monthly. WOB also provides free transportation to its employees to and from work, owning 17 buses and renting 90 buses more for this purpose at a cost to the Company of about 17 million cruzeiros a month (say, $50,000 at the then going rate). WOB also has a Company store which buys basic food items, clothing, shoes, household supplies, etc., and sells them at cost to employees.

Both IKA and WOB have modern accident prevention and safety programs, with large medical departments equipped to handle any type of emergency. Besides treating the employees, the medical staffs also engage in general health programs for the families of employees and communities as well. Often employees need loans in case of illness in the family. A medical loan program is provided by which any employee can borrow from one month's salary up, depending upon his length of service. No interest in charged, although in these countries the normal interest is 3% a month. Several hundred employees are thus benefited each month.

In general, both Companies have modern industrial relations departments with well-oriented personnel and labor functions. There exist job descriptions and job evaluation systems to assure intra-plant equity. Every effort, apparently, is made to carry into effect the American policy of mutual respect between labor and management. In this connection the gap between the American style firms and others is enormous.

Despite this general excellent performance on the part of certain of U.S. businessmen these people are still vulnerable to attack and remain the target for popular resentment because of the other side of the picture.

The basic contradiction troubling American managers and investors living in South America is that they come in as revolutionists in relation to their adopted country but carry with them their conservative postures and attitudes as though they were still in the United States where they are not revolutionists. Although they are distinctly aware of their revolutionary role in transforming an agricultural society into an industrial one, with all the social and political innovations that such transformation entails, they fail to draw the necessary conclusions.

When they first come into such countries as Argentina or Brazil they feel they are there on sufferance and must not offend anybody, especially those in the ruling groups. They must be gracious to the native aristocracy, even though it is ridiculously outmoded; they must not irritate the military, even though these warriors have fought no wars except against relatively unarmed civilians. They must support the traditional system of bribery and corruption. They must never call for political and social change that in fact is an inevitable part of their very entrance onto the scene.

For example, they know that the growth of industry can be accomplished only if there exists a basically educated labor force that can be trained. The American manager is compelled to spend money on education which in industrial countries is done by each and every community but for which in South America the ruthless Oligarchy refuse to tax themselves on the ground that the wealthy American investors should pay for it.

The American manager never comes out in public to say that there should be direct property taxation to create the necessary schools and educational facilities so that the wanted industry can operate. He keeps quiet so as not to offend his wealthy friends. He lets the Alliance for Progress advocate such ideas but he himself refrains from supporting this Alliance "from below," so to speak, even though such forbearance on his part means the Alliance can not properly function.

Again, the American manager knows that his markets and his business are gravely hindered by the mountain of sales taxes, transaction taxes, hidden taxes, custom charges, fees, licenses, surcharges, monopoly prices, etc., loaded on to the consumer, nevertheless he does not think he should "interfere" to advocate progressive legislation. He protests only where his own plant or industry is discriminated against. He does not act here as he would at home, even though he would be listened to and even followed by a large bloc of native capitalists, middle-class layers, and even the people as a whole.

Were a stable democracy to function in these countries, American businesses there might boom greatly. But the American manager, professional, technician, and others all watch one military putsch after another and never threaten to close down their plants were the military to continue holding their dictatorial power against the wishes of the people. What the American conservative would never tolerate at home, his political timidity and fear make him tolerate abroad—without a sound of protest!

The big point is American business is no longer a small economic force sneaking into a Latin American country. In the important countries of South America it is the heart and soul of the entire industrial system. American businessmen could not possibly be driven out of the country by the military or any political force, once they espoused a truly democratic viewpoint with their own workers rallying to their side. But these American managers were brought up never to be on the side of their workers at home and they fear to be on the democratic side espoused by their workers in the countries they have entered.

Certainly in Argentina, for example, the Americans there could have made it plain that they could not function under the military dictatorship of a tiny handful of conspirators thoroughly detested by the people. And yet it is these very Americans who make deals with the military and run to the President of the United States to help get loans to sustain that regime as long as possible. In Peru, when the U.S. State Department came out against the military coup there in 1962, it was the American Chamber of Commerce in that country that rushed to advise Washington not to interfere but immediately to recognize the new military Junta regime.

At home the American manager would strongly resent his workers being dominated by government controlled unions, headed by open agents of the regime. He would denounce his having to check off union dues and send them not to the union but to the government to be used as the government willed; but in Brazil he says nothing about this system. In Argentina he pays large sums into Government funds, knowing that the workers are not receiving the benefits they are paying for and that there is no public control over the thieves.

Often, even in matters directly concerning his own company, he is too timid and fearful to take a proper stand. He is very careful, for example, in many of his plants to have excellent sanitary conditions and accident prevention training, but in the hundreds of concerns grouped around his, owned by native capitalists but tied to his plant as subsidiary bodies, he pays no attention to whether his practices and principles are being carried out, with the result that the workers in the subsidiary plants, believing they are really working for the American plant—which in fact they are—blame the Americans for their actual miserable working conditions.

If one speaks to the American manager about taking a position— the normal position of an American business man for democracy, anti- militarism, free labor unions, adequate public education, health and sanitation measures, he will tell you he is only a "stranger" in the country and will return home soon. And with this hope that he will re- turn home soon he keeps aloof from the "natives," forms his own clubs and colonies to live apart, detested by the rest. And he will stick to this position even though his corporation has now become a native one and he himself a life-long resident, perhaps even a naturalized citizen of his new land.

If they wanted to, however, the Americans could become a great force for progress in the backward lands they are changing. They could revolutionize the country politically, as they are doing economi- cally. But these businessmen from the United States are neither con- querors nor reformers, nor do they care much since it is only their company that is apparently involved and not themselves personally. So they become isolated and the cry "Yanqui Go Home" becomes louder.

Very significantly, the Bank of Boston published the following sequel to IKA's labor relations: "When Industrias Kaiser Argentina's (IKA) management announced its decision to suspend vehicle manu- facturing operations in Córdoba for a short period to limit inventory accumulation in the face of reduced sales, the plant was forcibly occu- pied by certain union elements who took hostages and threatened both them and the plant with physical harm."[31]

We close this section with the following report pertaining to 24 lead- ing American companies in Brazil:

Table 21A[32]

BRAZIL: REPORT OF 24 AMERICAN COMPANIES

	1957	1961
Number of Employees (thousands)	46	61
Wage Payments (billion cruzeiros)	4	19
Charity etc., Contributions (million cr)	9	104
Total Taxes (billion cruzeiros)	3	21

[31] Bank of Boston: *The Situation in Argentina,* January 28, 1963.
[32] "Brazilian Business," July, 1962.

During the five years given in the table, the number of employees increased by one-third, but the average pay increased about 3½ times, charitable and similar contributions increased over 11 times, and total taxes paid 7 times. The average wage apparently was far higher than that paid elsewhere, amounting to about $20 a week when the legal minimum pay on the countryside was about $12 a month (not obtained by many), the minimum pay in the city about $16 a month, and the average pay in industry about $25 a month.

The share of U.S. investments and financing to the total registered capital is given below:

Table 21B[33]
DIRECT U.S. INVESTMENTS IN BRAZIL IN $ MILLION AND IN
% OF TOTAL CAPITAL REGISTERED

	Investment		Financing	
	Amount	%	amount	%
1959	$23.3	35.4	$93.9	25.4
1960	36.5	34.2	72.3	23.7
1961	10.8	27.6	59.5	45.7

The present problems facing Brazil and shaking it to its foundations can be broadly classified as follows:

  I. The agrarian problem;
 II. The problem of industrialization, including that of foreign economic relations and foreign domination;
III. Financial problems;
IV. The problem of poverty and social discontent.

  I. The agrarian problem is no easy one; it is not simply a matter of redistribution of the land to the landless. It involves such matters as the too-great parcellization of land in uneconomic units, the necessary increases in agricultural productivity, the formation of collectives and cooperatives, the supply of fertilizers, use of irrigation, need for farm machinery and equipment, the problem of erosion, matters of credits, financings, investments, price protection, marketing and care of harvests, transportation, better standards of life, safety, health, education, medical care, housing, social services, protection of the rural wage workers through minimum wages, proper labor contracts, etc., etc. But above all agrarian reform involves the elimination of the old Oli-

[33] Alberto Tangare and Waldir Mesquita: "North American Collaboration in Brazilian Industry Development" in *Brazilian-American Survey,* No. 18/19 (1962).

garchy as the ruling decisive force in the country. All the other problems are secondary to this; this is what must be accomplished first and fundamentally.

The difficulties in the way of accomplishing such thorough-going reform in the countryside are tremendous, if not impossible, without revolution. First of all, the United States itself stands in fact behind the Oligarchs and will not see them removed, since it fears revolution from the masses and a definite drift toward communism. In the second place, the Brazilian Government is as yet not strong enough to enforce any such expropriation of the old master class by peaceful parliamentary means. Nor can the present Government take revolutionary means to accomplish these ends.

Thus, so far the plans of the government are timid enough. In regard to agrarian reform they seem to include:

1. To assure free exploitation of virgin lands by those who have already been cultivating these lands during one complete agricultural cycle;

2. To guarantee to squatters and tenants who have been working on the land for two years that they will not be deprived of this land or of the results of their work without just compensation;

3. To see that the agricultural worker gets the minimum wage already decreed for unskilled industrial workers in the region;

4. To expropriate all lands considered necessary for agricultural production at present either not used or poorly used, with compensation spread over many years.

As can be readily imagined such a timid program will not at all remove the large landholders from power, but in fact will really increase the value of their lands, and will certainly not be able to solve the problem, so far as the agrarian poor are concerned. The last word, however, has not yet been said.

II. The problem of industrialization is no longer a matter of exports and imports, of simple loans and repayments. Among the intellectuals of Brazil, at any rate, the prime matter here is one of national planning on a broad and equable basis without overweening concern for individual private profit. Related problems are whether the State should directly take over and nationalize basic important industries, and to what extent, whether industrial development should be controlled or simply allowed to pursue its classic capitalist course with the drive for profit as the sole criterion, what sort of curbs should be set to prevent foreign domination of Brazil's economy, etc.

In a country where the tradition of king, emperor, slavery, and plantation oligarchy has lasted so long, the cause of Adam Smith with its classical laisser-faire theories has no easy sailing. In fact industrialization comes too late upon the scene for such theories to play any real part whatever. In a society where the intellectual's only role has been a servile one, secondary to family nepotism in charge of private enterprise, there is no great desire now on the part of intellectuals, engineers, economists, technicians, managers, and such to continue to fill the miserable part they would always have under Brazilian family control when they might become managers of large State economic entities which would put the businesses of their former masters to shame. Many of these intellectual elements are in the Students Union controlled by the communists.

By themselves the rising native bourgeoisie would be absolutely too weak to counter the growing power of State capitalism and nationalization of the basic, heavy, key industries of the nation: power: electricity, petroleum; transport: railroads, merchant marine; communications: telephone, telegraph, radio, television; utilities, mines, steel, chemicals, etc. Only foreign capitalist intervention can save the day for private capitalism: thus the question of foreign economic intrusion becomes one of transcendental importance, welcomed by some, hated by others, but all having their own particular interests in mind.

As has already been noted, President Vargas wanted industrialization but for the benefit of Brazilians only. It was under his regime that protective tariffs became a national policy as distinct from English laisser-faire. Before his death he charged that foreign importers had been engaged in illegal practices swindling Brazil of large sums of money. Specifically, he charged in 1954 that the declared differences in bills given by Brazilian importers to exporting countries in eight months of that year alone amounted to $250 million tax evasions. He also accused foreign companies of cheating in regard to remission of money allowed under the law. He alleged that they overdeclared their capital by more than 100% so as to be able to send out more than the law allowed (20% of the capital investment and 8% of the profits each year). Already noted have been his charges that foreign interests were sabotaging Petrobras and Electrobras and

were pushing their foreign petroleum as a motivating source for transportation instead of the railroads, or instead of hydro-electric power.

Following Vargas, after some hesitation, Kuibichek was allowed to
take office. Inside the Kuibichek Government the fight for industrial
control continued to rage. Electrobras development was hindered,
gasoline prices were raised, mixed private-State enterprises grew, private capital developed further in the distribution of products under
State control and in ferro-manganese mining, private airlines were
allowed, etc. Kuibichek had been elected on the program of Vargas
but he too was not quite able to withstand the great strain put upon
him.

This strain was continued under the next President, Quadros, also
elected within the Vargas tradition. Under Quadros, however, the conflict went much farther. Quadros repelled special American Ambassador Berle and American Ambassador Cabot; he wrote Soviet Chairman
Khrushchev affirming Brazilian neutralism and sent emissaries to
neutralist conferences, such as those held in Cairo and in Belgrade;
he refused to compromise in the United Nations on Algeria and on
Tunis, as the Western diplomats wanted him to do; he advocated the
entrance of China into the United Nations and sent special missions
to Mao tse-tung; he sent the Dantas Mission to East Germany and
commercial missions to Czechoslovakia, China, and the Soviet Union;
he received a Soviet Union goodwill mission and warmly welcomed
Cosmonaut Gagarin; he gave support to Captain Galvão in the Santa
María incident against dictator Salazar of Portugal and expressed
moral support to Angola in her fight against Portugal, as well as to
the independence movement of all former colonial African countries;
finally, he came out strongly against American intervention in Cuba
and received and decorated "Che" Guevara, one of the Cuban revolutionary leaders, second only to Fidel Castro.

As if this were not enough, further strain on Quadros was produced
by his allegedly inconsistent actions attacking the so-called radical
"Left." He organized a military expedition against the radical Recife
University students; he placed the Peasant Leagues under military control; he closed down the Radio Journal of Brazil; he fought hard
against the demands of the university students for one-third control
over their universities and closely censored the publication of theses
adopted by a student congress, etc. As a so-called puritan he antag-

onized the general public with his tantrums against cock fights, horse racing, bikinis, fashion shows of bras and of bathing suits, and such relative trivia.

The pressure at last became unbearable when the Russians offered Brazil goods with 20 years' financing at very low rates of interest. At this point Quadros collapsed and resigned in 1960 without there occurring any relaxation of the tensions he passed on to his vice-president successor, "Jango" Goulart.

At first parliamentary enemies and the military tried to interfere to prevent Goulart from taking office and there was danger of civil war for a time. But with the Army split, Goulart was permitted to become President only after some traditional Presidential powers had been taken away by Congress and bestowed upon the legislature.

Goulart's first test came soon enough. Although it was the traditional duty of the President to designate his Chancellor, when he designated Francisco Dantas as such, the appointment was rejected, the Chamber controlled by the National Democratic Union and Social Democratic Party (this last not a socialist body) refusing to invest the new candidate into office. In order to compromise, Goulart then designated Sr. Moura de Andrade of the Social Democratic Party as Prime Minister who was approved. Disdaining the wishes of the President, the Prime Minister then began selecting a cabinet of his own so reactionary in political content that Goulart refused to accept the nominees. The Prime Minister then resigned. At once all Brazil was paralyzed by a general strike called by the labor movement and the Brazilian Labor Party, at the end of which strike occurred the bloody hunger riots around Rio. The military now agreed to take orders only from Goulart, the opposition parties were put in their place and Goulart won the day, appointing Brochado da Rocha as his Prime Minister, quickly approved.

The leading political parties today are those which were founded around the time of the 1946 Constitution. They are the PTB, *Partido Trabalho do Brasil* (Brazilian Labor Party), the party of the masses headed by Goulart and whose organ is *Ultima Hora;* the PSP, *Partido Social Progressista* (Social Progress Party) whose chief organ is *O Dia;* the PSD, *Partido Social Democratica* (Social Democratic Party —but not a socialist party) controlling *Diario de São Paulo* and *Diario do Norte;* and the UDN, *Unión Democratica Nacional* (National Democratic Union) whose chief is Lacerda controlling Rio de Janeiro. Its paper is *Estado do Brasil*. In the last election the UDN elected 8 or 9 governors out of the 22 governors to be elected. Besides the above parties there is a host of local parties also important since they run candidates to the National Congress and make deals with one or the other national parties by which they hope to further their own interests.

Under Quadros and Goulart the governmental parties have been faced with the great problem of what to do in relation to the foreign penetration of Brazilian industry. Even before this time there had been passed laws curbing even the naturalized Brazilians so that at present some 53 restrictions limit such persons. The naturalized citizen cannot become President, vice president, senator, congressman, governor, attorney general, judge in most courts, or hold a number of other elective or appointive government offices. Such persons are also barred from holding positions of responsibility in newspapers, radio and television. They cannot be stockholders in mining companies or directors in cooperatives or in trade unions. They cannot become directors in a number of enterprises in which the Government has an interest, such as railroads and steamship lines, etc. They cannot head rural schools or be teachers in primary schools, cannot teach either the geography or the history of Brazil. Musical and theatrical programs given by naturalized persons must include work by native-born Brazilians. The only naturalized persons who may work in chemical plants or for airlines are those who have served in the armed forces. The number of naturalized Brazilians in a ship's crew cannot be more than one-third of the total, etc.

On the other hand, neither the Federal nor the various State Governments want to turn down genuine foreign aid or reject the Alliance for Progress Program offered by the United States. Only recently, in December 1959, in order to help the Northeast region, Law 3692 was put into effect providing the following additional advantages for foreign investors:

1. No imposts or taxes would be placed on imports of new equipment essential to basic food processing industries, if such equipment was not attainable in Brazil;

2. A 50% reduction in income and profit taxes would be enforced through 1968 for industries producing certain regional materials, pro-

vided Brazilian industry was not already there filling more than 30% of the consumption needs;

3. Expenses for mineral research by foreign firms would be deductible from income tax.

In addition to these Federal advantages, the State of Pernambuco added its own effective 1961 through 1965:

1. Real estate tax exemption;

2. Total exemption from State taxes for 6 years and 50% exemption for the following 3 years;

3. Special technical assistance offered free including preparation of plans for Federal exemption, financing through the National Development Bank, the industrial portfolio of the Bank of Brazil, or through the Bank of Northeast Brazil, various market studies State-wide or regional in scope, permanent contact with the Superintendencia for Northeast development, and contact with CODEPE, the agencies approving areas for the location of such industries;

4. A special industrial development was created in Cabo in Pernambuco, only 32 kilometers from Recife, where there was allocated plenty of land near an airport, concrete highways, etc.;

5. Still more, various municipalities offered land without charge under special law;

To curb the foreign control of industry in Brazil some of the "leftist" adherents of Goulart advocate the formation of more State monopolies, self-sufficiency in petroleum, nationalization of production and distribution of electrical energy, abolition of the privileges of foreign investors, rigorous control of remittances of profits abroad, and State monopoly of foreign exchange.

To this has been added the following program:

1. Suspension of new cruzeiro exchange devaluation and establishment of a gold price for exports;

2. Elimination of market obstacles and winning of new markets;

3. Selection of bank credits and elimination of unproductive and speculative credits;

4. Maintenance of the level of investments;

5. Maintenance of the purchasing power of the wage worker;

6. Tax on excessive profits;

7. Improvement of collection of indirect taxes;

8. Reduction of superfluous expenses;

9. Fight against foreign monopolies;

10. Drastic reduction of luxury consumption;

11. Program of national development with priority for bodies furthering national ends;

12. Aid to small and medium industries;

13. Strict control over foreign securities ranging from control of imports to limitations on exports of foreign capital.

According to present plans of the Government the industrial growth of production is to be 11% a year, or 37% at the end of the period. The country is to produce 70% of all capital goods needed. Ingot steel production is to increase from 2.7 million tons in 1962 to 4.3 million tons in 1965; tractor production is to increase from 8,000 units to 18,000 units, auto production from 190,000 units to 270,000 units. Electric power capacity is to grow from 4.75 million kilowatts in 1961 to 7.43 million kilowatts in 1965.[34]

The fight is continuous within the Goulart Government on all these questions. We have already discussed how some of the problems in the field of agrarian and industrial economics are being resolved. We can now continue with the other principal fields: finance and social life.

III. The financial problem facing Brazil has many sides, each perilous for the nation's future. The aspects of this problem include:

1. Great foreign debts and extreme budgetary deficits to be met with no money to pay them;

2. Drastic increase in paper currency, fall in valuta, rise in prices, and in the cost of living;

3. Vast funds required for advancement of industrialization and for desperately needed improvements in infra-structure.

All these problems are intertwined.

Briefly, the present facts are as follows:

1. The Brazilian Government now has little gold reserves for foreign payments. Only recently it was able to get an emergency loan from the United States of $84 million, a mere drop in the bucket. Brazil was also able to get a promise for a further loan of $312 million if she fulfills her plan to end the financial crisis (along the lines of reducing public expenses, slowing down industrial growth, freezing

[34] See *Brasil Constrói,* Vol. XIV, No. 17, 1963.

wages, discharging excessive employees, etc.) and if she comes to terms with the International Monetary Fund.

2. Brazil has a foreign debt of $1.5 billion to pay before 1965 and has no means to pay it. This debt has already a long history. From 1940 to 1956 the net transference of government assistance to Brazil in various forms—loans, grants, food supplies from all sources—Eximbank, ICA, IDA, Food for Peace, Peace Corps, Social Development Trust Fund, Public Law 480—have amounted to $1,024 million or about $50 million a year. Between 1945 and 1956 total grants and credits to Brazil from the U.S. amounted to $431 million of which $30 million was in grants. The following table gives the money in grants and credits to Brazil by U.S. and international agencies up to 1960:

Table 22
GRANTS AND CREDITS TO BRAZIL BY U.S. AND INTERNATIONAL AGENCIES
($ MILLION)

	1955	1956	1957	1958	1959
U.S. Government non-mil grants	$ 6	$ 6	$ 7	$ 7	$ 9
U.S. Government Credits used	48	37	76	190	87
IBRD Disbursements	14	13	4	2	21
IMF Draw			37	55	
IMF Repayments		28		17	20

In February, 1960, short-term loans which had to be paid to foreign creditors amounted to $1,008 million dollars, while other loans made for specific financings for equipment, etc., loans made by one government to another, private national loans and private foreign loans amounted to another $1,464 million for a total of close to $2.5 billion. Of these 71% were due the United States.

3. In 1962 a new foreign trade deficit of $190 million accrued because of disadvantageous ratios of exports to imports and of terms of trade. This deficit is but the last in a whole historic series of such deficits.

The next table gives an historic review of the relationship of exports to imports for Brazil.

4. From 1954 to 1955 while real production increased about 80%, paper money emission increased by almost 700% and prices rose 350%. From 1949 to 1954 real production grew 23% while means of payment increased 112% or at a ratio of 4.8 to 1; in the 1954-1955 period the means of payment grew by 133% and real production

Table 23
BRAZIL: EXPORTS AND IMPORTS IN VOLUME AND VALUE
(1953 INDEX LEVEL EQUALS 100)

	volume exports	value exports	volume imports	value imports
1954	86	101	142	124
1955	100	92	126	99
1956	108	96	119	94
1957	100	90	145	113
1958	96	81	145	103
1959	117	83	160	104
1960	118	82	161	111
1961	128	91	151	111
1962	118	79	140	112

Notes: 1. The base year of 1953 is not a good one, since it reflects too closely the effects of the Korean War. Nevertheless the table is better than no table at all, and is adequate in reflecting annual changes.

2. While the volume of exports increased moderately the volume of imports increased sharply and remained at a much higher level than that of the volume of exports.

3. The moderate increase in exports brought no moderate increase in the value of the exports, but on the contrary a sharp decline so that in 1962 the 18% more of the exports brought 21% less payments, making it evident that unit values of exports must have fallen about 33% or so.

4. The volume of import index is distorted because the base year 1953 taken as 100 was really a subnormal year for imports, the imports for the years 1951 and 1952 being 135 and 131 respectively, the level having fallen in 1953 to 100 only for that single year. Imports had regularly been greater than exports and had been paid for at times by favorable terms of trade and at times by influx of foreign capital.

5. The difference between the value of exports index and the value of imports index had reached 30% by 1962 to the disadvantage of Brazil, in comparison with the base year 1953.

17%, or at a ratio of 7.6 to 1. During this latter period the paper money issued increased by 72 billion cruzeiros.

5. From 1954 to 1955 public budget deficits rose 136 billion cruzeiros (110 billion cruzeiros for the Federal budget, 23 billion for the States, and 3 billion for the municipalities). In 1962 the Federal Treasury deficit more than doubled over that in 1961 and reached the total of 290 billion cruzeiros. The deficit for 1963 is estimated at 370 billion cruzeiros.

6. The Government, refusing to tax the wealthy or even to issue bonds, which with its growing bankruptcy would soon become worthless anyway, has met the problem of deficits by emissions of paper money.

7. While Brazil is now striving to maintain her cruzeiro at the

official rate of 475 to the U.S. dollar (at the time of writing just changed to an official rate of 645 to the dollar) on the free market by the end of 1962 one could obtain 800 cruzeiros to the dollar. The historic series of such ratios is as follows for the end of each given year:

Table 24
BRAZIL: FREE MARKET RATE OF EXCHANGE, CRUZEIRO FOR U.S. DOLLAR

1954	40 cruzeiros
1955	55
1959	100
1960	230
1961	318
1962	800
1963	1050

Note: In 1964 it had already reached 1500 cruzeiros to the U.S. dollar in the early part of the year.

Naturally, the purchasing power of this Brazilian paper money has rapidly fallen. In 1962 the Government issued new paper money to the amount of 195 billion cruzeiros, although the Government had promised the lending agencies in the U.S. that it would stop printing more new money.

8. One of the basic causes of the fall of Brazilian currency is the fundamental law of capitalism that colonial countries producing prime materials in relatively inefficient ways must have their money fall vis-a-vis the money of industrial efficient countries whose units of production are constantly being produced in less and less labor time. The fact of the matter is that Brazil's money fell relatively even before she was industrialized. According to a United Nations report in the period of more than 70 years, from 1876 to 1947, on the average, the quantity of primary products exported by Brazil paid for only 60% of the manufactured articles at the end of this period than the same quantity paid at the beginning. From 1815 to 1914 Brazilian money fell to 1/40th of its previous international exchange value.

Furthermore, as the prices of the goods exported by the primary materials colonial country fell abroad, the value of the currency of that country fell while the internal prices rose. This is best illustrated in Brazil by the history of coffee prices. Given 1953 as 100, the following tables show how on the one hand the price of a sack of coffee fell in terms of U.S. dollars on the international market and how the same sack rose in price in terms of cruzeiros at home while the cost of living rose simultaneously.

Table 25[35]
BRAZIL: PRICE OF SACK OF COFFEE (60 KILOGRAM)

Year	$	Index	Cruzeiro	Index
1953	69.93	100	1394	100
1954	86.84	124	2273	163
1955	61.62	88	2217	159
1956	61.28	88	2244	161
1957	59.05	84	2164	155
1958	53.37	76	1967	141
1959 (½ yr)	43.00	61	2516	180

In the case of Brazilian coffee it should be noted that the big exporters did not lose by the fall in foreign exchange since they received payment in hard dollars for their exported coffee. Ordinarily in industrial countries any increase in prices at home would favor industry rather than agriculture, but not in this case in Brazil where the coffee exporters in this manner could tax the industrialists in their own behalf. Furthermore, it should be noted that Brazil has been suffering from a chronic surplus in coffee which ordinarily should lead to lower prices. But with the purchase of the entire crop by the Government this subsidy only led to inflation and fall in Brazilian currency on the international exchange markets.

9. The runaway inflation in Brazil is marked by the great and rapid increase in prices, and the great fall in the value of the Brazilian currency unit. The next table shows the rise in the price index:

Table 26A[36]
BRAZIL: RETAIL PRICE INDEX: 1948 LEVEL AS 100

Year	Price Index	Year	Price Index
1944	63	1953	180
1945	72	1954	228
1946	84	1955	265
1947	92	1956	317
1948	100	1957	362
1949	107	1958	409
1950	119	1959	574
1951	140	1960	730
1952	156	1961	1101

Given 1953 as 100, the wholesale price index stood at 221 in 1958, the cost of living at the index number 237 (although manufacturing

[35] Nelson Werneck Sodré: Work cited, p. 307.
[36] Caio Prado Juniór: Work cited.

Table 26B
BRAZIL: PERCENTAGE RISE IN COST OF LIVING OVER PREVIOUS YEAR

1954	22.1%
1955	23.3
1957	16.6
1958	14.2
1959	25.9
1962	52.0

Table 26C
BRAZIL: CHANGES IN PRICES IN SPECIFIC NECESSITIES—3 MONTHS 1962

	Beginning Spring	End Spring
Milk	25.3 cruzeiros	55 cruzeiros
Bread	13	15
Meat	180	240
Butter	380	440
Potatoes	40	65
Eggs	120	200
Beans	85	95

production stood at 129 and manufacturing employment at 123). Because of the inflation nominal wage increases have been given the workers every four months in some plants in order to help them meet the rise in the cost of living. By the end of 1962 prices rose 52.7%, a record for one year! Given the price of meat at the freezers in 1948 as 100, then these prices jumped to index number 555 in 1956 and to 2,027 in 1960.

Table 26D
BRAZIL: GUANABARA STATE: COST OF LIVING INDEX: 1963 LEVEL AS 100

	Index Level
1954	122
1955	151
1956	182
1957	212
1958	243
1959	338
1960	437
1961	583
1962	884
1963	1530 (July)

10. Because of the inflation there is no long-time credit as in the U.S. In order to get an automobile, for example, one must put 60% to 70% down in cash and pay the rest in 4 to 5 months. Savings bring 3% a month; if one wants to borrow the rate is over 4% a month, although the legal maximum rate has been fixed at 18% a year.

11. Discounts average 25% or even more and are mainly worked

through finance companies who now have vast sums (20 billion cruzeiros) to work with. When a dealer sells an automobile, for example, say for 1 million cruzeiros, he marks the car price at 1.3 million cruzeiros and then discounts his receipts for 1 million with one of the finance companies which sees to it then that the customer makes his monthly payments until the car is entirely paid for.

12. Every State has a turnover transaction tax over and above the Federal tax. These State taxes amount to an average of 5% of the value of the article sold. The São Paulo tax is 4.8%, for example, but applies to each and every transaction so that for a single commodity such as an automobile that may go through a number of transactions before it is finally sold, the tax can accumulate to about 25%. This means that all other States must pay a tribute to São Paulo. Over and above this is the Federal tax of 3% on a Jeep and 15% on a passenger car. There are also import taxes on steel, foundry coke, aluminum ingots, and other raw materials needed for the automobile industry.

The Willys-Overland Company, for example, paid in 1961 taxes of 6.2 billion cruzeiros, not counting the taxes paid by the suppliers and by the dealers. Thus an automobile costs as much to buy in Brazil as in the U.S. despite the fact that the average wage in the automobile factory may be $450 a month in the U.S. and in Brazil about one tenth that wage.

12. In 1962 the rate of industrialization which had been estimated at over 7% in 1961 apparently fell to 4%. Should the Government place a further pinch on easy credits, as the U.S. has demanded as a condition for its future loans, the situation might well become critical, repeating that now prevailing in Argentina or in Chile where a depression exists with large-scale unemployment and suffering.

In order to get out of the dangerous situation in which they find themselves the nationalists in the Goulart Government did not hesitate to look for new markets even with the communists. In this they have been much encouraged by the increase in the sales of coffee to the Soviet Bloc illustrated by Table 27.

13. The bourgeois radicals in the Goulart Government have also made efforts to reform the income tax law and make it more progressive as well as to reduce cheating by corporations. Under the new income tax law the maximum tax is now 65% on incomes 800 times the basic minimum wage, or incomes of 11.2 million cruzeiros. In addition

Table 27[37]

IMPORTS OF COFFEE IN 60 KILOGRAM BAGS RY THE SOVIET BLOC
(ROUNDED FIGURES)

	1957	1961
U.S.S.R.	85,000	404,000 (92,000 of this to E. Germany)
Czechoslovakia	86,000	232,000
E. Germany	202,000	451,000
Hungary	35,000	56,000
Poland	26,000	70,000
Yugoslavia	47,000	159,000

there is a surtax of 25% but the total taxation is not to exceed two-thirds of the income. The tax on business profits was raised from 18% to 25%, with an additional temporary tax of 5% more and a surtax of 20% on profits from real estate deals.

To reduce cheating, while the taxes on identified bearer shares and funds remitted abroad increased from 28% to 33%, those on unidentified bearer shares were taxed 45% plus a 50% surtax. In addition many other measures were taken to check tax evasion and tax payment delays. There was no income tax for those with less than 336,000 cruzeiros a year, with further exemptions for spouse and children.

As to how the government has been traditionally cheated on excise taxes can be seen by the fact that the tax collections compared with 1948 prices were only 10 times higher in 1962 than in 1948 when they should have been 15 times higher. The government, however, is now increasing the pressure to collect the taxes at the very source of income so that the chances of cheating are less. The following table shows the problem and the change in this respect:

Table 28[38]

BRAZIL: REVENUE COLLECTED AT 1948 PRICES: (BILLION CRUZEIROS)

	1948	1961	1963 (estimate)
Total Revenue	4.2	8.4	10.2
Private	1.3	1.0	1.4
Business	2.1	4.4	4.9
Retention at source	.8	3.1	3.9

IV. A great deal of speculation in food exists, one of the results of which was the outbreak of the great hunger riots around Rio de Janeiro in 1962. The immediate cause was the lack of rice and beans, the staple food of the poor in Southern Brazil, due to hoarding on the part

[37] *Conjuntura Economica:* Vol. X, No. 6, June 1963.
[38] *Conjuntura Economica:* Vol. X, No. 6, June 1963.

of the distributors. The food was there in the warehouses, but the businessmen declared that they were unable to sell at the prices fixed by the Government since the Government agency, COFAP, had fixed a price of 3,120 cruzeiros per bag of rice when the minimum cost was 3,115 cruzeiros and the transportation costs from Rio Grande do Sul to the São Paulo and Rio markets were 850 cruzeiros a bag more. To this was added the stupidity and red tape of the Government men who had put a ceiling on colored beans which they eat in São Paulo and no ceiling on black beans which they eat in Rio, while in Rio the ceiling was placed on the black beans. This allowed for a great deal of evasion of the price ceilings and cheating in both places. Furthermore, it seemed that two different Government agencies had placed two different prices on sugar creating greater confusion, cheating, and hoarding.

The results of such confused governmental policies were tragic. Coming as they did in the midst of a general strike called to insist that the military did not hinder Vice-President Goulart from functioning as President as his predecessor had done and paralyzing the country, the hunger riots were an unmistakable warning that the political situation could easily degenerate into popular revolution.

The extremely rapid growth of industrialization with the aggravated contradictions it brings between cities and countryside, has created a situation of unbearable tensions. No matter how fast the cities grow, the slums around them grow at the same pace or even faster. These slums of unbelievable squalor with no water, light, or sewage are made up in the main not of the city poor but of the vast hordes of peons and country wretches who come on foot in filthy rags to find some job or some place in which they can possibly make a living. These people are easily led into hunger riots and into fighting for a change in their terrible lot.

Here is another reason for the master move of the country's capital from Rio de Janeiro to Brasilia, a city five or six hundred miles in the interior, far from the revolutionary turmoil existing in the more populated sections of Southern Brazil. It was the same motivation that helped choose Albany instead of New York City, Harrisburg instead of Philadelphia, Washington, D.C., instead of a large metropolitan center, and Ankara, Turkey, instead of Constantinople.

Thanks to the intense inflation and rise in the cost of living, strikes have been common for wage increases of 50%-55% at one time. On the one hand economic minister Francisco San Tiagas Dantas promised the U.S. to make a 40% cut in Federal spending and hold down pay raises in Government for both military and civilian personnel. On the other hand the Brazilian Labor Party pledged that real wages will grow at least on a par with the growth of productivity.

The 1963 wage bill of the present Government provides for increases ranging from 25% to 55% for the armed forces and from 40% to 56% for the civilians. On this basis the increased outlay for Federal wages would be 140 billion cruzeiros, a staggering amount which could be met only by new issues of paper money starting a new spiral of inflation.

Under the Goulart Government's announced Three-Year Plan, 1963-65, the basic goals included the following points:

1. The rate of growth of the national income was to be 7% to make the per capita rate of income growth 3.9% (3.1% being the annual increase in the population);

2. Prices to be stabilized so that in 1965 they should increase no more than 10%;

3. Wider distribution of benefits, real salaries to grow at least as much as income grows;

4. Rapid improvement in health and public welfare;

5. Disparities in regional growth and in regional living standards to be reduced; etc.

It is highly doubtful whether any of these goals will be reached in any substantial manner.

There is no doubt that the organized labor and agrarian toiler movements are growing larger, stronger, and more vociferous. More and more they are being led by Soviet oriented intellectuals who already control the powerful students movement. Brazil recognizes Castro's Cuba, as does Chile. What happens in Argentina will also affect Brazil.

All the contradictory forces seem to be heading for a showdown: U.S. penetration versus Brazilian nationalism, regional discrepancies versus Federal equable planning, city versus country, Oligarchy versus industrialists, industrialists versus proletarians, Government and armed forces versus the people. Brazil itself is headed for an imminent explosion.

Index